W9-AZG-750

COOKING
WITH
GREASE

 Stirring the Pots in America

DONNA BRAZILE

Simon & Schuster Paperbacks

New York   London   Toronto   Sydney

SIMON & SCHUSTER PAPERBACKS
Rockefeller Center
1230 Avenue of the Americas
New York, NY 10020

Copyright © 2004 by Donna L. Brazile
Afterword copyright © 2005 by Donna L. Brazile

First Simon & Schuster paperback edition 2005

SIMON & SCHUSTER PAPERBACKS and colophon are
registered trademarks of Simon & Schuster, Inc.

For information about special discounts for bulk purchases,
please contact Simon & Schuster Special Sales:
1-800-456-6798 or business@simonandschuster.com.

Designed by Elliott Beard

Manufactured in the United States of America

10   9   8   7   6   5   4   3   2   1

Library of Congress Catalog Card Number: 2004048116

ISBN 0-7432-5398-1
        0-7432-5399-X (Pbk)

For Jean Marie Brazile (1937–1988)
Frances Harriett Brazile (1887–1975)
Lease Douglas Brown (1915–1994)
Lionel "Teddy Man" Brazile Jr. (1961–1997)

Contents

Prologue

THERE ARE FEW EVENTS as exclusive as a Gridiron Club dinner. The Gridiron Club is one of the oldest and most prestigious national press clubs in the country. The invited guests at the annual dinners include only the crème de la crème—presidents, vice presidents, congressional leaders, Supreme Court justices, and media elite. Growing up in Louisiana, I had big goals, but I couldn't possibly have imagined being invited to speak before an audience of some of the most important people in the world.

When Ron Cohen, columnist for *USA Today*, called me in the summer of 2003 to invite me to serve as the Democratic speaker at the winter Gridiron Club dinner, I was as gratified as I was stunned. For years, I begged my journalist friends to invite me simply as a guest, but to no avail. Tickets for these events were reserved for the political elite. After I was offered to speak at the dinner, I became so worried that I would make a complete fool of myself, I went into temporary shock.

After years of being one of the most quotable political operatives around, I developed a case of political laryngitis. I have long had to speak publicly to large crowds as part of my job, but little could prepare me for the inevitable stage fright that comes from having to impress those who have seen and done it all.

When I want to get comfortable while working a crowd, I'll survey the room, looking for my mother. She isn't there, of course, but I'll often see a glimpse of her in a waitress or a cleaning woman, someone unassuming, just trying to do her job. At the Gridiron dinner, this was more important than ever. I was one of the youngest people in the room, and certainly one of the few African Americans.

Finding some "regular" people there helped me to get in touch with the values that shaped my desire to go into politics in the first place.

For nearly her entire life, my mother worked as a maid. Never in her wildest dreams did she imagine that her daughter would one day grow up to influence national politics or manage a presidential campaign or be the first Black woman to stand before an audience as exclusive as the Gridiron Club. Yet the lessons I learned growing up in Louisiana did, in many ways, prepare me for such feats. From the time I was nine years old and helped a candidate who promised to build us a playground, I understood that politics really was local. Growing up in a tight-knit community taught me the importance of making and keeping personal connections. The sacrifices and hardships that people like my mother faced taught me that the best thing politics can do is make people's lives just a little easier. Standing before the Gridiron Club, I realized just how far I had come, but also how I had never really severed the roots that took me there.

You'll find a lot of New Orleans food metaphors in this book. A lot of lessons I learned in the kitchen, watching the women of my family stir the pots and season things just right. I'm still working to do the same.

—Donna Brazile
June 2004

CHAPTER ONE

JEAN'S KITCHEN:
FINDING THE RIGHT POT

Jean assigned every meal a different pot. Eggs could be scrambled in the frying pan but not in the black cast-iron skillet that was used for heavy-duty frying or to make her favorite roux. No one dared stir anything other than the assigned meal in one of Jean's pots, pans or skillets. My mother taught me how to cook with grease.

I WAS BORN ON December 15, 1959, at 8:53 AM, Donna Lease Brazile, in Charity Hospital in New Orleans. I was the third child. My older sisters, Cheryl and Sheila, had arrived in 1957 and 1958. Two years later, in 1961, my parents, Lionel and Jean Brazile, had my brother Lionel Jr., whom we called "Teddy Man." My mother gave birth every year after that, until there were nine—six girls and three boys. The doctors at Charity Hospital tied something in a knot in October 1966. I am sure my father lit a candle and read a novena to St. Michael before the procedure was completed.

HOT, SWELTERING HOT, that's my hometown of Kenner, Louisiana. Back then the city of Kenner was a bedroom enclave located in the suburbs of New Orleans, about a twenty-minute drive west of the historic French Quarter. It was a small town and the neighborhood in which I grew up in the 1960s and 1970s had the feel of a closely knit village. Kenner is bordered by Lake Pontchartrain to the north, the Mississippi River to the south and an unnamed nest of swampland to the west. Along with the terrible heat and scorching humidity, God blessed us with daily showers—enough rain to wet the sidewalks, quench the thirst of our vegetables growing out back, and moisten our beautiful rose bushes in the front yard, but not enough to alter the blazing temperature. After one of those delightful showers, Kenner turned into a reptile farm, overrun with frogs, turtles, snakes and other small, ugly creatures.

I grew up afraid of these swamp creatures (about the only living things that managed to terrify me), especially after a nice downpour. When the coast was clear and the kids were allowed to go out and play, someone would scream and holler "snake!" and panic would set in all over the house. If my father was home, he would go to his room and pull out his old rusty gun, a Colt .45, and shoot the slimy creature, all to the delight of my brothers and sisters and me. My mother never bothered to come to the door to look at the reptile. Instead, she'd yell, "Get y'all asses back in the house."

In Kenner, where you lived in relation to the railroad tracks was your destiny. My family didn't just live on the proverbial "other side of the tracks." No, we lived behind *two* sets of tracks. The middle-class Blacks lived between the main highway—Airline Highway—and the working poor, like my family, lived behind the double railroad tracks. So in a way, if you really do the math correctly, we lived behind *three* sets of tracks pushed up against the banks of the Mississippi River.

We lived at 529 Filmore Street, and every now and then the train heading from New Orleans on the way up north or west would stop and people in their cars had to wait for the train to pass. White people would be stuck on our street and we would sit on the porch and study them. We studied their cars, their hairdos and their demeanors. We wanted to know if they were afraid of us, and we tried everything we could think of to get them to talk to us, but they never even looked our way. Back then, Kenner was about 30 percent African American and 70 percent Caucasian. Segregation was fading as law but was still in place as practice. There was definitely a White Kenner and a Black Kenner.

The airport when I was growing up was called Moisant, but it was later renamed Louis Armstrong International Airport after the world-famous jazz trumpeter who was one of Louisiana's most famous sons. Everybody in Kenner, just about, had some connection with the airport. Whites lived in its immediate shadow near Williams Boulevard, the center of commerce and Kenner's main street.

But on my side of town most folks were poor or working class. My mother did domestic work for the Hilberts, starting out at about fifty dollars a week and topping off near the end of twenty years of service at maybe one hundred dollars, without any Social Security or other benefits. My mom started work at 7:00 in the morning and got off at 4:00 PM. She had to clean, cook and get Mrs. Hilbert's children ready for school. Some of Mrs. Hilbert's children thought my momma was their momma because, in fact, she raised them. My mother went to work with a group of other women in our neighborhood, Miss Lois Jean and Miss Beulah, all of them domestic workers who cleaned and kept house for the wealthy White families who lived uptown, around St. Charles Avenue in the city. St. Charles Avenue was a beautiful area of stately homes that had once been plantations, with streets lined with trees dripping with moss. The men in my neighborhood were often day laborers or longshoremen. I grew up around men and women who worked long and hard with their hands and who never had too much to show for all their hard work, except an occasional new car.

There were men like Mr. Jumel Gant who lived next door to us— he was a bricklayer. My parents didn't have a car, so every time my mother was about to give birth, Mr. Jumel, who somehow was always home, would take my mother to the hospital in his truck—after he'd go and get her a pack of Salem Light cigarettes. The only time my mother smoked was right before and right after she gave birth. And Mr. Jumel was always there. He was there for the birth of at least seven out of the nine kids, including me, always getting my mother to Charity Hospital on time. There was also Mr. Paul Davis who lived across the street and drove the yellow school bus, and Mr. Joe Daigs who was a preacher and owned the corner grocery store on Filmore Street. Mr. Joe sold penny candies, pickles, pigs' lips, soft drinks, cold meats, aspirin and liniment for the older folks. He also owned a yellow school bus and had a church, the Community Missionary Baptist Church, up the street from our house. Although Mr. Joe and his wife, Mrs. Mary, had no children of their own, they were like surrogate parents to all the kids in the neighborhood. These were the people who made my part of Kenner often feel like one big extended family.

Poverty was a fact of life when I was growing up. Poverty meant we ate government "commodity" food, like yellow cheese, canned meats, grains, peanut butter and other surplus items. It meant my paternal grandmother, Grandma, made all the clothes for us kids, and I mean everything except our underwear! My parents never told us we were poor. We never discussed it, because they could usually make ends meet between paychecks or borrow from someone in the family. If we lacked something important, we got it when they got paid or during the holidays when our aunts and uncles would pitch in. We learned to wait and that patience was a virtue. We learned to do without and it never bothered us or consumed our daily existence.

One way to somehow feel rich even when you weren't was to cook delicious meals and share with other families in the neighborhood. My mother or Grandma would prepare a big pot of red beans and rice every Monday (laundry day), along with ham hocks, smoked sausages, garlic, onions and bell peppers. After we cooked the rice and made lettuce-and-tomato salad, the neighbors would bring over their plates and talk about their day at work. Cooking was therapy for women and men alike. The cook got a chance to work out his or her private blues and talk about the local news and politics. I enjoyed sitting in the kitchen helping my mother or Grandma cook up dishes and listening to the gossip.

When times were bad, especially around the holidays, we could always find something to prepare for dinner by fishing in the Mississippi River, Lake Pontchartrain or one of the many local gutters. Catfish, trout, croakers, crawfish or plain old shrimp—my mother would just batter it up and fry it in the old black skillet. It always came out spicy good and tasty, especially with some Cajun hot sauce on the side. Life seemed to revolve around cooking, sharing meals and telling great stories about the old days. We learned so much in the kitchen about life listening to those stories from our parents or grandparents about growing up in the South.

We had little, if any, money. Not only did my parents not own a car, they didn't even have driver's licenses. We caught the bus everywhere or walked. To visit our maternal grandparents, our mother instructed us early on how to get around Kenner and New Orleans. For the nine of us, learning how to catch a bus downtown was a big deal. Back then, the hour-long bus ride out of Kenner using the Jefferson or Airline Highway, along with a transfer to one of the uptown buses on Claiborne or Tulane Avenue, became a major highlight of my life.

If we were lucky, our mother, who was raised "in the city," would call up her dad or one of her relatives—like Pa Henry, Cousin Sullivan, her sister Aunt Gwen or brothers Uncle Johnny, Uncle Floyd or Uncle Douglas (and one of his many girlfriends)—to come pick up all nine of us, plus my mother, and drive us to her mama's house on Valence Street, between St. Charles Avenue and Freret Street in New Orleans. If we traveled by car, I, as one of the oldest kids, had to sit close to the window. Once in position, I had to allow two of my younger siblings to sit on each knee. We never complained about being packed into a car. It was great to leave Kenner to see our relatives in the city.

Poverty affected nearly every part of my childhood, even my mother's attitudes about playtime. As soon as she came home from work, she forced all of us inside the house. This seemed like a contradiction. How could we enjoy our childhood while forced to stay inside most of the time? If it wasn't the scorching heat or the unpredictable downpours, my mother was afraid that we would get hurt from playing rough games or catch a rare cold during the winter months. She made it clear that we could not "afford to get sick." This bothered me no end as a child. If we did get sick, Grandma would take out one of her old homemade remedies and force it down our throats, and she also believed in taking the necessary precautions, like castor oil in the late summer to rid our bodies of toxins. Another favorite was using spiderwebs to heal a deep cut or placing a piece of fatback in our shoes to avoid swelling from a rusty nail or splinter.

The fear of having to go to Grandma for a remedy was enough to scare me and my siblings into good health most of the time, or at least keep us from complaining of being sick.

We couldn't waste money. We couldn't mess up our school clothes or our play clothes. Our mother made us aware of the fact that we could not waste anything because there were people even poorer than us, which we couldn't believe. Gluttony was a sin my mother preached against all the time. She set an example of generosity, even under pressure, by feeding the neighbors' kids even when we didn't have enough for a second helping of corn bread and collard greens or shrimp jambalaya. My mother never missed an opportunity to tell us we had to learn how to share and give back in order to receive God's blessings. We were poor, but it wasn't the kind of poverty that made us go out on the street corner to beg for money or become a ward of the state.

WE LIVED PAYCHECK to paycheck, even with my father working two and sometimes three jobs. We had no rainy-day fund or savings account, but we had credit—lots of credit—with various corner stores. We managed because my mother was extremely disciplined and raised us to be quite frugal. Living in Grandma's house also helped. Grandma was a rock. She was always there to pitch in and help my parents fill the gap.

I DIDN'T CARE MUCH about toys—we couldn't get what we really wanted anyway until they were on sale. Instead of store-bought Easter baskets we used shoe boxes and filled them with boiled eggs, chocolate, candy and treats. Sometimes, to get a little extra money, my mother would take out a loan for five hundred dollars and pay it back at 20 percent interest. With terms like that, we kids simply did without. We learned at an early age the thing that was most important—family.

There was one Christmas when we got lucky. The driver of a Schlitz beer truck was speeding down Filmore Street and didn't see the train coming. Attempting to avoid hitting the train, the truck driver slammed on the breaks, hit a nearby post and landed in the ditch. Fortunately no one was hurt, not the passengers, the train conductor or the driver of the truck, but cases of beer spilled out all over the tracks. The train had been carrying bags of flour, which were also now spilling out. Word spread like wildfire and everybody brought wagons, bicycles, boxes, anything they could rustle up quickly to haul off their share of the beer and flour. That was a good Christmas. Aunt Adele and Pinkey, my father's older sisters, came over to get a couple of cases of beer. The adults had beer and the kids had buttermilk biscuits and we all felt like the richest people on earth.

OUR HOME WAS BUILT in 1947 by my father's older brother Ebbie and his friends. My dad's father, Grandpa Louis, had purchased the lumber from the Holloway Home Wrecking Company, which sold used wood from Camp Plauche Barracks located down the road in Harahan, near the river. It was an old, two-bedroom white wooden house. My parents paid most of the bills and made all the repairs while Grandma kept up the property taxes and kept the phone in her husband's name. Aunt Ethel, my father's oldest sister, and her family built the second home in 1956 next door. Aunt Ethel was also my godmother and she treated me as one of her own grandchildren. Her only child, Ethel Mae, and her five children lived at 531 Filmore with Aunt Ethel. This made us—the Brazile and Henderson clans—one gigantic extended family.

EARLY ON I SLEPT with Cheryl and Sheila, my two older sisters, in the bottom bed and Teddy Man and Chet, another brother, slept above us. And the baby of the year would sleep with my parents, plus the baby to come or the baby who had just been born. My grandmother would always allow one of us to sleep with her. I eventually slept in my grandmother's wooden four-poster queen-size bed with her until I was about twelve. Sometimes my little sister Lisa, whom we called "Little Red," would squeeze in with us or anyone who felt sick and needed Grandma's special medicine.

The center of the house, maybe even the soul, was our *bouvetroire,* or den. In Louisiana lingo, the *bouvetroire* is the room in the house where people go and kick back, relax, get their groove on, drink beer

and spend the evening telling tall tales and lies. Children were allowed to sit and watch TV, but if company came we had to depart.
And as hard as my father worked, when he was home, he played
music all night long in his *bouvetroire*. If he was in a good mood, sometimes he would let us kids come in while he listened to Otis Red-
ding, The Platters, Sam Cooke, Nancy Wilson, Aretha Franklin—all
the records that my mom had bought on Canal Street or Uptown on
Magazine Street. Music and laughter filled the house on those nights.
My parents loved showing us off and our visitors would watch us
dancing and showing off for their entertainment.

Being a good Catholic, my father had his altar right outside
his *bouvetroire*, in a little alcove. There was the altar and there were
two tiers so you could kneel and pray before it. It was a little scary,
but no one dared drink or curse in front of the altar. My father built
it himself from looking at some religious magazine. It was a long,
narrow piece of wood covered with a nice piece of linen. He had all
sorts of statues of St. Anthony, the Blessed Mother Mary, St. Michael
and several crucifixes all throughout the house. With twelve mouths
to feed, Lionel Brazile needed all the prayers and all the help he could
get. Prayer was a daily act for all of us. It was mandatory.

Despite his prayers, my parents still argued a lot about money. My
father would get home on a Friday afternoon or when he got paid
once a month, on the twenty-fifth. He would give my mother his
check and she would cash it at Lloyd's Furniture Store or Burton
Pharmacy. Later, he would come back home and tell her that he
wanted his cut. My mom would always shortchange him, giving him
five or ten dollars. If he asked for more to buy a new pair of working
shoes or a new pair of khakis or jeans, all hell would break loose. My
mother would grill him about whether he really needed them, reminding him that he had nine kids to feed and clothe and they came
first, but he wanted his money and he would start cursing until he got
what he wanted. These confrontations usually started in their bedroom, but they quickly spread through the house. There was Jean—a
tiny woman with a big voice—hands on her hips, begrudging Lionel
an extra dollar that she feared would take food out of the mouths of
her children. She was facing off against Lionel—tall, muscular and

six foot four—who probably just needed to feel like he controlled some small part of what happened to his paycheck. They argued, loud and long. And sometimes they fought. My father liked to throw things—always missing his target, but the point was made. He was in control. My mother never backed down. She threw things back. We watched in horror.

Early on I became the mediator, the peacekeeper between my parents. I was a big kid, a leader among my sisters and brothers, and everybody thought I was strong. My big mouth, my take-charge ways, my bossiness, and my "old" spirit earned me this often thankless task no one else felt up to. In the wake of or just before one of their arguments, I would sit in the kitchen and listen to my father, half sleepy and mumbling, complain about my mom. My job was to sit and listen and absorb his pain and anger. When I got older I would let my mother sleep in my place with Cheryl until he calmed down, and then I would wake her up and tell her it was safe to go to bed now. The next morning it was back to school or work. They rarely stayed mad with each other.

My father was so angry, so angry. But it wasn't about my momma. It was about his life as a Black man who spent eighteen months being cold in the hills of Korea. He was a proud army veteran and often talked about the war. Hell, I didn't care, but someone had to listen to him. He never complained about the White man, about racism, but his drinking and the fights with my mom said it all: what it meant to be a proud veteran locked into low-paying jobs, locked into poverty, and not being able to see any way out. He'd look at me and say, "I spent eighteen months in the hills of Korea. I don't take shit from nobody." He'd survived Korea but no one cared about that now, and this made him very upset.

On the worst nights, my father would remind us that he had a gun, and how good he was with it. In response I would tamp down my own fear and meekly agree, saying, "That's right, Lionel, you have six rounds in that gun and there are nine children, Jean, plus Grandma. I'm sure whoever is left standing will shoot you." And I'd keep him talking. He had worked for Boh Brothers Construction Company helping to pave roads and repair bridges. Then a crane hit him, injuring his back, and he was off recuperating for almost a year and a half without any workers' compensation. I don't think he ever recovered from that. Afterward, when he could no longer work in construction, he had to work two and three jobs in addition to his job as a cook at Dobb's House at the airport to come near to what he had been making at construction work. It took a lot out of him. There were times we didn't see my father until late at night because he worked literally from sunup to sundown. But I was the one who was the linchpin, keeping him and my mother from falling apart. Our family, in order to survive, had to stick together.

MY MOTHER, JEAN, came from a middle-class background. Although she enrolled at Southern University in Baton Rouge, she was the only one of her six brothers and sisters who didn't graduate from college. She had completed two years of college at Southern University, but dropped out to marry Lionel, a lean, handsome basketball player and veteran, a ladies' man with an outrageous sense of humor. They met, fell in love, married and moved into my father's mother's house on Filmore Street. They met just upon his return from Korea, where he was sent at eighteen. He was still in high school when he received his draft papers. Healthy but a poor pupil, Lionel was drafted into combat and came home to start his life all over again.

My dad was a star basketball player. He was a good ballplayer with many scholarship opportunities to play at area colleges before leaving for Korea. Upon his return, Grandma persuaded him to go back to school to get his high school diploma, and this is when he met Jean. One sunny day, my mom was walking across campus to class and saw my dad. She walked straight up to him and asked him out to the prom. He said, "I'll think about it." Later, dressed up in their fancy clothes and new shoes and car-less, my parents started courting and fell in love. Two years later, they were married.

My mother's family definitely felt that she had married "down." They felt sorry for her and for us, too. Some people marry for money or for lust, but my momma married for love, there was no question about it. She preached to us not to marry beneath ourselves, but we felt that's what she had done. My mother's family, the Browns, and the Braziles couldn't have been more different.

It always seemed as if my mother's brothers and sisters had perfect lives. We liked them. With so many aunts and uncles on both sides, we could always play favorites. Whenever we went to visit her mother, whom we called "Jean's mama," Jean made us promise to tell everyone that we had eaten before we left home. We could never appear to be greedy. Jean's mama always arranged for someone to bring us to her house in a car, and my mother would stubbornly turn down the offer, saying she didn't mind bringing us to 2304 Valence Street on the bus.

They say charity begins at home and with Jean's family it did. Aunt Zeola (nicknamed Trish), one of Jean's younger sisters, every Christmas would send us crushed-velvet dresses that she bought at Sears. She lived outside of Chicago in Kankakee, Illinois. Both Trish and Uncle Joe, her husband, were schoolteachers. We had to go parade in front of Jean's mama with our new dresses and clothes. I hated it. Trish always sent me a red or purple dress and I hated loud-colored clothes. At Jean's mama's house we couldn't sit on the good furniture and almost everything was covered in plastic. We'd sit on the floor and wait until the grown-ups told us we could come to the back where they were talking and drinking. It wasn't like at our house, where we could run around the house and be in the company of the grown-ups and listen to their conversations.

Food was always plentiful when the family knew we were coming. My mother fed us before leaving home because she didn't want us to act like we were hungry; we were well behaved and followed all of Jean's rules. When we visited her brother Uncle Johnny, his wife, Marva, made the most delicious cakes and sweets, which earned her the nickname Cupcake, but Aunt Marva's Creole gumbo was always weaker than our gumbo, which was made with okra and andouille sausage. You could always see straight through Aunt Marva's gumbo pot, which is a bad sign. When you stirred it up there was hardly any stock or roux to keep the ingredients together. Sometimes her shrimp or chicken parts floated to the top. So we barely ate Aunt

Marva's gumbo, not after eating the real thing at home. Uncle Johnny would make the most delicious-looking shish kebabs for the grown-ups but us kids got hot dogs. When we visited Jean's relatives we were always full of pride because we didn't like anyone talking behind our backs. So as we got older and were able to eat more, my mother just told us to take po' boy sandwiches, fresh fruit and canned sodas when we visited her side of the family.

But when we visited the Braziles they had feasts. A little laid back and comical, their attitude was get as fat as you want to, as Black as you want to, drink as much beer as you want to—we don't care. Do whatever you please. And Lionel's family cut a rug. We'd arrive and they'd say, "Uh oh, it's time to shake a tail feather." The Braziles could drink you under the table, force you to eat everything they cooked and then send you home with leftovers.

Although my mother was raised Baptist, she raised us in a very strict Catholic way. We had to work every day; our chores were laid out, from washing dishes to hanging up the clothes outside. No exceptions were made. We were well disciplined and there was no room for error. Jean was the commander in chief, that's the phrase she used, and she would tell us in a minute that if we didn't like it, we could leave. We called our parents by their first names, Jean and Lionel. My sister Cheryl started it, the rest of us followed suit, and as strict as they were on other things, my parents didn't mind this unconventional way of addressing them. Jean never went to church but sent us to Mass every Sunday, regardless of the weather. The ten o'clock Mass was our favorite because the priest often talked in Latin. Jean sent us off on Sunday morning with a nickel to put in the collection plate. But we'd go to the store on the way to Mass, break that nickel down to five pennies, put our pennies together and buy a snowball and share it. We gave God a penny. We loved Him and promised to give more when we could afford it.

Jean began her day at the crack of dawn. The rooster out back was our alarm clock. Like most of our neighbors, we had chickens, roosters and ducks out back. Jean, the city girl, had learned to cook from her mother. Whenever she went in the kitchen to cook, I tried to spend quality time watching her stir the pots. I was full of questions about everything going on in the world, the neighborhood and her family. Often she simply wanted to be alone. I am sure that being alone in the kitchen was one of the few ways my mother ever had any solitude, any mental rest. She could just be with her thoughts, away from her army of children.

Preparing the morning meal for a large family was hard work. In addition to knowing the right ingredients, my mother liked her kitchen warm. No matter what the temperature was outside, every morning Jean padded slowly from her bedroom in the front part of the house into the kitchen and turned on the gas stove to heat up the house. I often thought she kept the oven on to get her juices flowing for the day. After looking through the cabinets to find her old black cast-iron skillet, which she hid from us every night, Jean placed the pan in the warm oven to season it before cooking. While it was heating, Jean paced around the kitchen checking on her other pots and pans to see if anything was out of place. After lining up her cooking utensils on the counter, my mother would begin making up the breakfast menu in her head. A typical breakfast was scrambled eggs with onions and green peppers, toast, bacon or hot sausage, buttermilk biscuits and Tang, the popular powdered orange juice drink of the sixties. Jean and Grandma, who was a great cook, kept the kitchen fires burning from morning to night. They were always stirring up something, frying something, smothering something, smoking up the kitchen. I know now that the secret ingredient Jean put in everything she cooked was love.

WE WERE ALL about sharing. In a family as large as ours, we had to be. Jean drilled into us that we had to stick together—unity. It was hard to argue with her.

Jean's family history had made family loyalty and family ties very important to her. In 1832, when her family was sold into slavery in Richmond, Virginia, her great-great-grandparents were split from their children. The four little children—Pauline, Amelia, Benjamin and Julia—were put on a boat and shipped to the port of New Orleans. Jean told us, later one morning her family was displayed on a block at the slave terminal located on Drive and Melphomene

Streets. Colonel Charlie Welch, a wealthy plantation owner from West Feliciana Parish north of Baton Rouge, went out that day to purchase one "buck." But when he saw Benjamin, a tall, stocky Black man clinging to and holding on to his three little baby sisters, he decided to buy all four of them. The family worked on that plantation until slavery ended in 1863. Julia, one of the youngest girls, married William Brown, who also came down from Richmond and worked on the same plantation. Gradually, the family moved back down the river to New Orleans. And so, after such a start, the family story says we stick together.

Everywhere I went, I had to hold the hands of my younger brothers and sisters, since I was one of the oldest. If my older sister Cheryl was with us, she had to hold my hand. We'd walk along the train tracks heading to school, our hands locked together, in the Brazile family formation. As kids we thought the rule was stupid. But Jean had enrolled everybody in the neighborhood in enforcing the rule, and if anyone saw the Brazile kids walking without holding hands they reported us and Jean gave us hell.

GRANDMA, FRANCES BRAZILE, was born in Magnolia, Mississippi, in 1887. I was in awe of her. She walked with a cane with her head up all the time as if she were in control of the world. She stopped working early on to take care of her children. After giving birth to thirteen children, she retired to a small seamstress business that earned her enough to work from home. After my grandfather's death just months after my birth, Grandma lived off his pension from the Illinois Central Railroad, the IC, and a small allocation from Social Security. Grandpa Louis Brazile Sr. was born in 1882 in Tarboro, North Carolina. Grandma called him "Pappa" and had met him when she was getting off the train in Baton Rouge in the early 1900s. Grandpa was a fireman on a train that once carried federal troops from Illinois to the South during the Civil War. At the time, my grandpa was working for the IC with his good friend Austin White. One day while the train was held over in Baton Rouge, Austin set Grandpa up on a blind date with his girlfriend Mary Lou's sister Frances. Sparks must have flown, because my grandparents were married in less than six months. After the wedding, they made their way down to New Orleans.

My grandmother was really my best friend. I was her confidante. Thanks to her, I knew how to read before I started school. She'd use the daily newspaper, the New Orleans *Times-Picayune,* or the *Louisiana Weekly* to coach me. By six o'clock in the morning, Grandma and I would be lying across her bed reading the morning headlines. She'd make coffee—the strong kind, with chicory, and put Pet evaporated milk in it. I started drinking coffee at age five, imitating Grandma. We would sit in her bed reading the newspaper, drinking coffee and eating buttermilk biscuits, and then we would cut out our coupons and she would tell me the stores where I could go to get savings for Jean. My grandma would tell me stories about everybody on the block, so thanks to her I knew everybody's business—what Miss Olsie put in her hot tamales recipe and what was wrong with Miss Lucy's children. All the gossip was consumed with our breakfast.

I didn't know it then, but Grandma was my first mentor. I knew she loved me. She encouraged me to fly when others wanted to keep me grounded. She affirmed my big dreams and answered all the questions I asked and never told me they were crazy. She taught me how to manage money, listen to other people and to always respect my elders. Not until I was in my twenties did I grow to be as close to my mother as I was for most of my life to Grandma. Those mornings in bed with her were a kind of school for my spirit.

The only argument I ever remember my mother and grandmother having was over me. I was in the first grade. Thanks to Grandma, I was good with words and so I repeated every word I ever heard. One day I came home from school and asked my grandmother what is f-u-c-k. When Jean heard me say that she slapped me right across the room. Grandma picked me up, put her arms around me so my mother couldn't give me a second slap and told Jean, "You need to teach her these things. She can't figure these words out by herself. Jean, you know she likes to read and you've got to help her. You can't *tell* her that she can't say it. You've got to tell her *why* she can't say it."

Grandma was proud of me and loved me just as I was. When we'd all arrive at Jean's mama's house she would greet us outside and inspect us on the sidewalk for any change in size or color of our skin. Although we were all Negroes (being Black would come later in my childhood), Jean's mama lived in mortal fear that we would get darker than we already were, and that being so dark would make our lives even harder. My brother Teddy Man and I were the darkest of the kids, and we had a special bond. I think in part because of that Jean's mama would constantly lecture Teddy Man and me about staying in the shade or, even better, just staying in the house all day in the summer to avoid the sun. I hated it when she talked like that but didn't know what to say or do.

One Sunday during a July 4 outing at Uncle Johnny's house, Mama told Jean, "Donna and Teddy are getting too dark. Keep them inside or they're gonna have a whole lot of problems later on in life." I ran outside and told Sheila what Jean's mama said. Sheila told Cheryl and the whispering spread from child to child to adult. I was less than seven years old, and worried about how dark I was. I was a child, a Black child, and I didn't care about my appearance. I wondered even then how I would look with a wide nose, supernappy wirelike hair, and white skin. Jean's mama, for all her concern about color, loved us all deeply, and I know now that all her experiences as a Negro woman told her that her fear for Teddy Man and me was justified. But at seven I was hurt. I needed to cry. But I never did.

Later that night, back home in Kenner, I went to Grandma to tell her what Jean's mama had said. Grandma was dark, a deep bronze mahogany color, much darker than Jean's mama. I liked Grandma's skin color. It was my color. I didn't know how to begin the conversation, how to repeat what Jean's mama had said, so I asked Grandma, "What color should I be?" She laughed and told me that I was going to be a little darker than some of my brothers and sisters. She told me it was natural to be dark and reminded me that many of her thirteen children, including my father, were dark.

I chose to listen to Grandma instead of Jean's mama and played, jumped, climbed trees, ran on the train tracks, sat in the backyard and even tried to talk to the big bad sun. Nonetheless, until she died in 1994, Jean's mama constantly complained that I was getting "too

Black." At some point I learned that she was referring to my attitudes, my politics, even more than the color of my skin. Being Black and accepting my darkness became a powerful and potent weapon for me in a city whose Negro elite prided itself on their straight hair, light skin and White features. By their definition and according to their beliefs and the beliefs of a lot of other Blacks, I had neither the right color tone nor hair texture to succeed in life. But what was a curse to some made me different, and I liked being different. In a strange way I even grew to feel superior to lighter-skinned Black kids because they had to work at staying light and I didn't. Grandma called my color a blessing from God. I believed her. Besides, I didn't like getting my hair straightened with a hot comb and warm grease oozing over my scalp so my coarse hair could be combed out and braided. The entire process unnerved me. In my diary, which I started writing around the age of five, I wrote, "God give me an Afro."

I learned as a child to respect my parents' rules and their "laws of behavior." I respected those rules but I didn't always follow them. In fact, I was the leader of dissent, often organizing my younger brothers, sisters, neighbors and little cousins into mischief to defy our parents and their rules. As a result, as early as I can remember, every inch of my body had scars from the leather belt or wounds from the wet switch, a slender branch picked by Jean or Grandma from the weeping willow tree in our backyard. I wore my scars boldly and my wounds in defiance of orders I thought were inconsistent with the lessons my parents were preaching. In my diary I would write, "They hurt me badly today."

But despite all the whippings I got, I continued to be disobedient and "too smart" for my age. I was always big, tall, lanky and older-looking than I actually was. Looking older helped me to act older, too. I challenged my parents at times and caught hell for it. But the messages I got from my family were contradictory.

Grandma kept telling me I had to succeed at everything I did. There was no room for failure, which upset me because it meant that I couldn't make mistakes. And she taught me to stand up, fight back. Grandma told me early on that I was the strong one, the child who could bear any weight, do anything. Everybody, including my uncle Sporty, aunt Pinkey, uncle Johnny and aunt Ethel, reinforced this view. No one gave me time to just be a child. I had to grow up to listen to them and respond to their needs. But I was full of contradictions, too, for as much as I loved being "in charge," a tomboy and running and playing outside, my favorite place was to be up with the grown-ups listening to them talking, laughing, lying, as they drank beer, listening to music and cooking up something to eat. I knew even as a kid that there was something mystical, magical, about what the grown-ups were saying, and I wanted to hear their secrets. I wanted to know everything they knew. They used to call me "tape recorder" or "Nosey Nancy" because I could repeat verbatim whatever they said. Jean would warn her friends, "Watch out, Donna is listening to every word and she'll repeat it." Indeed, I was working on this book even then.

There was an irresistible rhythm to my childhood and a lot of that rhythm came from speech, from language, from talking. It wasn't just the rhythm of the music Lionel played over and over on Friday and Saturday nights to get over the workweek and steel himself for the one about to begin. It wasn't just the sounds from Aunt Pinkey's house, where she lived the life of the party every day. I was deeply influenced by the sounds of hearing old people talk—sounds of wisdom and joy. The old people were just plain ol' happy. Sure, they complained about their aches and pains. They talked up a headache or said they were getting tired, and the only way to stop the pain was to bring them an ice-cold Coca-Cola, a Goody's (powdered aspirin), some sweets like peppermints or a piece of pecan candy and sit down to listen to their stories. But they had such good stories to tell about growing up in Louisiana. Life was a daily adventure of running from snakes or looking for bait to go fishing. Everyone worked. No one sat home complaining. The old folks, like Ms. Dorothy down Filmore Street, drilled work ethics into me and the other children on the block.

Sitting on the porch in rocking chairs listening to wonderful little tales of their youth left us with the impression that our lives weren't so bad. After all, many of them knew the horrors of slavery or could tell you what it was like before people had electricity or running water. I thought the purpose of these stories was to remind us how lucky we were, because even though we didn't have much, we had more than they had had. The other stories always reflected their love of the Spirit and God. Yes, Jesus was famous in my neighborhood. We children heard all about God and the miracles and faith of the ancient people. In between stories, I recall them saying "Lord this and Lord that." So one day I worked up the courage to ask Grandma who the Lord was. "Grandma, you talk about the Lord all the time," I said. "What is he like?" She looked at me and said, "The Lord giveth and the Lord takes away. The Lord knows everything and everybody." So, Lord knows, I adopted the same language in my stories and speech. "Lord, look what I've done to my hair." "Lord, what about school?" "Lord, can you spare a dime and give us some money at home?" The Lord seemed to know everything on Filmore Street and my days were filled with the stories the old folks told of the families who lived on our street. But I was never to repeat or spread the stories. If I did tell anyone, the Lord would come after me and tell *my* secrets.

For all my bravado, I was a scared little girl who wanted to be accepted and to be told I was right. This was not the case in the Brazile household. The only time we children were given permission to talk was when an adult said we could. I wrote in my diary how unfair that was. I had a strong sense of justice early on. In my diary I wrote that children should be able to talk back to adults if they believed they were right. I wanted to talk. I had a big mouth and couldn't keep it shut. So my siblings and I developed a new rule: "no back talk." Simply, we were allowed to leave the room or the table without explaining our motives. It helped us to cope with our limited circumstances.

My first priority was school. I loved reading and I enjoyed going to school where I would just speak up every day. Grandma encouraged me to read everything I could. She gave me Bibles, novenas, and even her prescriptions to read. My other love was music. Jean's mama kept her kitchen radio on the gospel station WYLD-AM or WBOK-AM when we visited her. So I learned to enjoy music. I loved jazz, soul and gospel. My other major goal was to start working to make money to help out the family. I'd make a list of the things I loved. On another sheet of paper I would list the things I disliked about myself or that I knew I would have to change or overcome because they would stop me from reaching my goals. This was a very long and interesting list that included my hair texture, hair length, clothes, shoes, playing with baby dolls and games that made no sense.

I tried to encourage other kids to make lists of things they enjoyed doing. Teddy Man followed in my footsteps, but no one else cared. Teddy Man was my ace in the hole, a sister's brother. I included him in everything I did, including my adventures to the levee, my business to make money and my backup job of running errands for neighbors. As a boy he had tools—like hammers and screwdrivers—and toys I didn't have—like red wagons. And I could play with them when my older sisters weren't looking. Cheryl and Sheila often got on my last nerves. They were perfect; I was not. So I turned to sports while they spent their time being pretty little girls with long straight hair and colorful ribbons to match their clothes. The only way I could compete with them was to beat them at board games. Jean bought us games that involved multiple players, like bingo, checkers and Monopoly. I learned to play these games, often as the banker, and when I played I played to win.

Like most kids, during summer vacations my brothers and sisters stayed in bed too long. Not me, I got up early, picked up the newspaper, watered the plants outside, drank coffee with Grandma and began my day earning a living. Yes, I was an old spirit. After reading the news and clipping my store coupons, I was ready for a good day's work. The summer between my sixth and seventh birthday I wanted to make some additional money. After talking with Mr. Joe, who owned the corner store, I decided to recycle soft drink bottles and sell them back to him and Mr. Willie at the Kenner grocery store. In order for me to really succeed at this enterprise, however, I needed help. So after talking it over with Jean and Grandma, I hired my two brothers Teddy Man and Chet, my cousin Cedric Henderson, and my neighbors Marc Johnson from across the street and Jeffrey Conrad, who lived near the train tracks. They were younger but they had wagons, big wheels and more strength to lift the carton of empty bottles. Little girls weren't supposed to hang out every day looking in gutters for old bottles or in trash bins. So I hired them as my subcontractors and gave them a cut from the proceeds. Besides, I needed their wheels to carry the bottles home that we found so I could clean them up before returning them to the store for five cents a bottle. This business brought in an additional three to four dollars a week, enough to pay my helpers fifty cents apiece (big money back then) and give Jean her cut—one dollar. Everybody got a cut from me. I used my extra savings to buy candy for the little kids (key to winning support) and save for my Converse high-tops. I hated sandals—all types of sandals, especially the open-toe variety. One of my other businesses was a bait and tackle shop, digging earthworms from the ground and selling them for a dollar a bucket. This was slimy business, but my crew and I found fishermen and -women all over Kenner who needed our service. By the time I turned seven, I was putting aside about five dollars a week and paying the boys a dollar each, and I upgraded my mother's pay to two dollars. Still, I wanted more money to help out the family and buy my reading materials that now included *Ebony* and *Jet* magazines and the *Louisiana Weekly*. Those were magazines that I had Jean's permission to read. There were certain others that were off-limits and I would later learn a painful lesson about the cost of reading them.

At night, after reading children's books and the Bible to my little sisters and brothers, I pulled out some of the books about "the revolution" or pamphlets disseminated by the Black Muslims. One night, Jean caught me reading *Muhammad Speaks,* the newspaper of the Black Muslims and the Nation of Islam. The paper cost twenty-five cents and was cheaper than *Ebony* magazine. Like *Ebony,* the Muslim paper had great stories about Black people all over the country. That night I caught a serious ass whipping as Jean tried to beat the hell out of me for reading what she referred to as "hateful trash." I also got whipped for talking back to her, trying to defend and explain why I was reading the newspaper.

I will never forget that night. For the first time, as she raised her hand to hit me, Jean told me what I had long suspected, that she wanted me to act more like my sisters. "Shut up. Stay inside. Stop trying to run things. Behave!" The wounds did not heal quickly this time. I decided to leave the bodily marks as symbols of my courage and as evidence that I had dared to read about the problems of Black people, problems my mother didn't want me to know about. I was now eight years old, but I already had my feelings and opinions.

Yet the punishment only made me more determined to know the truth about what was happening to Black people everywhere—not only in New Orleans but around the country. I found adults and old people in the neighborhood who were willing to talk to me about the Vietnam War and the civil rights movement. Winkie, my friend Harlean's brother and the nephew of Lois Jean, who was Jean's best friend, arrived back from the war. He sat on the porch every day, staring into space and not talking to anyone about his experiences. Every day I walked out to the front yard and waved. "Hey, Winkie, you doing all right?" Winkie never struck up a conversation. He waved back and promised that after the revolution he'd discuss the war. I waited, but Winkie never stirred. In the newspapers and magazines and even some of the books I read, Black people, outside of Kenner anyway, were fighting back.

There were many who, like Jean, were afraid to discuss civil rights and Black Power. So I began to turn to God for answers. I wrote in my diary that all the adults were "too scared" to make a move or strike back. I wasn't scared, but I was unsure what I could do to help out. I was familiar with the words *civil rights, justice, freedom* and *equality*. But no one had a clue in Kenner. If they did, they didn't dare utter the words because I would have tape-recorded the conversation. God, I thought, was not afraid to listen. I did not know what to expect from my prayers, but I wrote constantly, based on everything I heard about God, that I would find the answers. The lesson I took from the beatings and the whippings was how to pray. It was a lesson that stayed with me throughout my childhood and adult life. That was a lesson my parents instructed us to follow and it was one of the few that I obeyed.

God, as Lionel constantly reminded us, was always with us. I liked that idea. I knew God and enjoyed praying all the time, as early as I can remember. Like most poor Black folks, we talked about God all the time. Lionel and Grandma taught us about angels and saints. We had statues and symbols of saints, angels and crucifixes all around the house, especially in my parents' bedroom where Lionel kept another altar. The family's Bible had colored pictures that we were told never to touch. Lionel's drawings of angels, like St. Michael and St. Anthony, and bottles of holy water filled each and every room of the house on Filmore Street. My first known prayer usually went something like this: "God, I know you made everything in creation—the birds, trees, flowers and everything underneath the stars. Yet my mother, who you created by creating her mother, is a little short on patience today. Please work with Jean and tell her to be gentle to her children, especially me, because I am trying so hard to please her." As always, I made a promise to God to give up something in exchange for my prayers being answered. Often the only thing I could bargain with was food. In exchange for one of my prayers being answered, I ate only one peanut butter sandwich. As I began to earn some money, I put more pennies each week in the "poor box" at Our Lady of Perpetual Help Catholic Church, located right near the train tracks.

We talked about God, but mine was not a household that talked a lot about love. My grandmothers affirmed me in so many ways, but the lessons were not personal; they were mostly about what we owed to others. In our home you were congratulated for getting the clothes off the line before it rained or for going outside to pick peppers or okra. When you "did good" God was happy. Lionel, Jean, and Grandma were happy. And because God was always watching, God was happy since he was always part of the conversation. Jean's Baptist upbringing and strong beliefs, which held sway over her although she didn't attend church regularly, and Lionel's Catholicism combined to create a heady Baptist/Catholic orthodoxy that scared us kids into obedience and faith. But because we were drilled with the notion that we had to be good to others and were taught to give back and sacrifice for our family, this shaped our character and, although Jean didn't know it, formed the basis for my sense of politics and social justice. They wouldn't have said it like that. Jean was afraid I'd be disappointed and hurt if I knew too much about what was happening beyond our little community.

She knew about the horrible slaying of young Emmett Till; about the civil rights workers Andrew Goodman, James Chaney, and Michael Schwerner, who were brutally killed in Mississippi; and that hundreds of children, some not much older than me, had been arrested in places like Birmingham, Alabama. She wanted to protect me from that fate. When she punished me she wanted to take the rebelliousness, the curiosity from my spirit—traits that could easily get a Black person in the South killed whether they were in the movement or not. But that didn't mean she didn't want me to care about people in need. She was simply sheltering me in the only way she knew how.

I prayed, I wrote and I read. And once I learned to read and understand what was happening around me, I wanted to participate in the struggle. I had fantasies of leaving Kenner, Filmore Street and "making something of myself." All so Grandma, Jean and Jean's mama could be proud. Living so close to the river, I thought the best way to leave home was to cruise down the Mississippi until we reached the clean, warm waters of the Gulf of Mexico. From the Gulf, I could explore the new world and see the Caribbean or go to Africa. I imagined the Mississippi River was actually the Nile, and from atop the levee, built to protect the city from flooding, I could see the giant Egyptian pyramids and talk to the pharaohs and the living gods of ancient Africans that I had read about. I enjoyed sitting on the levee. It was my mountaintop.

Other times I imagined leaving Kenner on one of the trains my grandpa and uncle Sporty worked on. The daily noise and movement of trains coming and going past our house sparked this fantasy. I'd leave home and go to some faraway city in old Europe. Sitting on the front porch we often watched Uncle Sporty, a porter on Amtrak, wave to us as the train pulled out of Kenner, bound for New York or Illinois. While the old folks talked, I would drift away and see myself in Vienna, Austria, boarding the Orient Express to Venice, a far more romantic trip than those Uncle Sporty made. I read about those cities in magazines. I wanted to leave Kenner and go to Europe. Perhaps the best way to leave, I thought, was just to catch a plane right down Airline Highway at the New Orleans International Airport. Years later, when I did leave Kenner, I sent Jean postcards from all over America, Africa, the Soviet Union and Europe. My imagination as a child helped to spark my interest in traveling and meeting people from all over the world. First, though, I had to finish my education. I wanted to learn everything about the world around me.

I spent my first few years at Ralph J. Bunche Elementary School, where a new Head Start program to teach poor kids was introduced. My mother signed up her three little girls to be part of the program and dropped us off, said hello to her old friends and caught the bus to Mrs. Hilbert's downtown. School was fun, but I soon learned it was for kids, not for someone like me. I wanted to grow up quickly and volunteer in the civil rights movement. By the time I turned eight, America was already changing. In 1964 the Civil Rights Act was passed by Congress, outlawing discrimination in public facilities. In 1965 the Voting Rights Act was passed, and in 1966, Lyndon Johnson launched the Great Society and the War on Poverty. These were the historical touchstones of my childhood and they created a charged, hopeful atmosphere in the neighborhood that encouraged my curiosity and inspired me. The leadership in the civil rights movement in my neighborhood came from the Clay and Burton families. One day word spread around town that Reverend Arthur Paul Clay, pastor of Mt. Zion Missionary Baptist Church on Clay Street, would host Dr. Martin Luther King Jr. Clay, a member of the Southern Christian Leadership Conference, was a prominent preacher in Kenner and a giant political figure. I hung out with Byron, one of his young sons. Byron taught me how to distribute leaflets about Dr. King's appearance. Naturally I wanted to get paid for it. Nevertheless, I got more than money by learning about the movement. Something was going on around me and everyone was talking about Dr. King.

A week later we got our chance to hear Dr. King on the radio, but my parents forbade us from working in any way with people involved in the movement. Of course, I didn't exactly follow Jean's orders on this one. At school my friends with parents active in the movement would bring me materials to read at night. I felt proud to know people who worked with Dr. King and it led me to ask the old people for stories they had heard or read about him. And so the day Martin

Luther King was shot in Memphis, Tennessee, changed my life forever. I made the decision to go to Taylor Street, the next block over,
to officially join the movement and work with Mrs. Rosemary Minor
and Mrs. Felice McMiller, who had become active in both politics
and the movement. I was only eight years old, but I wanted to get involved. I got tired of waiting to grow up. I joined the movement on
Thursday, April 4, 1968.

CHAPTER TWO

BLACKENED CATFISH

Some call blackened Mississippi River catfish hot and spicy, while others say it's greasy and delicious. It is a staple throughout South Louisiana. There is no stronger taste than fish blackened with strong Cajun seasoning. Throughout my early years, I, too, was learning of the power of Blackness—by watching the civil rights, Black Power and Black consciousness movements change American culture and politics.

LIKE ALL BLACK FOLKS around the country, we in Kenner were shocked and saddened by the news on April 4, 1968, that Martin Luther King Jr. had been assassinated. The shock quickly turned to anger. Just after nightfall on that terrible day, at the precise moment when the streetlights came on, word began to spread up and down Filmore Street that the Black Panther Party would burn down any house that didn't have a black flag or ribbon on the outside as a sign of mourning and solidarity. When Jean heard this from her friend Ms. Beulah, Harlean's mama, who lived around the corner from us, she was busy in the kitchen fixing our dinner of fried chicken, mashed potatoes, and creamed corn and dismissed the threat. I overheard her tell Grandma that the Black Panther Party was planning to start trouble. Grandma, always the mediator, listened to Jean's complaints and told her to watch TV and see what other folks were planning to do. We were glued to the TV for hours that evening and the days that followed.

It was a quiet time in our normally boisterous household. It reminded me of the days after John F. Kennedy's death, how quiet everybody and everything was. Grandma urged us to pray, to be still and to mourn. Jean, however, was in denial, saying we ought to turn off the TV because the coverage of the events was too sad, and that we needed to go on with our lives. But I know she was hurting inside—hurting deep inside. We all were. The Panther threat seemed outrageous, but over one hundred cities saw riots and protests by Blacks in the coming days, and the National Guard was called in to put down disturbances in Washington, D.C. Scores of people would be wounded or killed, and in Louisiana, hundreds of local students held marches in New Orleans and Baton Rouge to protest King's murder. Bobby Kennedy, a candidate for president, had been scheduled to come to speak at Dillard University on April 5, and the news soon reported that he had to cancel. The city was filled with all sorts of rumors. Our phone was constantly ringing with family members checking on each other.

As usual, I stuck my nose in "old folks'" business. What if the Panthers were serious? Back in 1965, Hurricane Betsy destroyed our home; we lost just about everything, including our barn, front porch, roof, and the tall "Joe Joe" tree out back. God knows, my family could not withstand another calamity. This was no time to ignore the real pain of Black people, pain even I felt at the age of nine. So that night I defied Jean, and after everyone was asleep, I snuck out the back door and hung one of Jean's black scarves on the front door, right under our address, 529, with a thumbtack. I know that Grandma saw me, but she never gave me up. On the night of King's assassination, I was baptized by the fires raging all over America. I took a stand. That night I cried myself to sleep. I was scared.

Several of the neighbors gathered out front to discuss the rumors. Mr. Joe and Mr. Jumel did not think much of them. Jumel, like my dad, carried an assortment of old guns and knives. He was ready. Mr. Joe tried to calm everyone and told Jean to keep everyone inside. My aunt Ethel, as always, was peeking out her front window looking up and down the street. Grandma did not bother to share her opinion. She was glued to the TV news. Something big was happening all over Louisiana and the world as I knew it to be.

The next day I heard from the Johnson family across the street that there was going to be a memorial vigil for Dr. King at their church, Greater Mt. Zion Baptist, which was four blocks from our house. Of course, I wanted to go and, of course, Jean said I couldn't. But it was too late. As far as I was concerned I was already in the movement. I had defied my mother with the scarf. Defying her again seemed inevitable and easy. I snuck out of the house and walked along the train tracks alone to the service at Greater Mt. Zion. It was cold that night. It started raining early that morning. Grandma told us that God "was upset about Dr. King." I felt a mixture of emotions welling up inside me. On the one hand I was scared. What about Lionel? He was a Black man, too. What about my mother riding the bus through Harahan—places where the old folks told us never to wander off to even during the day. I took the shortcut through the trail past the blackberries and strawberry bushes on Taylor Street, past the big pecan trees on Jackson Street, and the corn plants next to the tracks on Webster Street over to Clay Street. I took the backyard trail so that nobody would see me. This was the same path that I walked through so often with my brothers Teddy Man and Chet, along with my cousin Cedric, on the way to church or another one of our daily adventures.

When I got to the church I knew I couldn't go in. I was Catholic and Lionel had warned all of us that the Lord would strike us down if we ever stepped into any non-Catholic house of worship. The church was very small, but that night it was all lit up. People were coming in after work. The pews were full. I stood on the corner of Clay Street and saw my friend Byron Clay, the son of Reverend Arthur Paul Clay. I did not know much about preaching because the priest at Our Lady of Perpetual Help spoke in Latin. I stood in front of the church listening to the sorrowful but triumphant voices of the choir singing "This Little Light of Mine," and later I wrote in my diary "my light is going to shine too." The singing stopped and I heard this loud voice. Reverend Clay started to preach about the life of Dr. King, all he had done and the high price he had paid in the prime of his life. And he said that we would carry on Dr. King's work. I stood there for half an hour, scared of being seen but feeling a new kind of courage, a new sense of confidence at the thought of what I had done by coming to the memorial. I knew what awaited me at home if Jean found out, but I was willing to take the risk.

When I got back home, Jean was waiting for me at the back door. Before I could reach the bottom step she grabbed me by my collar and pulled me inside. "You better be glad Lionel isn't home," she said, "because he would whip the living daylights out of you." Then she jerked me and carried me out the door and told me to go out in the backyard and get a long stem from the weeping willow tree. Aunt Ethel was looking out her bedroom window but did not say a word. I walked across her yard and pulled down one of the biggest branches and picked a nice, firm switch. I didn't mind switches from the China ball tree, the oak trees or the myrtle bushes, but the weeping willow stems were very thin and they felt sharp as knives against your skin. Because I was a little wet from the weather and from running all the way home, the whipping was extremely painful. It was the worst punishment I had ever had. But the next day, before school, I showed my older sisters and little brothers my bruises; I was actually proud of them. To me they were symbols. "You see what she beat me for," I told them. "You all know why she beat me?" I asked them angrily, proudly. "Jean's not free. We're not free. No one is free. We must fight, too." I was fired up, not broken. And I told them that my little light was going to shine. The scarf, the memorial service, the whipping, all had combined to create a defining moment for me. From that point on, I vowed to take the lead inside our house and stand up for what I believed in.

Still, I had to nurse my wounds, and I talked to Grandma, who was reading the New Orleans *Times-Picayune*. I told her how sad I felt and that we had to do something. We all had to do something. Despite the whipping, my convictions grew stronger. The word was out that Dr. King was killed by a White man, and I just couldn't understand why anyone would want to kill him. Grandma comforted me and told me not to worry, that everything was in God's hands. But I kept hearing about the Black Panther Party, and they believed that some things were in our hands and that, just like Dr. King, there was something we could do.

Just like on the home front, at school my third-grade teacher,

Miss Pierce, sought to reassure us that everything would be okay. I felt like everybody was trying to hide the truth from us. Despite what the grown-ups whom I trusted told me, I felt that now that Dr. King was dead, things would never be okay again. Still, after King's assassination, Black people in Kenner became more vocal, more willing to talk about the long-standing social problems that plagued the Black community. Prior to King's death, the community was virtually apolitical. Nobody talked politics, community action or change. It was like they were asleep. The tragedy of April 4, 1968, had forced them awake. Suddenly political organizations sprang up and ordinary people wanted to see things change for Black people.

In New Orleans, the city people had been strategizing. Aunt Pinkey had grown children who were active in some of the protests and they knew what was going on around the city. My uncles Floyd, Johnny and Douglas were also active in various political clubs. I had heard a lot about the NAACP. Emmet Douglas was the state president and Reverend Clay was the Southern Christian Leadership Conference local chapter president. The civil rights movement up till then in Louisiana had been an intellectual movement of sorts. The middle-class Blacks who went to Xavier and Dillard, who lived on the other side of the tracks, had been talking about change for some time. They knew integration was coming. They knew that things had to change and that there was going to be a major shift of racial power, and they had to take part in the struggle.

The next week we stayed home for spring break. The kids gathered in our backyard, to play softball or marbles. No one was allowed to take trips into the city or to leave the general area around Kenner, especially not Harahan. After school ended that year, another tragedy hit. Bobby Kennedy was killed in California. The Kennedys were famous in our household because they were Catholic, too. Grandma told us we had to go to church for a special Mass to mourn Bobby Kennedy. When we arrived, the Black folks had to sit in the back—as always. I did not like sitting in the back and I vowed when I completed my first holy communion and made my confirmation that I would sit up front like everyone else. We prayed for Bobby Kennedy and the entire Kennedy family. Grandma had told me the Kennedys were "for Black people." I wondered out loud if they were killed for helping Black people. I could not figure it out on my own, and as usual no one was talking. That summer I did not make any money selling bait or recycling bottles. I was too busy praying and trying to read up on the civil rights movement.

Kenner was changing. On one of my prescription runs I overheard Mr. Burton talk about lawsuits. Burton Pharmacy became a gathering place for political news, and while in the store waiting for a couple of prescriptions for Ms. Olive and Mr. Jimmy to be filled, Ms. Rosemary Minor, who lived on Taylor Street, was sharing the news about her lawsuit for more public recreation centers in Kenner. I did not know Ms. Minor or her husband, Mr. Fred. They lived in a nice-size wooden house and had seven kids. Mr. Burton's wife, Shirley, a schoolteacher and administrator, was also sharing her news on the political front. As they talked, I pretended to look at the marbles. Mr. Burton's store had a little bit of everything, from books to toys for children. Once they completed their conversation. Ms. Minor looked over at me and asked, "Are you Lionel and Jean's child?" "Yes ma'am, I am. My name is Donna." She looked me up and down and said, "You come here by yourself?" I nodded my head and she smiled. Ms. Minor told the Burtons good-bye and walked out to her station wagon. "Hey," Mr. Burton said, "li'l Brazile, here's your package. Grab yourself a cookie and I'll see you tomorrow."

For the first time in a long while I was becoming excited again. The grown-ups started talking about filing lawsuits and stirring up people to get registered to vote. It was called politics and I liked hearing people talk about it. Soon, "voter education" and "voter registration" were the two words I kept hearing the activists in Kenner say again and again. Ms. Minor had a brown-and-white Ford station wagon, and she'd say, "Well, let's go to City Hall, let's talk about the things we need." Ms. Minor had a soft voice. She was cream-colored and of medium build. When she entered the room she often smiled and greeted people in a nice, loving way. I grew to like Ms. Minor a lot and felt that she was the kind of person I wanted to be. She was tough. She was strong. She had no fears. Ms. Minor was the only person who wasn't afraid to literally take on City Hall. She'd march down there and tell them that we needed a playground for the kids, better schools, paved streets, a sewage system and transportation. We had only one colored school and many of the roads in Kenner were dirt and gravel. Mrs. Burton was ready to assist in organizing the people of Kenner.

Transportation is a big issue when you're poor. You are literally stuck. And the buses that ran through Kenner had a drop-dead time. They would carry you from Kenner to New Orleans, but not to where the White people lived in the suburban areas. If you had to go where Black people lived you had to transfer to several buses, going miles around the White areas, out of the way, in order to get to Black neighborhoods. Kenner is a small city. When I was growing up, the population was less than 67,000 people. Before the big interstate system was built we had only two ways to get to New Orleans. We were sandwiched in between two great bodies of water. At times I felt isolated, lost and abandoned growing up on Filmore Street. I did not quite fit in. I wanted to be in the city where all the action was beginning to simmer. When I felt alone, I would walk down the street all the way to the levee that kept the Mississippi River from overflowing into our backyards and talk to God. I really wanted to leave Kenner and start working for the civil rights movement.

My cousin Ethel Mae, who had spent time traveling across the country, came back home and had her friends over to play cards, eat, drink and talk politics. I was excited sitting under the porch listening to Ethel Mae talk about the civil rights movement and what was happening all over the South. Ms. Minor came by the house one day to ask Jean if I could help her out with some projects. "What kind of projects?" Jean asked. Ms. Minor explained that she needed some help going from house to house, business to business, the barbershop and the corner store to engage people in conversations about getting registered to vote. Ms. Minor had already enlisted me to be the person who helped her recruit kids for the girls' softball league. She had several children; my little sisters Lisa and Demetria, and Elise from across the street, were my contribution to the team. She made me an assistant coach because I could help lead. So the year after Dr. King's death and the election of Richard Nixon, a Republican, to the White

House, I drove around Kenner with Ms. Minor soaking up every-thing she talked about. It was like having a private tutor in political activism. She told me that the mayoral race and the election of the city council were coming up in 1970. That fall we had to get more people registered. If Joseph Yenni won, we could get a playground built in South Kenner.

Yenni was White and he needed the Black vote to win. But he couldn't get the Black vote unless more Blacks registered. Everyone was now focused on voter registration, including the folks in the city of New Orleans. Reverend Avery Alexander was leading some of the protests down at City Hall, and I read in the papers that students at Xavier, Southern and Dillard were organizing voter registration drives. Now there was interest in voting in Kenner, and in having a say in the political process. And Ms. Minor wanted me to be a foot soldier in this effort. First, I had to read up on voting rights: what it was, how it was done, who was in charge and what I should say to people. It was then that I learned about Adam Clayton Powell and the rise of Black politics in New York City. All the Black magazines— *Ebony, Sepia,* and *Jet*—and the books about Black people I had hidden from Jean were an introduction to what I was learning now and a preparation for what I was about to do.

Ms. Minor turned her garage into an office, and that was her cam-paign headquarters. The garage was decorated with posters of Yenni, literature on home rule in Kenner and all sorts of materials and papers. I started out initially by myself, going door to door, telling people they had to register. When someone said they would register I took down their name and Ms. Minor gave me five cents a name.

After a while I drafted my little gang of workers—Teddy Man, Chet, Cedric, Jeff and Marc. The boys had bicycles. I often took over Chet's bike and he rode on the handlebars. Chet was very skinny and I could pick him up and carry him anywhere. Marc, who grew up in a large family across the street, was also a good talker and smart. I thought Marc would be the preacher in the group. Teddy Man wanted to be a stockbroker. Chet and Cedric wanted to be firemen. Jeff had no immediate plans but wanted to help us work. Marc, who is now a city council member from that area, was a natural leader.

We took on Filmore Street from track to track, over to Taylor, Jackson and straight to Webster Street, where we stopped over at Sneaky Bird's house to see if she really had monkeys, tigers and lions hidden away in the backyard to protect her big, tall pecan trees. We would make our way to Williams Boulevard, stopping by Burton's for candy, snowballs and marbles. This was fun. We enjoyed working for Ms. Minor.

The toughest part was going to the apartment buildings. To this day I hate to do voter registration in apartment buildings because the tenants seem transient. They didn't seem interested in community activities and rarely wanted to register to vote or bother with politics. But we had better luck with home owners. And the seniors were especially receptive. I think they knew how important a moment this was for Black people. They were old enough to have seen the worst of times for Blacks in the South, and believed that if we fought back with the ballot we could win. But there were people like Miss Olive and Mr. Jimmy. They didn't want to vote. Miss Olive told me "People die if we start voting." I remember begging Miss Olive to try. When I asked Miss Eddie Bee Battle, from Mississippi, if she was ready to register, she would change the subject and ask if my mother wanted fresh croakers or trout on Friday. Ms. Eddie Bee went fishing all the time.

I remember having only twelve names on my first list, people like Miss Lucie and Miss Olsie and Brenda Sullivan's mom. Then I got the Conrads. Jeffrey's dad, Charles Conrad, was a businessman who was already registered, but his wife, Eunice, wasn't. Not everybody got registered, but things were changing in Kenner and I was part of that change. I knew people who were registered to vote and those who were too afraid to get involved and that left a strong impression on me. At the end of the day I would come back to Ms. Minor's home office and give her the list of people I had talked to, who were registered and who needed forms. I felt that this was the most fun, the most exciting thing anybody could do.

Grandma had paved the way for this flurry of political activism by talking to Jean. I had learned by now how to make my mother happy. I couldn't make her happy with my appearance. Unlike my older sisters, I hated to dress up and I prayed she would lay off my hair. I was nothing like my sisters Cheryl and Sheila. They played with Barbie dolls, Easy-Bake ovens and sewing sets. My brothers had trucks and a red wagon, and I found those toys more useful to my business. The Barbie dolls couldn't do anything for me. Lionel taught me how to do carpentry work and I was good at building things—just like him. I knew I was a bona fide tomboy and if I forgot, my two older sisters reminded me every day of my life. It didn't matter. I thought they were jealous of me because I knew every boy in Kenner. Like boys, I enjoyed playing basketball, going hunting for wild game with home-made slingshots and fishing in the mighty Mississippi River. Of course, my tomboyish ways didn't sit too well with some of Jean's friends, who didn't mind telling her that she had to do something. Feeling pressure from her friends and worried about how unlike my sisters I was, Jean told Grandma in exasperation that at some point I was just going to have to grow up and be like the other girls. When I found out she'd said this, I told Jean that if I grew up to be like the other girls, then I'd be going after her husband, like all the other girls. You know, my mom never ever again talked to me about what she or anybody else thought of me.

I was doing very well in school and I was bringing home money as a result of several side businesses. I was bringing in ten dollars, some-times fifteen dollars a week, lots of money for a ten-year-old girl. I filed to start paying Social Security taxes when I was twelve. I was an ambitious entrepreneur. So my mother let up on her frequent criti-cism that I wasn't always neat, prim and proper in the way I looked and dressed, and just warned me as she told all of us daily "Don't get in too much trouble, because trouble will always follow you." Still, I began to enjoy my childhood doing things my way. Jean knew and respected Ms. Minor and liked that she was keeping me busy, but not so busy that I couldn't watch out for my younger siblings.

That summer, an average day for me consisted of rising early and performing a number of chores around the house—soaking the tow-els in the bathtub, rinsing and hanging them out to dry on the clothesline. Next, I'd go get the morning paper for Grandma and buy her a big giant cola to go with her Goody's powdered aspirin. Like a lot of the old people I knew, Grandma took her Goody's at the same time every day—before noon. These were people who lived into their eighties and nineties. Grandma even made some of her medicines from roots, tree drippings and herbs.

Before I devoted the afternoon to voter registration, I would do my prescription runs for the old people in the neighborhood. I was fast on my feet. My prescription runs brought in a dollar or two every week.

My grandmother and Aunt Ethel taught me how to garden. They both enjoyed flowers, especially in the spring. They taught me how to plant according to the moon and from signs that I could read from the trees. Mr. Jimmy taught me how to repair lawn mowers and how to cut grass, trim hedges and pull up weeds. I could landscape with the best of them. I knew about tulips, gladiolas, daffodils, the bulbs and what time you put them in. I had a lot of things covered, whether it was planting your garden, getting your medicine, cashing your check or picking up your liquor. I'd go to the Kenner grocery store on the corner of Taylor and Short Streets, a block away from my house across the double set of train tracks. Mr. Willy, at the Kenner Corner Store, got the calls and soon I was on my way over. He placed the beer or bourbon or wine in a brown bag and I ran home. Most people let me keep the change, so if beer was sixty-eight cents a quart and you gave me a dollar I would get to keep thirty-two cents. I kept a little safe box under my bed or in Grandma's cedar closet.

Then Shasta Cola built a plant near the airport and they threw away cans of soda that had dents. In the late afternoons we would go over to Compromise Street where the ice plant was and get a huge block of ice. My brother would ride his bicycle, I would run or walk behind him, and we would sell dented sodas to the men leaving the Pellerin Factory on Jackson Street. This was a quick moneymaker for us, and soon I brought some other kids like Bone and Winkie, who lived across the track, to help us out.

I now had employees to pay and materials to buy. While my brothers would be playing with their marbles, I'd be counting my change. Often Jean would borrow money from me and she didn't have to pay me back. Lionel worked two, sometimes three jobs to help ends meet. I felt sorry for my dad. I wanted to help out, too. The money I made helped the family and gave me a sense of independence and accomplishment. I don't remember being treated like a child or thinking of myself as a child. I was always a very old spirit. But there was a war going on inside me. I wanted to know everything the old folks knew, and yet I hungered to be treated like a child. I took on responsibility so easily. It was hard to resist telling my siblings about family woes or trouble in the neighborhood. Once I overheard Jean talking to her friends about Ms. Hermione. Rumors had it that she was pregnant again. Like an adult, I had to tell someone so I confided in Grandma.

This was the summer that I began to think about the stories that Grandma had told me about her life and her family in a new way. Whenever I would ask her if she had been a slave, or how her family had been treated by Whites, she always lowered her head. When I wrote about these conversations in my diary I recounted how sad I felt seeing Grandma's reaction. Around the time I started reading more than the morning paper, she began telling me stories about her mother, whose name was Harriet. Harriet grew up on a plantation in Mississippi where she was often beaten and scolded. Grandma gave me enough information to understand that slavery was bad and what followed wasn't better. At first, she told me her family's history in bits and pieces; she told me as much as she thought I could handle. It wasn't until after Dr. King died that she gave me a full account of her own pain and suffering. Grandma ran away from Mississippi to Baton Rouge, and Grandpa was introduced to her by her older sister. She was tired of being beaten by White people. She told me, "We used to get whipped and chased." She told me about how bad it was in Mississippi and how Blacks couldn't walk on the same side of the street as White people. She made me sad. I loved Grandma so much. As I moved closer to her in bed at night, I asked God, "How could anyone hurt a little girl like Grandma?"

I now know that so much of what I did and so many of my political beliefs spring from my grandmother's influence. Grandma taught me about love and about strength. She told me never to follow anybody, but to take my own path. She was all about affirmation. Ours was not a household that spent a lot of time talking about love; in fact, I don't think love was ever discussed. At times we'd get a pat on the back or a slap across the shoulders as a sign of approval or affection. But there was no hugging, no kissing and rarely even a simple embrace.

Ours was a household where you were congratulated when you did good. And doing good was good because God was happy and your parents were happy. God was always part of the conversation: "God is watching you." "God wants you to help others, especially the poor and hungry." "God's not pleased." I was and I am still so afraid of God. Lionel even went so far as to tell us that God would strike us down if we lied. Grandma told us that rain was a sign that God was angry, so every time it rained I thought it was because God had caught me telling a lie or something. Now, in spring, it rains almost daily in Louisiana, so you can imagine my anxiety level. But like always, my grandmother's message assuaged my anxieties. She taught us that if you do good work, like running errands for her friends who could no longer walk to the store, that was not only good from a Christian perspective, but it was also good because it taught me character. I could even get my blessings. I thought to myself, this is a bargain.

Grandma helped me to grow up after Martin Luther King Jr. and Bobby Kennedy died. She made me understand that the world was not black and white, and that our faith was important. When I showed my temper my grandmother would remind me that I was not of God. To bring home her point, she would quote Galatians 6:9, one of her favorite Bible verses, "Do not grow weary in doing good, for in due season, you'll reap a harvest if you do not give up." Despite all the pain of growing up in Mississippi, raising thirteen children with my grandpa and seeing America slowly move away from its segregationist past, Grandma never lost her patience or her faith. Along with Ms. Minor, Ms. Miller, Mr. Joe, Ms. Burton, Mr. Burton, my cousins, aunts and uncles, I was ready to fight for the underdog and for freedom. My family kept pointing me, the summer after King died, toward the road I wanted to take, a path that it seemed sometimes only I could see.

CHAPTER THREE

RED BEANS AND RICE

There are few dishes as synonymous with New Orleans as red beans and rice: red kidney beans mixed with Louisiana long-grain rice, ham bone, andouille sausage, cayenne, peppers and local spices. Traditionally, it was served on Monday—washday—so the red beans could simmer and cook all day while attention was paid to the laundry drying on the clothesline. For me, the dish also represented the mixture of dark and light, black and white, that I would encounter when we were bused to new schools to achieve integration.

THE PUSH FOR EQUALITY moved into the Jefferson Parish Public Schools in August of 1971. Orleans Parish had experienced it a couple of years before it rode through our neighborhood. It didn't sit well with the Black folks or the White folks. Both communities were in chaos over the timing and how it would be implemented. There was a lot of confusion about busing in the Black community of Kenner, and it wasn't welcomed as a remedy for generations of segregation in the separate and unequal school systems. We loved our local schools. They were located in our neighborhoods. The teachers knew our parents and they lived in the community. There was no transition period for us to adjust to the new system. Our parents were informed in the heat of the summer that they should prepare us to go to a different school. The White schools across town in Metairie and Harahan were better equipped, often more modern, and the students had newer textbooks. But the school I was supposed to have attended, Bunche Village Middle School, went from Head Start to eighth grade. It was named for the famed U.N. ambassador Ralph J.

Bunche. I was ready to take Mr. Marchand's history class where he wove Black history into American history and made it so interesting and challenging. In fifth grade, Mr. Marchand had told us to read up on the sixteenth president, Abraham Lincoln, and to learn about our history. Mr. Marchand was an inspiration. We were taught by teachers who were our neighbors, who knew our families and really cared about how well we did in school.

Busing was one of the worst public policy decisions ever made. We were bused past schools within walking distance of our homes, miles away into neighborhoods where we weren't welcomed, weren't liked and which were often inaccessible by public transportation. Only the Johnson and Conrad families had cars. Busing began for me at age eleven, when I was about to enter the seventh grade.

Lionel, Aunt Lucille and my cousin Ethel Mae had attended Washington Elementary School on Clay Street, also known as the Kenner Colored School. They did not know a thing about T. H. Harris Junior High, where I would be bused to in the fall, or the other schools in the predominantly White areas. There were some White students who were bused to Bunche Village Middle School in our neighborhood, but for the most part busing only went one way, taking Black kids into White neighborhoods.

Jean received notice in early August that Sheila and I would be attending T. H. Harris Junior High, on West Metairie and Elsie Avenue—almost four miles from our home. I knew nothing about T. H. Harris. Who was he? I went to the library to learn more about him and try to figure out a little bit about the school. I was only able to find out that T. H. Harris was somehow involved in President Theodore Roosevelt's Spanish War. From the very first day, life at T. H. Harris was horrible. When my parents learned that Reverend Williams would be our bus driver, Sheila and I were scared. From the first day we left Filmore Street, things were tense.

Metairie, like Harahan, was not a welcoming place for Blacks. Both Lionel and Jean had odd jobs on the weekend in the area working for the Wren family. Mr. Wren often came to pick up my mom early on Saturday morning or called the Blue Cab to bring them home. Blacks rarely crossed over Airline Highway to shop or visit

Metairie, a vast working-class White suburban area. David Duke, the former grand wizard of the Ku Klux Klan, called Metairie home in the eighties; he was extremely popular there. T. H. Harris was a big redbrick school with a large playground and nicely landscaped property. A week after we arrived at the school, lawsuits to stop busing were being fought out in the courts. On our first day, Vice Principal Causey was standing in the front of the school to greet us. Mr. Causey came up to the bus and thanked Reverend Williams for bringing us to school and told him when he should come back to pick us up. And then he walked away, grabbed his bullhorn and shouted, "Please get off the bus and follow me." God, we were nervous.

A week earlier the U.S. Supreme Court, with a written order from Thurgood Marshall, had ordered the Jefferson Parish schools to open to Black students. The leaders of the Stop Busing Crusade had appealed to President Richard Nixon to intervene. The leaders of the antibusing movement made it clear that they did not want any Black children in their schools. Every day I would read their comments in the *State Item* (the afternoon paper) or the *Times-Picayune* and tell Grandma something bad was about to happen.

Mr. Causey watched as we filed off the bus. Sheila, Baby Jack, the Lane sisters, who had a reputation for being tough, and I slowly stepped off. I walked behind Pamela Robertson, one of my childhood friends who lived on the other side of Mr. Jumel, her uncle. Mr. Causey told us, through the bullhorn, that we had to stand behind a bright yellow line until we were familiar with the school and neighborhood. The White kids just stared at us, their expressions a cross between bewilderment and curiosity. I got off the bus wearing my classic school attire—white Converse sneakers, blue skirt and white shirt—and carrying a book satchel filled with pens and paper. From day one I wanted to write about the entire experience: I put down in my diary that I felt humiliated by the whole process, which took place every day.

The White students were told to stand in a shaded area, where they were protected from the sun or the rain. The Black students stood in an open area surrounded by a tall fence. No sooner had we gotten off the bus than we were pelted with eggs. Groups of angry

White parents had parked near the school to keep an eye on their children, and they started lobbing eggs and tomatoes across the fence. We were horrified. Pam started crying and Baby Jack came to her aid to shield her from the bombardment. Sheila searched for me (we still had to stick together) and asked me if I was all right. I was afraid one of the Lane sisters would pull out a knife, so I ran to Mr. Causey and begged him to find us cover. The White parents started cussing us out in language we never heard at home. They called us monkeys, baboons and niggers. They shouted at us to "leave their schools and do not come back to Metairie." This was integration.

We were kept segregated by geography and race for several minutes before we were allowed to enter the school. Finally the bell rang and we went inside to clean up and go to our homerooms. In our classes we were integrated, but in word only. The atmosphere was tense and edgy most of the time, and even during recess we all felt segregated. In the lunchroom, the Black students sat together and discussed plans to get back home safely. We always checked on one another and made plans to talk in the evening when we were back on safe ground in Kenner. It was difficult to break down the invisible lines we had been trained never to cross.

After a couple of days of this I was fighting mad. I was a self-proclaimed militant. Although I was very eager to learn more about White people and to attend their schools, I was ready to start a revolution of some sort. I started to write poetry and essays about busing. One day I wrote a poem entitled "Black Is." I was proud to be Black. "Black is being who you are / Black is being a child of God / Black is 'cuz no body gonna love us, but us."

The White parents were hostile and mean. We did not want to fight, but in Metairie we were outnumbered, and finally we had to take a stand. I'd had enough, and so one day I brought some eggs to school. I brought duck and chicken eggs that I had stolen from Miss Eddie Bee and Miss Mary's henhouse on the side of our yard in the back. My friend Jeff, who was being held back a year, was always eager to join my causes. We were so close that some folks thought Jeff and I were an item. He was just one of the many kids I played with all the time. Our families shared backyard areas, along with the woods. I trusted Jeff with all my secrets and he shared his secrets, too. To this day we often laugh about the tricks and games we played on the rest of the kids. But I knew when it came to organizing, Jeff was a reliable ally in battle: I could trust him as I planned our counteroffensive. I would have told Sheila, but she would have given me up in an instant. She and I were often competitive, because Jean bought us the same gifts and clothes and often treated us as if we were twins. Jeff had the brilliant idea to bring duck eggs because they were bigger than chicken eggs. I was ready to make the point that we were not going to take it anymore.

That morning Reverend Williams looked us up and down as we got on the bus. He made the so-called bad children, like the Lane sisters, sit up front. I went straight to the back of the bus. I wanted to have an organizing meeting on the long ride to T. H. Harris. Baby Jack grabbed the last seat near the emergency exit and I sat next to him. I showed him what was in my book sack. In addition to the eggs I had some stones from the train tracks and a couple of unripe green tomatoes from the garden. I told Baby Jack that his role was to take a couple of rocks and tomatoes and throw them over the fence. I would take the eggs and aim for the kids standing and sitting in the shaded areas. We hand-selected our operatives and told the timid students, like Lynn and Pam, to stay near the bus until we finished.

Somehow Mr. Causey figured out that we were going to fight back. Before we could complete our assault, he called me to go to his office. He was tall and balding, with large brown eyes. Before he could say a word I told him, "No need to call my momma. She can't get here because there's no bus that comes out here. She'd have to catch a cab and we can't afford cabs." I didn't mention that Grandma was at home. I looked at Baby Jack, who was being pulled into the principal's office, and told him thank you. Baby Jack was going to get punished, and it was my fault. I was the mastermind behind the rocks, tomatoes and eggs. I took responsibility for launching the offensive but was able to talk myself out of trouble. I felt my actions were justified under the circumstances.

I didn't know it then, but by the time I completed eighth grade at T. H. Harris, Mr. Causey and I would be friends. I was summoned to his office so often because of something I said or did that we got to know each other pretty well. To his credit, and my good luck, he never once suspended me. I did frequently go home with notes to my parents, which I slid under the altar. I knew St. Jude would watch over the note and protect me from harm. Mr. Causey recognized my leadership abilities and thought that we could work together as allies to gain control of the revolts and protests that frequently rocked the school. I actually initiated a lot of the Black students' protests, and I guess he figured it was better to have me on his side. But when I organized protests to have our voices heard, or to have Black representation at some level in school decisions, they were defensive, not offensive. I couldn't let the White kids just beat us up. Grandma taught me to stand up and act.

But that day Mr. Causey asked me not to bring eggs or rocks to school anymore. I stared straight back at him and said, "Tell the White kids that, too, and their parents. If they stop throwing eggs and tomatoes at us, we'll stop throwing at them. But we're not going to come to school, stand in the heat and then get eggs thrown at us. No way!" I reminded Mr. Causey that he'd never once chastised the White kids for their behavior. In his defense, he told me that he'd summoned the White kids who were egg throwers to his office. "You never did it in front of me," I shot back.

For a couple of weeks after that incident, when we arrived at school, Mr. Causey would slowly allow some of us to stand under the shade—the first steps toward integration. He encouraged us to sit in mixed groups in the cafeteria. But the whole idea of busing, how it disrupted our lives, taking us away from our neighborhood, upset me to no end. And although I didn't throw any more eggs, I found other ways to protest. Changes were taking place all over the country and in New Orleans, and I began to think more seriously about the civil rights movement. When we had to stand to recite the Pledge of Allegiance, I stayed in my seat. When my homeroom teacher reported me, I initially told them it was against my religion. "What religion are you?" Mr. Russell, the principal, inquired. I told him that my family were practicing Catholics, but I was converting to Jehovah's Witnesses like Charmane and Janice from around the corner. But the real reason I refused to salute the flag was the last six words in the pledge: "with liberty and justice for all." I didn't see any justice in the way we were being treated. I even wrote an essay in my eighth-grade class entitled "What's Wrong with the Pledge of Allegiance." Of course, I got in trouble for that, too.

I was at T. H. Harris for two years, in the seventh and eighth grades, and for the first time my academic performance was poor. My grades didn't recover until I entered high school. Prior to busing, I had A's and some B's. Now my grades were suffering in math and science—I did quite well in literature and social sciences. I had always had pretty good relationships with my teachers, and to this day, I can say that I remember nearly all the teachers I had before busing—my first-grade teacher, Miss Collins; my second-grade teacher, Miss LeBlanc; my third-grade teacher, Miss Pierce; my fourth-grade teacher, Miss Eugene; my fifth-grade teacher, Mr. Marchand; and my sixth-grade teacher, Mr. Lee. Then there was Ms. Fox, Mr. Phil and later Coach Smith from basketball at Grace King High School in Metairie. They helped me a great deal in becoming a good student and an athlete. But some of the White teachers didn't challenge us. They brought nothing to the table. They didn't want to teach us. They didn't want us there. I do remember that Mr. Lockwood, my eighth-grade teacher, who I also had in ninth grade at Grace King, really cared. But for the most part, the White teachers didn't like us and we didn't understand them.

Of course there were no Black teachers, no Black guidance counselors, not even a Black gym teacher at T. H. Harris. This was a total culture shock coming from the neighborhoods where we lived. If a teacher called your home to speak to your parents, that conversation occurred in a vacuum because our teachers knew nothing about our lives. I was never the physical victim of any racial incidents (outside of the egg pelting), probably because I was so flippant with the White students. But they did try to beat me down, to tell me that I wasn't as smart as they were, that I wasn't intelligent, that I didn't know everything and I was not going to make it. In response to their taunts I spent evenings studying in the Kenner Library or reading *Ebony* to learn more so I would be armed and could talk back. But I had a huge barrier, and that was fear and anxiety. I felt as if we were under siege. We were in a war. It was a while before I got to know some of the White students, like Barbara O'Connor, who brought cookies to school and shared them with me. After a while, I stopped playing the Black militant role and settled into being a little girl and learning again. I wanted to play sports and get involved in school activities like before.

Metairie was a different world from Kenner. They had giant supermarkets like Schwegmann's, and shopping malls. Interstate 10 had opened the area up, and soon a shuttle bus system was created to transport folks from the Veterans Highway back to Airline Highway. In the beginning of school integration it was difficult for Black kids to get involved in extracurricular activities. And if we missed the school bus in the afternoon, well, we'd just missed the bus. We had to figure out how to walk all the way home, through neighborhoods where there was hardly a Black presence. And frankly, there was no safe route to walk back home to Kenner, because Metairie was a hotbed of racism.

If a Black person drove by and saw you walking, they would pull over to give you a lift back to the colored section of town. Harassment was a constant threat. Some of my friends were threatened and had all types of eggs, rocks and things thrown at them as they walked back to the Black section of town. Once or twice when these incidents happened, I told Baby Jack and Randy and all my kids back in Kenner, who were in high school at East Jefferson, that I was planning to walk home in protest. I did. It was one of those hot autumn days when I decided to stay after school to participate in a play, and then walk all the way back to Filmore Street. It took me two hours. I wasn't scared, but I kept my head down and stared at the ground. Grandma taught me never to look into the eyes of a stranger—Black or White—unless you wanted confrontation. I did not want confrontation, but I wanted the people on Roosevelt Boulevard and David Drive to know I was not afraid of them.

One of the things that kept me sane, kept me going, was my reading. I was reading everything I could get my hands on about Black people. Richard Wright's *Native Son* was one of my favorites, as well as poetry by Nikki Giovanni. Lerone Bennett's *Before the Mayflower,* and Lorraine Hansberry's *A Raisin in the Sun.* But there were certain books that Jean didn't want me to read, and she told the librarians not to let me check them out—*Die Nigger Die* by H. Rap Brown and anything by LeRoi Jones (now Amiri Baraka). Jean was a book banner. In order to get around her edicts, I simply "borrowed" books from the library that were on the banned list, hiding them in my book bag, sneaking them out and returning them when I was through reading them. I could not leave a trace because Jean would be hot on my trail.

I was still writing in my diary, in addition to my poetry, and had even authored a little pamphlet on my place in the struggle. Everywhere I looked there was struggle. Richard Nixon had been elected president the year King and Bobby Kennedy died. Then there was the war in Vietnam, where my uncles Johnny and Douglas were off fighting. Ms. Beulah's son Winkie went over, too. Down the street, Ms. Alma's son Junior went and came back, but some others never returned. We hated that war. It was on TV every night.

And like everybody else back then, I was grooving to Aretha Franklin's "Respect," Marvin Gaye's "What's Going On" and Freda Payne's "Bring the Boys Home"—songs that became anthems. While some kids dreamed of being movie stars, I dreamed of being an activist. I wanted to lead a march. I wanted to be front and center with the fiery, outspoken radical Angela Davis, whose books were banned in my house. One day Jean found me reading *Soledad Brother* by George Jackson, and she grabbed the book out of my hand and said, "You ain't reading that shit." When I shot back that Cheryl and Sheila were reading the silly, trashy girl magazines *Right On* and *True Confessions,* and that at least I was reading something educational, Jean smacked me with the book. From that day on, I hid my books under my bed or in the bottom of the closet. The only place where I could read in peace was under the weeping willow tree out back. There I read until dusk. It was always cool under the weeping willow tree, and I would often climb the limbs as high as I could so Jean couldn't find me. I'd open my books and escape, dream and plan my future.

I attended Grace King High School. I don't know what the system was in other states, but in Louisiana after the eighth grade, although students were racially integrated, high schools suddenly be-came same-sex. Grace King was a huge school, with nearly four thou-sand students. It was another two miles away from Kenner, near Lake Pontchartrain. Every day we waited for the bus, exposed to the bitter cold wind that swept off the lake. Miss Velma Kemp, middle aged, stern, with wire-rimmed glasses, was the principal and she started off each day saying to us "Good Morning, young ladies—shamrocks to all." Cheryl had warned me before landing at Grace King that I would not be in charge there.

About 15 percent of the four thousand girls at Grace King were Black. We came from both the north side (near the lake) and the south side (near the river). It was a mixture of working-class and middle-class Black families. Grace King had a citywide, if not statewide, reputation for being a good academic school that prepared students for college. I was very excited about going to school there.

I thought of the school as a kind of minimum-security prison. It was strict, very strict. It wasn't a Catholic school but it was run like one. Miss Kemp was tall and pale and wore colorful dresses. She pa-trolled the halls with a ruler. She would stop and greet us in the halls and measure the length of our skirts to see how high above our knees they were. A few of the girls even wore slacks, but I kept a pair of shorts on under my skirt all the time just in case I had to run off somewhere. The racial atmosphere at Grace King was a bit more welcoming—at least there were two Black teachers and some Black guidance counselors. They were young teachers, fresh out of college. They could relate to us.

My sisters Cheryl and Sheila, who were in the tenth and eleventh grades, had settled in at Grace King and were very popular. Cheryl was actively engaged in several school activities and was one of the founders of the Soul Sisters Club, which was a club of culturally and politically active Black students. Apparently I wasn't the only activist in the family. As soon as I could, I joined the club. The year before they'd wanted to help out Shirley Chisholm, the first Black woman elected to Congress, who was running for president, but she did not have a campaign in the state.

The club was important to me for a lot of reasons. It was the first thing I'd inherited from Cheryl that I was proud to call my own. It was the only thing I ever did where I followed my sister. Usually I went my own way, did my own thing. I was the family oddball. But the Soul Sisters Club brought us together as sisters. And it meant a lot to me because it wasn't trivial, nor was it your typical female social club.

And my relationship with Cheryl changed. By the time I turned sixteen she supported me in getting an Afro and even allowed me to come to her parties. I would read my poetry about Black love and Black families: "I remember the love and strong embraces / when Mom and Pop would see our faces." I don't know if they liked my poems, but I was tolerated and respected by the older kids. They knew I could organize and help them buy their booze and stir up pralines or pecan candy or frozen cups filled with our favorite kind of Kool-Aid.

The Soul Sisters Club was a way to ensure that Black girls were involved in every aspect of the school, and in that sense the club was more political than social. Cheryl was going to graduate in 1975, and she was grooming me for leadership. One of our main priorities was to keep the pressure on the school to hire more Black teachers. The administrators and teachers at Grace King responded pretty well to our requests. There were teachers like Mr. Lockwood and Miss Fox, who were White and very liberal. I was on all the sports teams—basketball, volleyball, softball and track. Miss Fox would often give me a ride home after the games or a meet. She felt sorry for me because I had no way to get home if I had to stay after school for a game. In my junior year another Black girl, Sharon Hill, joined the basketball team, and Miss Fox drove us both home after the games. Sharon lived on Acorn Street in North Kenner. One of her older sisters also attended and was a member of the Soul Sisters Club. Because my parents didn't have a car, nobody in my family ever came to see me play or compete in track.

Mr. Lockwood became a mentor for me at Grace King and someone I could talk to about almost anything. He was one of the nicest people I'd ever met. In his English class I learned so much about literature, poetry and philosophy. He had a great sense of humor as well as a real mastery of his subject. He also served as an adviser to the Soul Sisters Club. He'd often ask me to stay after class to talk with me about what I had written, usually something militant or provocative or angry. He really wanted to know why I felt the way I did. I wrote essays and poems about my grandmother and what she had told me about growing up in the South and what it was like sharecropping. I felt that I could be totally honest with Mr. Lockwood about how upset I was by what I saw around me, and how eager I was to be part of it.

By now I was active in sports and the Soul Sisters Club, but more important my grades had improved and I was back to making A's and B's in some of my subjects. While at Grace King I also began developing deep friendships, many of which have lasted my entire life. I remained friends with Sharon Hill. Martha Strong was a girl who lived in Metairie and became my first White buddy. She jokes that being my first White friend is the burden she carries in life. Her father was a pathologist at Ochsner Hospital, which is located on the outskirts of New Orleans. Her mother was well connected and very active in Louisiana politics. I gravitated toward Martha because she was working on the upcoming 1975 Louisiana governor's race and the attorney general's race. They needed help getting the Black vote and I told Martha that since I was very active in Kenner, I could help out. Martha was of medium height, slender, with brown hair and eyes and loads of personality. She reminded me of Mary Tyler Moore, she was so perky and energetic—and a bit wild.

Eventually Martha and I participated in a 1976 mock Jimmy Carter/Gerald Ford election. We helped to organize events for the Carter-Mondale team. When it was time to go off to college, Martha and I drove to LSU together in her car. We met when we were both running on the same slate for the sophomore class officers—Martha won. My slogan was "Make a deal with Brazile." I knew I couldn't win, being Black, but the whole point of my candidacy was to challenge the system. And at least I was able to present a platform, to argue, to stand up and let the White students and faculty know that I was willing to run. Despite my loss Martha wanted me to work closely with the class.

We grew to be very close. So close that she would laugh and call me a nigger bitch and I would call her a White honky. We could cuss each other out and still respect each other (we still do). If I went off on one of my rants Martha would joke, "Here you come with that Black shit. You know I don't care about your people." She'd just cut through my hostility so easily that it made me laugh. We could be totally honest with each other. As president of the sophomore class, Martha had clout—and the Soul Sisters Club needed her support and the sophomore class sponsorship for projects we proposed.

Martha was open to inviting me to go out with her friends— and she had a nice car, which meant that she took me to parts of Jefferson Parish and Orleans Parish where I was never permitted to go. I couldn't afford to buy the hamburgers and po' boy sandwiches at places in Metairie along West Esplanade. I didn't become buddies with many of her friends, and she wasn't buddies with mine. She never came over and sat at our kitchen table. Yet everyone in my neighborhood knew her because of her green Mustang. People would yell, "Donna, the White girl's outside." Nobody ever remembered her name. She was just "the White girl."

I helped Martha's mom on the campaign of Billy Guste. He was the Louisiana attorney general in 1976, the bicentennial year. That's the year I discovered Texas representative Barbara Jordan, when she gave her keynote speech at the Democratic National Convention. I had never heard anyone so passionate and articulate, and she immediately symbolized everything I wanted to do and be politically. I had followed the Watergate hearings, the entire drama, watching the whole thing on television and reading about it in the newspapers. I loved watching Barbara Jordan ask questions at the hearings. In her speech at the Democratic convention, I loved it when she said that we Black people may not have been written in the Constitution, but by a series of amendments we had finally got there. She was not only eloquent, she told her story—she told *our* story. I was at home watching the convention by myself and she inspired me so much that I decided right then and there "I'm going to run a presidential campaign."

I wrote in my diary after Barbara Jordan's speech that I wanted to help her become the first female and the first African-American president of the United States. I suddenly got very clear about my life and goals, and I saw Louisiana politics as a means to an end. Jordan was my new candidate. I began to learn everything about her career. I no longer saw myself as just being in Louisiana. All I wanted from Louisiana at that point was to learn the business of campaigns and politics. I started reading every history book I could about the American presidency and what it took to run for president. I wanted to get the kind of experience and credentials that would equip me for running a presidential campaign one day. Everything was changing. I had even begun to question poverty and injustice.

I felt so optimistic about my future that one day I told Jean, "Don't worry about me, Mom. I'll be okay. I'm going to be successful. I'll make a good living and I'm going to get deeply involved in politics." I knew by then that politics was about helping people, which I was raised to do. But it was also about giving back, which I was raised to do as well. Barbara Jordan just woke me up. My little light was shining again. This time more radiantly. I read her speech, printed in the newspaper, for days on end. I walked around quoting her speech verbatim for weeks.

While working on the Guste campaign, when I registered people, I registered them as Democrats because the Democrats were on the side of poor people. It was in 1976 that I began to identify myself as a Democrat. I was changing. I didn't know it then, but even more change was in store for me and for my family. Grandma had been the backbone of our family for so long and had always been strong physically, but when she turned eighty she began to suffer from terrible arthritis. She was still walking without a cane, although her knees were in bad shape due to the arthritis. We all thought she would live to be a hundred. We just knew she would always be there. In 1975, Uncle Sporty, her eldest son, died suddenly of a heart ailment. Uncle Sporty was my grandmother's favorite child. He came to the house every Sunday to bring Grandma an elegant gourmet meal. We'd sit around the kitchen table and talk about where he had been that week. He would tell us about what was going on all over the country with the movement. He'd entertain us with stories about the celebrities he'd met in his travels, like Fats Domino and Louis Armstrong. Uncle Sporty had retired but still worked occasionally for Amtrak. When his train passed by our house Grandma would say, "Go outside and wave to your uncle Sporty." He was always on his way to Chicago or coming back from Chicago. And sure enough, we'd see Uncle Sporty standing between the rail cars and waving to us in Kenner.

Uncle Sporty's death sent Grandma into a deep depression. She just couldn't get over it. And at the end of my sophomore year she had a stroke. Jean called Dr. Beamer, who'd been our family physician for years. She always made house calls for Grandma because no matter what ailed her, she never went to the hospital. Grandma was the one who taught us all the natural remedies. She wore a wrap behind her neck with Colman's yellow mustard to keep her blood pressure down. She drank red wine vinegar infused with garlic to lower her blood sugar and to prevent diabetes. She had remedies for everything.

But she grew weak physically and emotionally, and couldn't bounce back from her grief. I used to always press her hair every week—she had long, shiny gray hair. I would press and then braid it for her. She liked her hair brushed back; she was a very proper woman. Grandma always wore her glasses because she was a readaholic. And her lips were always soft because she kept them moisturized with Vaseline. She had pride in her appearance. But after the stroke she let all that go. Dr. Beamer told us that Grandma could no longer care for herself, and we had to decide whether we wanted to put her in a nursing home. Jean couldn't stop working, nobody could, so I volunteered. I said, "I'll cut back on my school projects. I'll take a shift and Lisa can take a shift."

Every day Lisa and I would wash and dress Grandma. She was so proud. She tried to help us, but we told her not to exert herself. We bathed her and combed her hair. We would help her sit up in her rocking chair. We were her nurses and her physical therapists. That summer Grandma became the entire focus of our lives. Dr. Beamer came to the house weekly and checked on Grandma, especially her blood pressure. But we would never let her go to the hospital. Grandma had told us over and over that when you go to the hospital you never come out the same way. Grandma believed that as long as you don't go to the doctor you were fine. To this day if I feel a cold coming on, I start drinking castor oil and hot tea with lemon, and I swear by my grandmother's folk remedies. They work.

Although Lisa and I spent the bulk of our time tending to Grandma, it was a family effort that involved everyone. Aunt Pinkey would come to visit. Aunt Rosalie would call from California. Aunt Anna and Lucille would call from New York. Aunt Ethel would drop in around lunchtime and give us a much-needed break. There came a point that summer when Grandma's health really began to deteriorate, and many family members thought it was best to put her in a nursing home. But all of us young people in the family to whom Grandma had been a rock, a surrogate mother, said no. "She's our grandma," we told the adults. "She raised us and now we'll take care of her." But by the end of the summer Dr. Beamer told us that Grandma, "Miss Frances" as she was called, would not live much longer despite our best efforts. She said Grandma had done extremely well by holding up all summer. But she told Jean that with fall on the way, and the need for us to return to school, it was time to put Grandma in a nursing home.

During the weeks leading up to Grandma's death, I kept remembering Hurricane Camille, which had torn through Louisiana in 1969. So much of our house was destroyed again in another bad storm—the roof, the front porch, the back, the barn area. Grandma decided not to leave the house. This time, she begged Jean and Lionel to stay and ride out the storm. That night, she baked us our favorite buttermilk biscuits, cooked a ham and stirred up some potato salad. The winds picked up and we were scared that the weeping willow tree would fall on the house. Grandma told us to pray, and we sat up all night in front of the kerosene light praying and begging God to spare our home and family again. When the storm had passed and the sun had broken through, the house was in pieces. Everything was everywhere. Eventually we found Grandma back in her room, in her rocking chair looking out a window that was torn loose from the seams. She calmly told us, "I told you we would still be here." She always kept the faith.

Jean came up with another plan for keeping Grandma at home.

I would change my shift to the afternoon, and Sheila would take classes in the morning. My grandmother was proud to the bitter end. We would go out into the garden and pick her favorite roses. She loved her yellow roses. She loved the smell of roses. Grandma had some of the healthiest rosebushes in town, and we would cut up roses and put them in vases all over her bedroom. Soon she started becoming senile and would mumble, telling us "Go outside and take the clothes off the line before your momma comes in." We'd tell her that we had already done that. Or she would start calling out for her dead children—Frances, Dorothy, Louis, Alice, Adele and Ebbie. We knew then that the end was near. So we kept her comfortable and fed her soup. Her favorites were vegetable and turnip bottom with chicken stock.

On the morning of August 7, Grandma started spitting up phlegm. Dr. Beamer came to the house, examined Grandma and told us that we had done everything possible. During my watch at 9:30 that night Lisa came in to take over. To this day if you ever get sick, you want Lisa by your side. She's strong. When I left Grandma's side I told Lisa that I was going to pray for Grandma because I thought her time had come. Grandma had already told us, and especially the girls, "When your time comes and you're ready, you go ahead and tell God you're ready because God knows you're ready. You've just got to be ready." And I went in my parents' room and stood before Lionel's altar. I had never, ever prayed at the altar because it was my dad's. I found my mom in the room and I told her that Grandma was ready to go. She asked me how I knew. At that point I felt as old as any adult in the house. I looked at Jean and said, "I just know. She taught me and she taught Lisa; she taught all of us when to know you're ready to go." Jean left me alone in the room and I fell on my knees before the altar and I said, "God, I don't want my grandmother to suffer anymore." I'll never forget that prayer. I said, "She's tired now and we've done all we can do. You can take her now. We love her, but we know it's time to let her go." As soon as I finished the prayer, Lisa called out to me "Donna, Donna, Grandma wants you, she's dying now." I ran back to Grandma's bedroom. It was 9:49 PM when my grandmother died. Lisa was holding her hand. I was there to see her go. She looked at me and then she went in peace. I loved my grand-mother so much. I held her hand. I cried. She was my best friend. She taught me everything. There was no stronger force in our family, and we all have our grandma stories to this day. We all have rocking chairs and we all like ginger snaps. We all like music and to cook up wonderful Creole dishes like filé gumbo and shrimp étouffée. We like buttermilk biscuits, creamy sauces and sweets. We're not afraid of raging storms. We're all just like Grandma.

For years after my grandmother died, I knew when people in our family were ready to go. They'd lived a lifetime of hard work raising their families, and they never had time to rest. They never had vaca-tions or time off, and when they did, they often found odd jobs to help make ends meet. They taught their children to work hard, play by the rules, stand up, take charge and above all else to keep the faith. Grandma was my inspiration—a strong warrior with a gentle spirit. From Grandma's generation we learned patience and loyalty. They taught us to pray for wisdom and guidance. They taught us to tell the truth and to never surrender. Most of all, they taught us to give back and to be responsible for others. For weeks after her death, I spent time on the levee thanking God for her love, patience and kindness. Then it was time to move on. I've made my peace with Grandma's departure from this earth, but I will never forget the stories and the lessons she left behind for me to follow the rest of my life.

CHAPTER FOUR

CRAWFISH ÉTOUFFÉE

Crawfish are known as mudbugs. Many different Cajun dishes call for the little swamp creatures, but only the tail is really eaten. Étouffée is a somewhat tangy tomato-based sauce, common to many Southern Louisiana dishes. Normally, you can find crawfish on sale throughout the spring and early summer months (crawfish season). When I left Kenner to attend Louisiana State University, I watched the swampy waters we passed and thought of the tasty crawfish just under the surface.

WHEN I GRADUATED from Grace King I knew that politics was going to be my career and my life. I spent my senior year working hard to improve my grades so I could get into a good college. Before I left Grace King, I was selected to attend Louisiana's Girls State, sponsored by the American Legion Auxiliary for future student leaders, in Baton Rouge, with all the best student leaders from across the state. This was a dream come true—an opportunity to compete in a mock election, with girls my own age. While at Girls State I decided to run for local positions and to get behind someone early to run for governor. My friend Martha was also selected to participate and she and I conspired to get girls from the rural areas to support someone from the city. There were not many Black girls there, so my first task was to find out if any of them wanted to run. A couple of them wanted me to run, and after some initial hesitation because I wanted to work behind the scenes, I decided to throw my hat in, for attorney general. At the time, I wanted to pursue a career in law, which could help advance my political ambitions. Martha ran for the state supreme court.

After a few days of speeches, hand holding and wild parties masquerading as campaign events, we both won. The victory was sweet and I told Martha that I was ready to work full time for statewide political candidates. Jimmy Carter was in the White House and several Blacks were appointed to his cabinet. In New Orleans, my uncles and cousins worked hard to finally elect our first Black mayor, Ernest "Dutch" Morial. Mayor Morial was one of my new role models; he understood politics and would help usher in a new era of Louisiana politics. During my research on the campaign, I learned something very important about Mayor Morial. He had helped to integrate LSU Law School years before. I liked his style of activism, which brought together the civil rights struggle and electoral politics, and I followed his career every day in the New Orleans *Times-Picayune, States Item* and the *Louisiana Weekly*.

One of my first major political decisions was to select a college to attend. Although I wanted to go to the predominantly Black Howard University in Washington, D.C., I knew my parents could not afford the tuition, so I did not bother to apply. Howard was the so-called mecca of Black colleges and where many of my political heroes like Ralph J. Bunche, Vernon Jordan, Andrew Young and Ossie Davis attended college. Even the novelists Zora Neale Hurston and Toni Morrison went there. I loved their books even if I did not understand many of their writings and the subjects normally went over my head. I figured I had to stay relatively close to home, so I called Aunt Pinkey's children and Jean's family to discuss their preferences and experiences. Then it was time to do my own research. I like the chaos of living in a major city, so I narrowed my choices to two locations— Baton Rouge and New Orleans. I chose to attend Louisiana State University.

Predominantly White, LSU was located eighty miles away in Baton Rouge—the state capital. It was the state's flagship university and everybody who wanted to be anybody in Louisiana state politics attended LSU undergraduate, graduate or law school. I was no exception. After years of getting my feet wet registering new voters and organizing small protest movements, I was eager to expand my horizons and was sure that LSU would give me a better understanding of how to deal with Democrats, Republicans, conservative Whites, rural voters and other minorities in the political arena. By this time I had gotten pretty good at going head to head with fellow students on politics. I had read the biographies of every American president and I was actively aware of the number of electoral votes needed to win the White House. I was ready to register to vote at the end of the year when I finally turned eighteen. It's a funny thing about Louisiana—we immersed ourselves in the local culture. We went to Mardi Gras events, celebrated funerals and made new friends along the way. I was already hanging out at bars and drinking, going to wild parties with friends in the French Quarter, watching R-rated movies like *Shaft*, but not of age to vote.

The most important thing I wanted in life was to be a registered Democrat like most Black people in the city. Grandma had told me that some people registered as Republicans because Lincoln freed the slaves, but I rarely met any Blacks who wanted to register as Republicans. Everyone I knew wanted to be associated with the party of Franklin Roosevelt or Jack Kennedy. Once, I wrote to Reverend Clay to seek his advice about voter registration and what political party I should belong to. I never forgot his response: He told me to stick with the party that accepted us, not rejected us. Another reason why I made the decision to go to LSU was that I wanted to intern for state representative Avery Alexander, who had led many civil rights protests in New Orleans, or Representative Diana Bajoie—both from the New Orleans area and family friends. As an intern, I could gain more experience in state government and gain more contacts across the state. LSU, in my analysis, was a good choice, and Jean agreed. Her only concern was transportation. We still did not own a car.

Martha also chose LSU, which some members of her family had attended. When she informed me of her decision, I knew I had my ride to Baton Rouge. I spent the summer telling just about everyone that I was off to LSU, bragging that I would have my own bed. My neighbors and friends grew excited for me. I left Teddy Man and Marc the business to run and I gave Chet and Cedric all my tools. I went to my baby brother Kevin to give him my marbles and athletic gear, but he wasn't interested in my junk. The Kenner Lions Club gave me a scholarship to pay for my books. I had saved up enough money to carry me over for a year. I spent the final weeks during the summer of 1977 going up and down Filmore Street to tell my clients that I was off to college. They all gave me money and gifts, along with prayers to succeed. I would never let them down or forget the people of Kenner.

Martha told me to be waiting outside at 2:00 PM—and she meant exactly 2:00 PM. I got up and went to church. Lionel gave me a dollar to light a candle. I told the priest not to expect me unless I came home on weekends, but I would continue to volunteer for the church's feeding and clothing drives during the holidays. That Sunday, the priest gave me a free candle. It was white and I placed it under the Virgin Mary and lit it. I prayed for luck and success in college. I also asked God to watch over my family and the house on Filmore Street. Martha was on time. Before she could get to the house, the news was already up and down the street: The White girl was coming to get me again. Martha laughed at my trunk and boxes. I did not have any suitcases, just a couple of gym bags and a large black trunk that Jean had gotten through layaway at McCory's on Canal Street. We left Filmore Street and took a left turn down Airline Highway to Baton Rouge.

It was an interesting ride along the mossy swamps, big plantations and dusty roads. Martha wanted to take Airline so we could stop and use the bathroom if needed. Frankly, I wasn't planning on asking her to stop anywhere. I still did not trust the back roads of Louisiana, but I wasn't in charge of getting us to Baton Rouge. Martha drove fast, playing Fleetwood Mac, James Taylor and Barbra Streisand songs in her cassette recorder. I wanted to play Aretha Franklin, the Commodores and Earth, Wind and Fire. No such luck. Martha was driving. When we got to the outskirts of Baton Rouge, she pulled over to Highland Road, where there are so many magnolia trees and stately homes. It was a great drive. We barely talked. Martha got us there in one hour and she asked me if I was thirsty. We were always thirsty and it was Sunday, so we immediately went to the local A&P grocery store off campus and bought an eight-pack of Miller Beer, which was our favorite drink.

Luckily, we were both assigned to Evangeline Hall off Highland Road across from the Student Union. Evangeline was in the horseshoe, along with Annie Boyd, Grace King, and East dormitories. We unloaded the Mustang. Jean had packed me a good lunch and dinner of fried chicken, jambalaya, salad, biscuits and some cookies. We tried to figure out how we could get the people from New Orleans to join us on the second floor. People from New Orleans are prejudiced against the rest of the state and vice versa. They hated us so we said jokingly no more "country bumpkins" moving into the dorm. Martha and I lived across the hall from each other. She was in 219 and I was in 222. I had a room facing Annie Boyd Hall. My roommate was a Black girl named Roxie Collins. Roxie was from Franklin, another mostly conservative, rural area of the state. She was definitely homespun. She arrived on campus with matching pillows, sheets, bedspreads—the works. By way of comparison, Aunt Ethel gave me Aunt Adele's blue towels and Aunt Pinkey's green sheets and Jean gave me a beige cover for my bed. Martha took me to TGY to buy a pillow. Everybody had given me something to bring to school. Nothing matched. But it was all clean. I started to unpack my boxes, my cassette recorder and my books. Mama had given me an electric popcorn popper and a Crock-Pot to cook my red beans on Monday. I was ready for campus living. I placed all my cooking utensils, seasonings, pepper, garlic powder, onion salt, parsley and paprika on another shelf. Jean had given me enough canned goods to last three or four hurricanes.

LSU's student population was 22,000, and about 500 of those students were Black. The campus was a huge spread of brown-colored brick buildings surrounded by a man-made lake where all the sorority and fraternity houses were located. At the rear of the campus was the big stadium with a tiny cage out front—LSU's mascot, a live tiger, also stayed on campus. I was anxious to get started on my college career and I did not have any time to waste. The next presidential campaign was coming up, but I wanted to get involved in the upcoming Louisiana gubernatorial race. Edwin Edwards was not running and I heard rumors that some Blacks were ready to run for statewide office. So I dove right in. During my first semester, Martha and Sharon Higgins and another friend from Metairie talked me into running for dorm president. When it came to running for office, I had mixed feelings. On the one hand, I could not get over the rejection I felt back in tenth grade when I first stepped into the political arena. On the other hand, I had won two elections at Girls State. Whites, although friendly, could not be relied on for votes, but Martha promised to help me try to galvanize the White vote. Higgins, too, signed up and I reminded them both that Black students in the dorm were outnumbered five to one. Back then we had to learn how to build coalitions. Martha and Sharon agreed to sign up Vivian, Suzanne and Gretchen—women from New Orleans and our neighbors across the hall. One night I ran into my old friend Janet Bezner and her roommate Lisa Erickson. Janet and I played basketball together at Grace King. She left Grace King before graduation because her dad, an oil executive with Exxon, had gotten a job elsewhere. Janet was a brainy, objective friend. Her roommate Lisa, who grew up in Metairie and went to private school, was difficult. When I asked for her help, Lisa just laughed at me. I wrote in my diary a poem to describe how cruel and evil her laughter was at the time. "Lisa, Lisa, you're no fun. / You laugh at me when you know I am the one. / You hate me 'cuz I'm Black. / Get over your hatred / because I am going to come back for your vote."

It was Lisa's laughter and the promise of help from Martha, Lisa, Sharon, and the other New Orleans girls that helped me win overwhelmingly. For days I walked the hall going door to door meeting girls from all over the state and some from Mississippi. No one said no. My platform was simple: bring air-conditioning to Evangeline Hall, open up the study hall to allow men to be with us, and encourage more dorm-sponsored parties so we can get to know each other. To win the White vote, I did not have a racial agenda. The only time I discussed race was in my room with Roxie or with my other Black friends on campus. Much of the job as dorm president was administrative, establishing the time that meals are available in the cafeteria, establishing dorm procedures and rules, but everybody got to know me pretty fast. When Elvis Presley died I organized a candlelight vigil outside the dorm in the horseshoe and collected money to buy beer, which we sneaked into the dorm. We smoked cigarettes. We cussed and sang his hit songs. Even Black folks like singing "Don't be Cruel," "Love Me Tender" and other hits. It was a fitting tribute to the King.

Martha had come to LSU to major in medical technology. She wanted to follow her father and pursue a career in medicine. I had no idea what I wanted to major in, but I flirted with becoming a history or sociology major. It took me months to decide, but I was determined not to stay at LSU a day longer than four years. I was eager to get to Washington, D.C., to work on congressional campaigns and to work on Capitol Hill. After becoming dorm president, I volunteered to get involved in student government. I had a partial scholarship to play sports, and several local charities, including Mama's church, Greater Rose Hill Baptist, gave me a thousand dollars. That first semester I really tried to adjust to LSU. It wasn't easy. There was a certain coldness to the place. It was hard to make new friends or get comfortable with my new environment. I took too many classes and, along with my outside projects and party time, I did poorly. Jean warned me to slow down and take it easy, to focus on making good grades. I did not listen and at the end of my first year I was behind. I went home worried about my future and reconsidered some of the decisions I was making in school.

The last thing I needed was to flunk out of school. Every week, Jean and Lionel would send me five dollars. She would tear a sheet of paper from the notebook of one of the younger kids and fold the five-dollar bill in the notebook paper and send it to my post office box on campus. There would be nothing, not a word on the paper. Just the money. When we would sit around the dorm reading letters from home I would joke that Jean had written saying, "Dear Donna get your Black ass up at five AM and stop wearing those funky clothes." After we had all had a good laugh, I'd look at the blank page and read what I knew was in my mom's heart: "Here's five dollars. Please use this wisely." I knew that the money, small as it was, was hard-earned and needed back home. I joked about it, but I appreciated it. When I got those envelopes from home with that money, it always reminded me how far I had come, how hard I had worked to get where I was and how much support I had along the way.

At LSU, money was tight. Even with my scholarships, financial aid and Jean's five-dollar weekly stipend it was a struggle to live away from home. I applied for a work-study job to help make ends meet, especially on weekends when I had to fend for myself to eat. Campus life was interesting. LSU had so much to offer—a large library in the middle of campus, big open classrooms where hundreds of students would sit for hours listening to boring lectures and of course football. Football was sort of a religion on campus. Everyone was supposed to attend to cheer for our beloved Tigers. "Geaux Tigers," we would chant. I went to every game with fried chicken, biscuits and a couple of Millers until the school banned drinking at the games.

My passion for politics did not blind me to the possibilities of passion in other areas. I was ready to start dating boys. After my rocky first year, I was allowed back on campus. Sitting on the levee, I promised God to cut out some of my partying and to stay focused. One day I was in the LSU library studying and I looked up and saw this tall Black man strutting through the door. I remember saying to myself, "He's not from around this campus." Most of the tall Black men played ball and I knew them, but this guy was different. He wasn't a jock. He looked like a youthful version of Paul Robeson, the Black actor, singer and civil rights activist. It wasn't love at first sight. I did not believe in love at first sight. It was a political sighting and I couldn't wait to meet him one day.

It took weeks for John Pierre to finally come sit near me to study. One day we were sitting upstairs in the music room waiting for Quincy Jones's new album *Body Heat* to return to the bin and John finally asked me a question: "Where are you from?" I did not look at him. Focusing on the floor, I said, "Kenner, outside New Orleans." I then asked him, "What's your name? I see you here all the time." He told me, "My name is John Pierre and I am from Lorriville, Louisiana." In the back of my mind, I said to myself, Where the hell is Lorriville? God, I was supposed to know the state of Louisiana, but I was completely dumbfounded. He went on to tell me that he was enrolled at Southern University and was an accounting major. John was also on an ROTC scholarship and was expected to serve his time in the army. I liked him a lot. We talked for hours about music, politics and sports. He wanted to be a lawyer and told me I should pursue a career in law. I told him that I was interested in attending law school. John and I spent hours together studying in the library, and we met daily to listen to jazz. After a month of talking, he finally asked for my number. Initially, I wasn't going to give it up. Dating took up too much of my time. I was focused on organizing and stirring up the student body. But "what the hell," I said to myself. He called the next day and told me he wanted to go out for a meal. I wasn't big on dating, but I told him to meet me downstairs the next day.

We were both poor, so our first date was at Burger King off campus. We talked about our families and the future. I quickly picked up that John was an only child and a momma's boy. He was so respectful—unlike most guys—and I did not intimidate him. He liked my Afro, although I knew it could use a trim from time to time. John had big dreams of being like Thurgood Marshall. He was so passionate about Black literature and art. We spent hours talking about books we both enjoyed reading as children and my all-time favorite topic: Louisiana politics. The gubernatorial season was beginning and another issue was brewing in the state: desegregation and the fight to save Black colleges. John wanted to enlist my help in the effort. Although I did not attend a Black college, I realized how important they were in giving Blacks a college education. Our next date was a community meeting at a local church on Government Boulevard. There he introduced me to Sybil Taylor, now Sybil Taylor Holt, of the Louisiana state AFL-CIO. All over the South there were rallies to keep Black colleges open.

I was a little embarrassed to be at the rally. Here I was, a Black student attending a predominantly White institution trying to rally students to save historically Black colleges and universities. The contradiction was getting the best of me. For a moment I felt ashamed because some speakers made me feel that I wasn't Black enough, that I was abandoning my heritage. But I also wanted to keep alive the tradition started by James Meredith and Charlayne Hunter, who had both opened up predominantly White state colleges in the South. I wanted to attend LSU to learn how to live in a multicultural society and to learn how to navigate the Louisiana political system. I stayed that night listening to speeches from Southern University's political science professor Jewel Prestage and others. I decided to go back to LSU to organize Black students to help save Black colleges.

While rallying to save the Black colleges, I began to feel disdain for the Black students at LSU who were apathetic. For the most part they were apolitical. They came to college to learn and to socialize. Some of them came from good families and did not care about the status of poor people in the South or of Black people in America. All they were interested in was the next party and pledging. By now I was working with a couple of Black students on campus to organize events. We needed an organization, so we started BUS, Black United Students. I became one of the officers. Our first project was to organize Think Week. Curtis Pittman, Steven Fauconier, Priscilla Daigle, Randy Cummings, Rhonda and Wanda Holmes ("the twins") and others worked day in and day out to put together our first political event. Our featured speaker was Warith Deen Muhammad of the American Muslim Committee. We wanted someone controversial who would inspire Black students to take a stand. Venetta Boyd was on the faculty and we appealed to her to help us gain status on campus. We needed money to bring speakers to school. I was famous for writing scathing letters to just about everyone, and I drafted one to Chancellor Paul Murrill and Dean Margaret Jameson to support our programs. Dean Jameson responded and asked us to come to a meeting. She did not offer much but told us to write a proposal for funding. Priscilla and Curtis took the lead in drafting while I worked on an op-ed article for the *Daily Reveille* to explain our position. Randy and Steven decided to make flyers and the twins came back with warm bodies to spread the word. We were ready to help save Black schools like Southern and Grambling.

I received a lot of support from the Black faculty—there were about ten while I was at LSU and I got to know them all and they knew me. Huel Perkins, who was vice chancellor for academic affairs, was a tall, smart Black man who encouraged me to widen my horizons. He told me, "You can't attend LSU and only be involved in politics and protest. Get involved in the honor societies, travel." He was very helpful to me as a mentor and guide. I wanted to make a direct appeal to the Student Government Association (SGA), whose leader was Mike Futrell, a young man from Baton Rouge.

I met Mike Futrell during one of my visits to a student government meeting. Elaine Smith, one of my roommates, was with me, as were Priscilla and Randy. After a couple of hours, I was recognized and spoke up for a greater role and voice for Black students on campus. "You all support the football and basketball teams and the great contribution of our athletes. I know, I am one of them, but today I am asking for your support to bring more Black speakers to campus." The room was silent. Afterward, Futrell, a tall, White kid with dark hair and a big round face, came up to me and said, "We'll help you, but you have to do the work." Fine. I shook his hand and thanked him. Mike, who is now a conservative state representative, became one of my best friends. As student body president, he appointed me to serve in his administration. I became his statewide representative for external affairs and he designated me as his contact person on the regional board of the U.S. Student Association (USSA). Mike not only supported BUS, he wanted me to help out with local politics.

Ben Jeffers, one of Governor Edwin Edwards's top lieutenants, had decided to run for secretary of state. Jeffords, like A. Z. Young and Sherman Copelin, had worked alongside Edwards and had a lot of Black support across the state. Congressman Dave Treen, a Republican who represented the suburban New Orleans area including Kenner, was also running. Treen understood that in order to win he needed the Black vote. His campaign was eager to appeal to young Black students. They sent representatives to campus to recruit workers. With the encouragement of Mike Futrell and others, I went to a couple of the meetings as a representative of the SGA. I was still helping Martha's family out with local races. My uncle Floyd and Johnny were active in BOLD (Black Organization for Leadership Development, founded in 1968) and SOUL (Southern Organization for Unified Leadership, founded in 1965). My cousin Josie and her husband, Nat LaCour, had plugged me into the Black political clubs in New Orleans. I was finally coming into my own. I was writing pieces for the *Daily Reveille,* serving on the chancellor's Student

Advisory Committee and on the Baton Rouge Mayoral Advisory Committee on Housing.

I had gone from registering voters at age nine to being a young political player at age nineteen. In one decade of my life, I had gone from seeing Blacks locked out of the political system to witnessing Blacks serving as mayors and state representatives and running for statewide office. All across America things were beginning to change. More Blacks were being elevated to major positions in government and more Blacks were going to college. There was a feeling of acceptance that we no longer had to protest in order to make progress. On weekends, I started to go back home to New Orleans on the Greyhound bus to visit my folks, get something to eat and then shoot back to LSU.

By the end of my second year I decided to major in psychology and not political science. I had to make money. My first love remained politics, but I knew that I had to get a job so I could help my family back home. I'd gotten fixated on companies like Xerox in New York and Procter & Gamble in Cincinnati. I'd look at a map and see how far away from Kenner a corporation was. The farther away from Louisiana, the more it piqued my interest. I figured I would work in the human resources department or eventually go to grad or law school at Howard University, anything to help my family out once I got my degree.

In my junior year I stopped sports because I wasn't focused on it anymore and my political work had begun to take up all my time. An athlete must dedicate 100 percent of her life to the pursuit of the game, and I realized that there was no future for me in athletics. I thought to myself, "My butt got me in, but my brain's gonna get me out." I then focused on writing columns for the *Daily Reveille*. I wrote on everything from Black English—"It Bes That Way, Don't Fight with Fire"—to urging LSU to drop standardized tests for admission, to apartheid, abortion and anything else that might rattle the student population.

Every Friday on campus there was a Free Speech rally held outside the Student Union where I would rally students to register to vote. The right-wing student group Young Americans for Freedom

(YAF) would preach the ideology of David Duke, who was very popular on campus. Affirmative action, welfare and school desegregation were just some of the issues they rallied against. You could not reason with them, and Mike's friend and right arm, Kirk Gasperecz, a tall, lanky White guy with braces, would sometimes come with me to check to make sure nothing got out of hand. It infuriated me that the Black students never stood up with any kind of rebuttal. They just watched me walk up and stand in line to shout back. I was the campus rabble-rouser. The rallies would last two or three hours and there might be two or three hundred students. I'd stand in the audience and listen to them and I'd get up on the podium and with every bit of knowledge I had, remembering all the books I'd read, I would condemn the racist views of the speakers. Sometimes I would get things started, arriving at Free Speech Alley an hour beforehand to be the first person in line. Surprisingly, despite my militancy, I was never booed.

There had been a time when I had really thought the revolution would come. By the time I graduated, though, Ronald Reagan was president and a conservative tide had begun sweeping the country. Reagan made a surprise visit to campus in 1980 and spoke at the large gym on campus. We tried to get Jimmy Carter on campus to fight back, but he did not come to Baton Rouge. It was the first presidential election in which I could vote, and I cast my ballot for Carter. That night, sitting in my dorm room with my new roommate Seitha Duplessis of New Orleans, we watched the returns and talked about how America was going backward. It was sad. Reagan had campaigned on the states' rights platform. While in the South, he went to Philadelphia, Mississippi, where Chaney, Goodman and Schwerner had died in the summer of 1964. We worked hard on November 4, 1980, to get out the vote all across Baton Rouge, especially in the projects near campus. No one cared. There was so much apathy both on and around campus. We could barely get people to the polls. Reagan won Baton Rouge by a landslide.

My time at LSU was coming to an end. I entered my senior year eager to tie up loose ends on campus and to start looking for a job. After years of fighting the sororities and fraternities, all the Black social groups developed a unified strategy that brought us together under one umbrella. That way, we appeared to have more power than we actually possessed in numbers. With one central organization to articulate our values and our position, I believed we could get more accomplished on campus. This took a lot of hard work and energy to pull off. Some of the social organizations did not want to come under one banner. We insisted. More than anything, I wanted to leave a legacy of campus activism and the involvement of Black students in areas beyond athletics. Venetta Boyd urged us to begin a drive to send excess books to Angola, Louisiana's notorious prison, and to write letters to our brothers in prison urging them to keep faith. In one of my last memos to Black campus leaders and organizations, I urged them to stick together, to plan more projects that would get them more active in the Baton Rouge Black community and to build ties to Southern University. I urged them to take their seats at the political table and to volunteer to work on campus projects.

Although I was active in student government I didn't want to hold an elected position on campus for fear of losing because I took strong positions. Mike kept me on his team and I began to organize important campus projects ranging from an apartment guide for LSU students to organizing to get more streetlights and after-hours transportation for women students. I became the liaison between the student population and the university, so I had an important role with the Black students as well as the larger student body. I made sure we had minority students on practically every governing board at LSU. I did my research and I could make my case. I was a hell-raiser. At the national level, I started traveling on behalf of the U.S. Student Association (USSA) and the National Coalition for Third World Students. This gave me an opportunity to work with other campus leaders, especially in the South. We used these ties to strengthen our hand on campus and to network with other student leaders.

In 1981, I was invited by the YMCA to the World Youth Conference on Peace, Détente and Disarmament in Helsinki, Finland. When I told Jean, she asked, "Where is Finland?" "In Europe, near the Soviet Union," I told her. After discussing the trip with Lionel, they agreed that I could go, and I went down to Canal Street to get myself a passport. This trip, which first took me to New York, was one of the most amazing trips of my life. I met people from all over the world, including Africa. I wrote in my diary about what it felt like to be a member of the world where you're not designated as colored or White but simply as an American. I was an American. This was unsettling because it meant I had to defend my country and I wasn't always quite sure how.

The election of Ronald Reagan shook up the world. Many of the delegates from other countries lined up and denounced the United States for fueling the nuclear arms race. To make their point, the sponsors invited representatives from Hiroshima to address the conference and they told of how America dropped the bomb. I looked around the room and said, "We did not drop the bomb, the White man dropped the bomb." All I could say was that I did not vote for Reagan. It didn't matter how much we distanced ourselves from the president, we were still Americans. Here I was, in this bitterly cold country where the sun burned day and night and the people walked around looking at us as if we were from another planet. I wanted to go home. But we had another day added to go to Vienna, to debrief and thaw out before returning to the United States.

I became very active in the USSA and was elected to the board. Soon, I lined up a job with the National Student Education Fund (NSEF) as a lobbyist. Reagan's election, especially the Republican Party's sweep of Southern states and the low voter turnout, really confirmed my belief that I had to go to Washington to work for change.

I often thought about the many hours I had spent as a child sitting on the levee, on the banks of the Mississippi River near our house, dreaming and plotting my life. I'd sit there alone for hours at a time, looking at the muddy dark waters of the river trying to understand where my life was headed, how it would flow. More than anything, I wanted to help. I had a tremendous weight on my shoulders. I wanted to help my people, not just my immediate family, but everyone I loved and Black people in general. I had a really strong sense of history and a sense of responsibility that I wanted to be part of the struggle. I told Jean over and over again that I wanted to get involved in national politics. She was skeptical. She wanted me to use my education to earn money. All my life I had worked, saved my money and shared it with others. I was ready for a different path. Sitting on the levee, I dreamed for three years of political activism at the national level.

I finally graduated in the summer of 1981. Jean, her mama, her sister Gwen and my uncle Johnny and uncle Floyd and all the kids came up to Baton Rouge in a blue Ford Taurus. When my name was called to get my diploma I told Chancellor Wharton, as I shook his hand, that I was glad to be leaving. He smiled and told me that he was glad I was graduating, too. He was relieved to see me leaving campus because I had spent four years writing editorials criticizing him for how slow the administration was to accommodate the growing number of Black students, how insensitive LSU was to the needs of students on campus and how weak he was in his support of scholarships for financial aid. We drove home that evening, somehow getting my trunk and all my stuff into that small car. We had a great family dinner of smothered pork chops, collard greens, potato salad, crawfish étouffée, red beans and rice and bread pudding. And later that night, Lionel allowed me to sit on the porch to see my friends. Everyone came over to congratulate me. Then, after all the food, after all the joy of the day, I sank into a depression. I did not want to leave home. My family was all I ever had. It was a crazy childhood, but my parents worked hard to get us all in school.

My sister Lisa saw me sitting under the weeping willow tree playing with our dogs. The year before, Lisa had given birth to a little girl, Janika. She was now living in the room formerly occupied by me and Cheryl. Lisa asked me what was wrong. I told her I was depressed because I had no way to get to Washington, D.C., and the job that was waiting for me because I didn't have the money. Lisa looked at me and reached into her blouse and pulled out a handful of bills. Lisa was working two jobs to support Janika. She counted out four twenty-dollar bills, five ten-dollar bills, three five-dollar bills and five one-dollar bills. "Here," she said, "a hundred and fifty dollars will get you there." I didn't know what to say. I was so grateful. I jumped up and hugged her (something we rarely did in my family) and said. "I'll pay you back in two months. I promise." Lisa looked at me and said, "I know you're good for the money." She was right. I always made good on my promises. I ran back inside and told Jean. She told me to call her mama right away. We had some cousins in the Washington metropolitan area and they could put me up until I found somewhere to live. I called Mama and told her. She told me about my cousins Thee and Anita. Mama told me to call my uncle Nat in New York, who would help me plan my trip. Uncle Nat was a cop. When I called his home, Jenetta, his wife, told me about the airlines going on strike because Reagan fired the air traffic controllers. She told me not to cross the picket line and to make a reservation to take the train. I did.

Jean told all her friends about my trip. Once again, I started to receive all sorts of odd gifts and good wishes. The week before my trip I received a credit card from Sears—my first. I was still cash poor, but I used the credit card to purchase a suitcase and a new pair of shoes. Next, I bought a washing machine and dryer for my parents. For years, I had watched my mother soak her clothes in the tub, rinse and hang them up outside. I wanted to leave my parents something for all they had given me. Lionel tried to give me one of his rusty guns for protection. I told him that I would be okay. That Sunday morning I went to church, lit a candle, prayed in the front row, walked back home along the tracks and told Ms. Minor, the Johnson family, the Conrads and Burtons good-bye. My train was leaving after dinner and I had to go to Providence Memorial Park Cemetery, where Grandma was buried, to put roses on her grave and say good-bye. Before I left home, I went down to the levee. I wanted to take one last look at the mighty Mississippi River and to pray. God had gotten me through college. He kept His promise. Now I wanted to pray and ask for strength and faith to keep my end of the bargain. For now, I was saying good-bye to my home and the people who raised me to give back and help others. I would soon miss Kenner, Louisiana.

CHAPTER FIVE

GARLIC GRITS

Grits in Louisiana are stirred with butter, and sometimes cheese, but rarely plain. When I got to Washington, D.C., however, I tasted some on Capitol Hill made with onions and garlic and they were delicious, too. I discovered that maybe I'd stir the pots in D.C. after all.

I ARRIVED IN WASHINGTON, D.C., on September 20, 1981. I was twenty-one years old and excited about being in the nation's capital and starting my career in national politics. When I got off the train and looked around Union Station, I felt completely grown up. No one was there to greet me, but I saw a line of cabs nearby and asked a young Black man to help me carry my trunk and suitcases to the car. As we walked over to put my life's belongings in the cab, I saw the dome of the U.S. Capitol. I was in awe of its size and the building surrounding it. The young man walking with me was not impressed. I thanked him and gave him three dollars and told the cabdriver to take me to 2000 P Street, N.W. The cabdriver was a foreigner. I could tell from his thick accent. "Where are you from?" I wanted to know. He told me Africa. "Have you been there?" he asked. "No sir," I replied, "I'm from New Orleans, Louisiana." "Oh, why are you here?" he asked. "I have a job and now I must look for an apartment," I said to him while I stared out the window as we drove past the Capitol, the Justice Department and the Mall. When I arrived at the headquarters of the NSEF, Kathy Downey, the executive director, was standing at the door waiting for me; she knew what time my train was to arrive and she was expecting me. I spent the rest of the afternoon discussing my job, which was to promote and train women students on college campuses to be leaders. The job would require traveling around the country, recruiting students to lobby, attending meetings in D.C. and organizing political events. The NSEF was the education and training arm of the U.S. Student Association, which was a union of sorts of all the student governments across the country. This was a natural for me because I had been active in all the student government movements nationwide. It was my ideal job—the pay was okay, but I mostly kept thinking of the experience I would gain. As the sun began to set, Gwen Benson Walker popped into Kathy's office and told me to wait around. Gwen was a maverick, a petite, chocolate-colored sister, a firebrand of a woman and a single mother of three children. When Kathy left the office, Gwen found me in the hallway looking over books. "Donna, do you have a place to stay?" she asked. "No ma'am," I said. "Well," Gwen hollered, "come on with me." My cousins Anita and Thee were upset that I failed to check in with them, but I wanted Gwen to fill me in about my new position. I would catch up with them later on in the year. During the car ride home, up Thirteenth Street past Georgia Avenue to New Hampshire Avenue, Gwen invited me to stay with her family until I had enough money to rent my own place. I was extremely grateful. Kathy had made a similar offer, but I was missing my own family, so staying with Gwen would help me settle down.

After two weeks I received my first paycheck—$435. I went over to the Madison Bank on M Street and opened a checking account, depositing the entire check. For weeks I lived off the free food at receptions and meetings, plus whatever Gwen fed us at home. In less than two months I saved up enough money to rent an efficiency apartment in the Minnette, a yellow-brick apartment building at 320 Constitution Avenue, N.E. I paid $285 a month for a rent-controlled furnished efficiency. I would live in that apartment for ten years. I quickly made friends with Barbara Covington and Al Bowie, two African Americans who lived in the building. Another African American lived on the first floor, but I rarely saw him or smelled anything coming out of his apartment. This was not the case with Al and Barbara. Al was from Monroe, Louisiana, and I met him one day after a long walk from work. I was starving and too tired to trek up to Capitol Hill for another round of receptions. When I opened the door to the apartment building I smelled greens—collard, mustard or turnip. It didn't matter. I was hungry and I desperately needed an invite. So I pretended to lose my keys and went back out to buzz apartment 12. When this man walked out, I said to myself, whoa, he's skinny. "Hi, my name is Donna Brazile and I live in apartment eight, but I lost my front-door key," I said in one full breath. Al stood there for a minute and said, "Where are you from?" "Louisiana," I said. He looked surprised. "What part?" he asked. Al, whom I would later call Bowie, grabbed me and pushed me inside his apartment toward the dining room table. Pam Grisham, his co-worker at Chamberlain Career Center, was sitting at the table with a drink and together they welcomed me to Washington with a big plate of collard greens, macaroni and cheese, corn bread and a nice cold beer. After dinner, he called Barbara, who lived in the basement apartment, to come up to meet me. They became my nucleus, not just my friends but also my family away from home. No other tenants opened up their apartments to welcome me.

In Washington I started a career pattern that I have followed all my life. I have never worked just one job. I have too much energy, too many ideas. I have never been a nine-to-five woman. I have always been someone more likely to work from eight in the morning to ten at night.

That first year I also became active in the effort to make Dr. Martin Luther King's birthday a national holiday. During the day I organized students to make them more effective in lobbying for their own agendas, including fighting to save student grants and loans. At night I organized students—frequently the same ones I met during the day—to be an effective constituency in support of the King holiday.

In the spring of 1981, Reverend Ralph David Abernathy, chairman emeritus of the Southern Christian Leadership Conference (SCLC), was a guest speaker as part of the Think Week series that was the focus of our Black History Month programs at LSU. After Dr. Abernathy's speech, I spoke with him at the faculty lounge where he was staying and encouraged him to tell Mrs. King that I wanted to help out in the national effort. I told him that I had spent time with the Louisiana Survival Coalition helping to lobby the state to observe King's birthday and that I was ready to go national.

Still, I had also come to Washington to learn the ropes of working on Capitol Hill and soon I was. Gillis Long, my home-state congressman, had an intern position open and Willy Meaux, his chief of staff, encouraged me to apply for it. I wanted to work with Gillis to keep a hand in Louisiana politics, and I wanted to learn the legislative process so I could become a more effective lobbyist for students. They hired me with a small stipend to spend time at the office helping his wife, Cathy, with correspondence. Cathy Long became one of my good friends and to this day remains a part of my life in Washington.

There were so many people and members of Congress that I met and began working with during those first months in Washington—Representatives Henson Moore (R-La.) and Lindy Boggs (D-La.) met with me to discuss politics in Washington. I also took time to meet my senators, Russell Long (D) and J. Bennett Johnston (D). Soon I ventured away from my Louisiana roots and met Representatives Patricia Schroeder (D-Colo.), Claudine Schneider (R-R.I.) and Peter Peyser (D-N.Y.), who were championing legislation to help students. I got to know many members of Congress and became very good friends with John Conyers (D-Mich.), who was leading the effort to make King's birthday a holiday. John Conyers introduced me to Walter Fauntroy, who was the nonvoting delegate representing the District of Columbia. I wanted to become more involved in the politics of "Chocolate City," as D.C. was often called by Blacks then, and I thought that by working closely with Fauntroy I'd be more actively engaged in the civil rights struggle.

Walter Fauntroy had been one of Dr. King's main lieutenants in Washington. He spent much of his youth working to register African Americans to vote and was one of the key organizers of the historic 1963 March on Washington, along with Bayard Rustin. Fauntroy's office was in the Rayburn House Office Building and his staff—Wayne King, Johnny Barnes, Alfred Jones, Clifton Smith and Yvonne

Green—were all very accessible and allowed me to come around to help out.

So I had all these bridges. I would bridge my student politics to the civil rights movement, my civil rights movement work to congressional politics, and back to student politics. I was also, in a sense, adopted by people like Jack O'Dell, A. C. Byrd, Maurice Jackson, Phyllis Jones, Ivanhoe Donaldson, Teresa Cropper, Cora Masters, Damu Smith, Adjoa Ayitero, Beverly Dehoniesto, and Cathy Powell—all of them local activists. I was this kid with all this energy and they would give me projects to work on, from stopping the Klan to organizing Black empowerment events at local churches. No matter what they told me to work on, I was fast. I was efficient. If they said, "Donna, we need five hundred people for a rally," I brought seven hundred. If they asked me to put together three different types of meetings, I put together six. And then Walter Fauntroy would keep me in his office until one or two in the morning typing up lists, so I got to know all the names of all the important people, not just in D.C. but all over the country. I had a photographic memory, so if I typed in Coretta Scott King's address in Atlanta, Georgia, it would stay in my head for the rest of my life. And so I became indispensable to the movement because I had a good memory and I was scrupulous about keeping a paper trail. I kept all my notes and materials in files. My trunk became a bookshelf of sorts, with records of important events and the people who were actively involved in organizing the political empowerment of African Americans. I got so wrapped up that I forgot to send home a Christmas card and Jean called me, upset. Christmas meant a lot to Jean. She wanted her children to come home, get a good meal, and rest up for the New Year. I was too busy trying to mail enough letters to get people to attend the January 15 march on Washington to make King's birthday a national holiday. I was on a mission again.

The civil rights movement was seen by the mainstream media and political thinkers as dead. But to the many African-American leaders and organizers I met, including Howard University's Ron Walters (now at the University of Maryland), the movement was in transition from being one that "tore down the walls of discrimination" to one that "opened up the doors of opportunity." I knew that the movement was not dead—it had a pulse, albeit weak, and the moral voice and conscience of the movement was still needed. America had turned a page, but the chapter on racial reconciliation was still being written. This was a chapter I understood and wanted to be a part of. So I worked day and night to find my place in the struggle. At times it was depressing because many of the leaders did not accept me because of my young age, but I made up for it by maintaining a good work ethic and completing every assignment in a timely manner—without complaint.

There was a groundswell of support building for the King holiday, but there was considerable congressional opposition as well. Senators Jesse Helms (R-N.C.) and Strom Thurmond (R-S.C.) were working with various conservative groups to oppose the initiative. And there were others who said that Dr. King was not a patriot. Stevie Wonder's song "Happy Birthday" in support of the initiative really galvanized the effort as well. It was really quite amazing that in the midst of the conservative tide that had swept Ronald Reagan into office in 1980, we organized people all over the country around the idea of making Dr. King's birthday a national holiday.

But there was a geographical split in this movement. People like John Conyers felt there should be a huge march on Washington in support of the drive, but Mrs. King wanted a celebration in Atlanta. In 1982, I served as the director of mobilization for the second march on Washington in support of the King holiday. We drew 150,000 people and we were able to pull it off thanks to Mayor Marion Barry, who gave us office space at Ninth Street and Pennsylvania Avenue, S.E. We had no money, but that didn't stop us. Mrs. King's celebration down in Atlanta made national news with a large parade filled with celebrities and a wonderful church service at Ebenezer Baptist. Teresa Cropper, an entertainment lawyer from Chicago, was our leader. She kept both teams working together under the same umbrella. Tree, as we called her, was also our liaison to Stevie Wonder and his manager, Abner, who helped bring in celebrities and communicate with the King family.

Mrs. King wanted the focus to be on the events taking place in the South, not in Washington. Like many others in the civil rights movement, Mrs. King did not support the idea of national marches to achieve the goal of a national King holiday. There was always the fear within the leadership of the movement that we could not generate the crowds of the past. I took the opposite view. Maybe it was because I was young and did not have a long history in the movement, but I felt, what did we have to lose? Why not have a march for King's birthday. The King holiday gave the progressive movement a voice. People were so demoralized and felt so powerless after Reagan's election, and this drive brought progressives together again. It gave people a focus. It was a positive issue, something we could stand for rather than just always being against Reagan cutting social programs.

Bringing 150,000 people to the Mall was a major accomplishment and I started with my base—students. My job was to make sure that on each campus we had a committee devoted to the King holiday drive. I had campus coordinators all along the East Coast and the Midwest. Their job was to raise money to get a bus and to fill that bus with students going to the march. I'd begun organizing as a child, when we had to decide how all of us would fit into a car or get on the bus to go downtown to Canal Street. I came from a large family and Jean was the first organizer I ever saw in action. I just thought back to how skillful she was at getting us around.

I figured out how many buses it would take to fill up a quadrangle. I know for a fact that you need fifty thousand people to fill up the west front of the Capitol, or you could fill up the east front with ten thousand and it will look like a huge crowd. I took my plans, my diagrams, and my message to all the campuses where there were USSA leaders and chapters. For NSEF and USSA, this gave them another coalition to support student issues; for the movement, it gave us more foot soldiers. I helped raise the money for buses and vans and then I would report back to Teresa and she would ask how many buses I had gotten committed each week. Buses were literally rolling in. They were so impressed that I could organize so effectively and so fast that they gave me even more responsibility.

Weeks before the march, celebrities—among them Stevie Wonder, Gladys Knight and Gregory Hines—came to D.C. to hold press conferences and attend area churches. We needed the churches behind us to house all the students coming into town. Nobody had hotel money; these were kids. Stevie Wonder provided the financial resources we needed to get materials, posters and literature out. He would come to town as the main attraction at these great events that would prepare people for the actual march. Then Reverend Jesse L. Jackson came on board and that gave us even more legitimacy. Then members of the Black Caucus—Parren Mitchell (D-Mich.), Shirley Chisholm (D-N.Y.), Harold Washington, Cardiss Collins (D-Ill.), William Clay Sr. (D-Mo.), Louis Stokes (D-Ohio), Charlie Rangel (D-N.Y.), Walter Fauntroy and others—began pulling for us, pitching in, helping us out.

Mrs. King still held her official celebration in Atlanta, but in Washington, our goal was twofold: to put pressure on Congress to get more co-sponsors for the bill and a presence in congressional hearings, and also to pressure the states to make Dr. King's birthday a state holiday. The day itself, January 15, 1982, was cold, and there was snow, but the crowd looked beautiful. The buses roared in and parked along the route. We tried to get the vans to go past the Capitol and park at RFK Stadium for access to the Metro. My logistics team found vacant lots and cars carrying marchers from across the East Coast. By noon the crowd was large enough, diverse enough, and warm enough for the speeches to begin. I felt a sense of pride. We did it. Later, Teresa Cropper told me she would give me a glowing recommendation to help out on the next major march on Washington.

All the organizing I did for the King holiday helped me to understand the importance of local grassroots organizations and community-based leaders. We got people to call their governors, to lobby state lawmakers for legislation to be introduced in state legislatures in support of the holiday, to conduct write-in campaigns. We had petition drives across the country. We had an army of volunteers working to make the King holiday happen. And after the march we continued to lobby not only for the King holiday but also for legislation to create a million jobs for the long-term unemployed.

The following year, 1983, was the twentieth anniversary of the historic 1963 March on Washington. I went to Atlanta to meet with Mrs. King about the planned anniversary march and once again I was appointed youth coordinator. The theme of the march was not only to honor Dr. King but also Jobs, Peace and Freedom. We also wanted to spotlight President Ronald Reagan's disastrous record on the poor and working people.

RONALD REAGAN WAS ONE of the most conservative presidents in modern history. After his election in 1980, Reagan went about cutting taxes for the wealthiest Americans and dismantling programs for the most vulnerable citizens in the land. The civil rights community disliked all of his domestic and international policies and vowed to defeat Reagan at the polls in 1984.

During Reagan's tenure, African-American unemployment skyrocketed to almost 20 percent. Rather than address issues of inequality and injustice, Reagan often ignored pleas by civil rights leaders to show some compassion. The administration's massive buildup of the military diverted resources from inner cities and public education. The King holiday was about more than honoring a man who stood for peace and justice; it was an organizing tool to energize citizens in time for the 1984 presidential election—a campaign in which I was eager to serve as an active participant.

When I was tapped to help organize the anniversary march, I knew that I had to quit my position at the National Student Education Fund. It would be a financial sacrifice, for I wouldn't have a salary for the months I was working on the march. I would have to survive on unemployment benefits and my friends who could cook. But it didn't feel like a sacrifice to me. It felt like a mission I had to be part of. In the movement you were hired but rarely paid.

Our first office was at 1542 Ninth Street, N.W. This was Operation PUSH headquarters. PUSH was headed by Reverend Jesse Jackson. Jack O'Dell and Mary Bates Washington worked out of the D.C. office. Jack had been active in the 1963 march. Mary was the secretary and PUSH gave us a little office space upstairs. Our office was down the street from Shiloh Baptist Church in the historic Shaw neighborhood. We worked there for months until we were able to raise enough money to begin our groundwork organizing the march.

From the start I was told to focus on organizing students, the buses and local contact people. As a former representative of USSA, I was given the task of being one of the national conveners of the March on Washington. Mrs. King was comfortable with me working directly under congressional delegate Walter Fauntroy, who was in charge and was going to "hire" someone to serve as national coordinator. Until then, I ran the day-to-day activities in the national office and helped to hire other staff members. The biggest joke was that while I was indeed the national student coordinator, I was doing most of the work pulling the whole thing together. There was little or no salary, so nobody wanted to take on the job. It was a Catch-22.

Pretty soon Peter Parham, Cathy Powell, Carol Page, Lezli Baskerville, Thomas Atkins and Steve Miller were hired to assist me. When we grew out of the office space at PUSH, Sam Etheridge of the National Education Association (NEA), which had endorsed the march, helped us to get larger office space at 1201 Sixteenth Street, N.W. Because of the success I had with the previous march, I used the same formula for organizing support on the campuses. In addition, I started organizing Black churches and Black organizations like sororities and fraternities. I also got grassroots Blacks and progressive Whites like Chad Dobson, who was involved with the nuclear freeze movement, and Brady Tyson, who was close to Andy Young, to become actively involved. We had key people all over the country working with us. If you said Durham, North Carolina, I would say Lavonia Allison. If you said Philadelphia, I would say Henry Nicholas of Local 1199. If you wanted Cleveland organized, I would call Otis Moss. I knew every person in every city who could organize and get Black people on the bus. That was my specialty. I had no other portfolio inside the march machine, but I understood that organizing was key to its success, not to mention fund-raising.

WHEN I WROTE or called Jean, I found it hard to describe exactly what I was doing. I didn't have much of a salary. It was because of friends like Al Bowie, Pam Grisham and Barbara Covington that I survived. I was literally eating out of cans. To pay my rent I did odd jobs for friends. I was a great cook so I would cook for parties and earn $50 here and there by making seafood platters, gumbo, beans and rice. Now and then Walter Fauntroy would give us $20 or $50 or whatever he could spare. And there were my unemployment checks, but they ran out after a while, yet somehow I survived. I walked everywhere because I had no money for the Metro. People would buy me lunch. Employees of NEA like Warlene Gary and Teresa Rankin came on board to help and they found ways to get lunch inside the building. People just took care of us.

By the beginning of the summer of 1983 I was running the Twentieth Anniversary March operation. Whenever the other conveners met, someone made the statement that the committee should hire me. Delegate Fauntroy tried to get Guy Draper and Thomas Todd, two well-connected African Americans, to move to Washington to play a role. But they could not break away from their busy work or families. I just went on doing my job. I hired Cathy Powell to assist me with local organizing. Her job was to interact with the D.C. community as well as colleges, universities and public schools in the area, raising awareness of the march. (Cathy's son Scott died on 9/11 at the Pentagon. He had been one of our young volunteers.) I was running the march by default because nobody else would step up to the plate. Then one day attorney Lezli Baskerville and Shelia High King, who worked for the National Alliance of Postal and Federal Employees, informed the executive committee that I needed a title and a salary. "Donna," Baskerville said, "needs a promotion and a paycheck." They told the group to officially designate me for the job that I was doing unofficially. But there was resistance. Behind my back I heard some leaders complaining that I was just "too young." Eleanor Holmes Norton, at least, had the decency to tell me to my face that she was opposed and had told Coretta "you must be losing your mind to hire someone so young." All this talk about my role and my salary took me off my game. I wanted to organize and so I left it to others to defend me. Meanwhile, I had to get my bus totals up.

Dr. Benjamin Hooks, who was the executive director of the NAACP, came to town three weeks before the march. There was a meeting with Bill Lucy, representing the Coalition of Black Trade Unions, Norman Hill of the A. Philip Randolph Institute, Jack O'Dell, Walter Fauntroy and A. C. Byrd. Brady Tyson, a professor at American University and a good friend of Mrs. King and Andy Young, sat next to me. Brady and I worked on the Call to March. He often took me to Hunan Dynasty on Capitol Hill for dinner. We would talk for hours about how to get more Whites involved in the civil rights movement and struggle.

Finally it was the big meeting—the last meeting of principals before the march. Dr. Hooks arrived late. He sat next to Reverend Joseph Lowery, president of the SCLC, and looked across the table and asked me point-blank: "Donna, how many people are we expecting on August 27?" Without hesitation I told him 250,000 plus. Everyone at the table looked at me in disbelief. I told them, "We will match what you all had twenty years ago." I was feeling confident and a little bit in control as I had finally raised enough money to actually pay my staff. And I took a modest salary to cover my rent. The Twentieth Anniversary March was my turning point in the movement.

At that meeting we went over all the plans for the day of the march and the program. There was a lot of nervousness about the decision to bring in Arab Americans, gays and lesbians and other nontraditional associates of the civil rights movement as part of the march. The tension in the room was thick. While everyone argued about their position on the podium, their place on the front-line camera angle, I focused exclusively on expanding the outreach to include Black Republicans, giving local leaders some events to sponsor and working with students, who did most of the work. Dr. Hooks said that if we failed to produce a crowd of 250,000 or more, we would be laughed out of town. Immediately, everyone looked nervous. Walter Fauntroy finally spoke up and said he could find the money to hire a coordinator at a really high salary. This made me extremely upset. Here I was working day and night. Yes, I was only twenty-three, but I knew what I was doing and I had plenty of experienced people like Jack, Lezli, A.C., Brady, Chad and Leslie Kagan, a peace activist who organized over a million people in New York in 1982, helping and guiding me. I asked, "Why hire someone this late in the game? The march is days away." They looked on and I kept my focus on planning the march.

Reminding everyone how the sound system had been sabotaged at the 1963 march, and how the organizers had to call President Kennedy, ironically an early opponent of the march, to get a new sound system from the Park Service, I said we needed to raise money for state-of-the-art sound equipment. I was able to get a good sound system practically on credit from Myles Clark of Events, Inc.

After the meeting, I got embroiled in fighting over who would deliver the keynote speech. Reverend Jackson wanted to deliver the speech, and the keynote address had grown from one that would talk about jobs and peace and freedom to one that included the environment and a nuclear freeze. The Arab community, led by Jim Zogby, wanted to have a voice in the march and speak on behalf of the Palestinians, and the Jewish community, led by Rabbi David Saperstein, expressed strong reservations. The lesbian and gay community wanted poet/activist Audre Lorde to speak on their behalf. They even staged a protest at Delegate Fauntroy's Capitol Hill office and got arrested. I got involved in all the warfare swirling around who would speak, when, for how long and what they would say. I was too young to fully understand the politics of all this.

In the end, I typed the final version of The Call and faxed it to Mrs. King's office for edits. The Call was our organizing document that was supposed to answer questions about why we had to march again. At times, I felt as if we were working on a new draft of the Bible. Everyone wanted to see the final document before they would endorse the march. It went through hundreds of drafts. This was before the Internet, so we had to type it up and send it to every participant overnight. We would have conference calls at night with Mrs. King, Ben Hooks, Joe Lowery, Andy Young (when Andy couldn't make the calls Brady Tyson would represent him), Reverend Jackson, Judy Goldsmith from NOW, Rabbi Saperstein and Walter Fauntroy.

During these calls they all offered their ideas on how the program should proceed; my job was to take notes, type them up, and fax them to everyone for additional input. Two days before the march I turned the program over to Barbara Williams-Skinner, a friend who worked on the Hill for Congressman Ronald Dellums (D-Calif.), because I needed to focus on the buses and the crowd. I was haunted by a warning from Ben Hooks. A few days earlier we held a final meeting at the mayor's office with Joe Yeldell and Sam Jordan. Ben Hooks looked at me and said, "I hope you're ready for this because if there is any violence, if there are any problems, you'll be held responsible." This was an enormous burden and one I felt was unfair. I went cold inside. First my projection for a crowd of 250,000 was questioned, and then I was told that if there was any violence I'd be blamed. Hooks said if I failed to get a big crowd or if there was any violence, my career as an organizer would be over. Over fish dinners that evening in the cafeteria at Shiloh Baptist Church, Jack O'Dell told me stories about the history of the movement and the role that different people played in it. He told me that the NAACP wanted to "legislate Black people into history," while SCLC, SNCC and CORE were using nonviolent tactics of direct action. After the meeting, while I was still bristling from Hooks's warning, Jack had pulled me aside and reminded me that the NAACP did not like confrontation. He tried to raise my spirits and remind me that regardless of the size of the crowd we would still make our points about the need to continue Dr. King's dream of a just society. I wrote in my diary that night, "The civil rights movement will never accept young people without a struggle."

I called Barbara Williams-Skinner and told her, "You know what? I don't care who speaks." Louis Farrakhan had become the latest issue. He was coming to the march. I had survived the Arab/Israeli conflict and the gay and lesbian movement versus the Black church, and now came the Black Muslims versus the civil rights leadership. I had had it. I couldn't handle any more interpersonal skirmishes and I returned to what I did best—organizing. I didn't sleep for the two days leading up to the march. By August 15, we estimated that 2,600 buses would come to D.C.; representatives from every state and over 200 foreign countries would attend. The Twentieth Anniversary March had struck a chord in the hearts and minds of a wide spectrum of people. People wanted to attend to honor Dr. King's legacy and to hear the powerful message he articulated on August 28, 1963. They also came to stand up and be counted at a time when so many people had lost jobs and dreams despite Reagan's promise that it was now "morning in America."

On the day of the march, based on our bus totals and the number of people who rode the Metro that day, we estimated that we had 400,000 people in attendance. That's 150,000 more than attended the original march. We filled not only the perimeter around the Reflecting Pool at the base of the Lincoln Memorial, we also filled every available grid along the Reflecting Pool, all the way to Seventeenth Street, to the Washington Monument, and to Fourteenth Street. And there was no violence.

Once the speeches started, I walked around to shake hands with my staffers and others who had volunteered to serve as marshals. The speeches were too long. Too many voices. Many criticized the Reagan administration for turning its back on the poor. I did stop working long enough to watch the main attractions—Ben Hooks, Jesse Jackson, Joe Lowery, Andy Young and Louis Farrakhan—all give their long speeches. When it was finally over, Susan Kidd of Channel 4 interviewed me about the march. Later that evening, sitting in Al's living room feasting on ham, turkey and dirty rice, I saw myself on television looking dead tired but talking about the enormity of the moment. The next day, the *New York Times* coverage of the march included a quote from Leslie Cagan saying of me, "She's the one who holds this whole thing together." And I was quoted on what kept me going on a project of such proportions: "I recognized that there is a great need for us to catalyze the nation, stir the conscience because people are really affected and hurt by policies of injustice and inequality."

I always prided myself on the fact that it never rained on my marches. Sunday, the day after the march, it rained. After church I went back to the Lincoln Memorial to make sure that all the trash had been picked up, including the Sani-Jons, Don's Johns and other portable toilets. I wanted to make sure that we left the Lincoln Memorial the way we found it. I spent an hour picking up trash myself. Then I sat down on the steps of the Lincoln Memorial with a cup of coffee and looked all the way over to the Washington Monument, remembering how this same space had looked the day before, filled with people. I savored the memory and the moment. I was now truly a part of the struggle. I had been baptized by fire.

More than anything I wanted to go home to see my family, but I had neither the time nor the money. Since I'd come to Washington, whatever money I had been able to spare I sent home to help out the family. I missed them. I longed to climb up the weeping willow tree or sit on the levee and watch the big ships and barges go up and down the Mississippi River. My family needed me. If the pressure of organizing the Twentieth Anniversary March wasn't enough, in the weeks leading up to the march, Jean called and told me that the family had to move out of the Filmore Street house. I couldn't believe what she was telling me. Jean said that since Grandma had not left a will, the other family members had decided to file a succession for the house. Lionel did not have the time or money to bid on or buy it. His brothers and sisters sold the house right from under us.

His sister Lucille had tried to give him a heads-up, but it didn't come in time for Lionel to prevent what happened. They filed for succession on the West Bank, it was announced in the daily papers, but Jean and Lionel did not know what to do. Uncle Johnny tried to find them a lawyer, but it was too late. The house was on the market and was quickly sold, and they got the notice to vacate. It was too late for me to help my family. All I could do was help them with rent.

It was the saddest moment for me because I knew all these important, influential people—Mrs. King, Stevie Wonder, members of Congress. I knew everybody, it seemed, but I couldn't save my family home. I didn't know who to turn to so I kept it to myself. I borrowed some money from my friends and told them I would pay them back as soon as I had a job. I was able to send $1,000 home to Jean, and with the help of her sister Gwen, she was able to move the family from Kenner to a nice-sized house off Jefferson Davis Highway in New Orleans.

Because my parents were given less than twenty-four hours to move, we left so many of our childhood mementos behind. There were still six, maybe seven kids living at home. It was very traumatic because the younger kids still attended school in Jefferson Parish and had to catch the bus back and forth to school. I was very bitter, but I decided to let it pass. I still liked my aunt Ethel and my cousins, but Jean took it hard. So did my other siblings.

After the march, Ben Hooks and his wife, Frances, gave me five hundred dollars to take a vacation. I used the money to pay my friends back. Mrs. King called to thank me. But it was Eleanor Holmes Norton, Dr. Mary Frances Berry and Vernon Jordan who really reached out to me. Suddenly I had an entirely new status with them. They wanted me to go to law school. And after the march I became good friends with Reverend Jackson.

Then I took a trip to the Soviet Union sponsored by the YMCA. This was another remarkable international journey to Moscow, Leningrad and Baku, located in the Azerbaijan region. It was a small group and there was only one other Black person, Cassandra Pye, a dear friend who now works for California governor Arnold Schwarzenegger. The delegation of fifteen Americans had been selected from all the major student groups. It was a great trip because it gave me a very different worldview, especially of the Cold War and its impact on both our nations. This was my second international trip and I wanted to know more about international politics. The Russian people were indeed curious about our culture and wanted to know why we hated them. I had no idea at the time because I was not familiar with the cold war, but this time I defended America. I spoke up about how the civil rights movement was transforming our country, despite Ronald Reagan and the conservative movement.

Later we stopped in London to debrief, and by the time I came home, I was ready to do something totally different. In fact I had recently stepped down as president of the National Third World Student Association. I had received good job offers from the labor movement, women's groups and civil rights groups to come and organize. I had great job offers to work on Capitol Hill and in the upcoming congressional elections. Everybody wanted to know what I wanted to do next.

Finally, there was movement on the King holiday bill. Congresswoman Katie Hall (D-Ind.) was on the congressional committee that moved the legislation to the full House of Representatives. And on October 19, less than two months after the march, the Senate approved the measure 78–22. On November 2, flanked by Mrs. King, Katie Hall, John Conyers, Walter Fauntroy and others, President Reagan signed the legislation. I was there, too. For the first time I looked at President Reagan, whom I loathed, and smiled at him.

The King holiday drive unleashed an even more ambitious design for the movement. The day after Reagan signed the bill, Reverend Jesse Jackson announced plans to run for president of the United States. Prior to his announcement, Jackson and Reverend Joe Lowery of SCLC had convened meetings all over the country to discuss the possibility of an African American running for the highest office in the land. But there was a big split between the politicians and the ministers. Some of the politicians wanted to identify someone who would make a run similar to that of Shirley Chisholm in 1972, and they put together a short list. Although many of the civil rights leaders and elected officials had endorsed Walter Mondale, there was a growing number of African Americans who, after the march and the passage of the King bill, wanted to revive the movement and make the transition to electoral politics. We had reconstituted ourselves as the civil rights movement and we wanted to take the kind of bold action that would help us to increase the number of African Americans who were running for political office. Harold Washington had won the election for mayor of Chicago in a grueling but inspiring campaign that captured the imagination of Blacks all over the country, and it made many of us think that anything was possible. We wanted a seat at the political table. For the first time, many Black leaders were openly critical of the Democrats taking us for granted and the Republicans for ignoring our community completely. Our time had come. This was our moment to seize the national agenda and demand inclusion in the electoral arena where all the decisions that affected our lives were being made. The momentum was finally on our side.

CHAPTER SIX

JAMBALAYA

A literal fusion of flavors, colors and textures, jambalaya is a thick and hearty dish of tomatoes, rice, ham, andouille sausage, chicken, celery, peppers, onions, garlic, parsley and other Louisiana seasonings. Much like Reverend Jackson's Rainbow Coalition, it combines many disparate elements into a satisfying whole, greater than the sum of its parts.

THE CALL FROM REVEREND JACKSON came early on a Saturday morning. "Donna," he said, "this is your brother. You did a good job organizing those marches. Can you help me pull together some people to kick off my campaign?" He wanted me to help pull together the formal announcement of his intention to run for the 1984 presidential election. I said, "No problem, but I've got to call Mrs. King."

Mrs. King, along with some influential members of the Congressional Black Caucus, Andy Young, Joe Lowery and much of the Black political and civil rights leadership had all decided to endorse former vice president Walter Mondale as the Democratic candidate to run against President Ronald Reagan. They felt the resources were not available to support a Black candidate, and the rift in the leadership that had grown when Congresswoman Shirley Chisholm ran in 1972 had not healed. I had become extremely close to the entire King family during my work on the march and although I supported Reverend Jackson's decision to run, my personal allegiance was to Mrs. King.

This was one of the first times that I had to make a major decision about working for one faction versus the entire movement. I turned to prayer. And later that day I knew it was time to call Mrs. King. I didn't know how I was going to break the news to someone I had come to really love. Before I made the call, I reached out to Teresa Cropper to get her input. Teresa and I had become very close working on the King holiday events and I valued her opinion and support. Earlier in her career she had worked with Reverend Jackson and she knew his inner circle. I also called Eleanor Holmes Norton, then a law professor at Georgetown University. Eleanor wanted to think it over, but she said, "Go on, you're still young."

I called Mrs. King after 10:00 that night. All civil rights people were night owls. You could never call them in the middle of the day. They were early-morning and late-night folks, doing some of their best work at night, which is how I operate to this day. I was nervous. We talked for a few minutes about my trip abroad and what I had learned. I told Mrs. King that I had boxes of material, including lists of activists and others, and I was shipping it down to the King Center in Atlanta. Finally, she broke the ice and asked me what was going on with Reverend Jackson. I broke down and said, "I need your advice." I really didn't want to break away from helping her because I knew how she felt about Reverend Jackson. Mrs. King thought that Reverend Jackson was going to make up his own mind without much input from the other civil rights leaders. I finally explained to her that he was offering me a great opportunity to continue organizing and to help him build a movement through political participation. Although at that time I had neither a title nor a promise of pay, I told Mrs. King that his campaign would continue the work we had started—rebuilding the civil rights movement, registering new people to vote and energizing young people. The Reverend's candidacy, I assured her, would not be just about winning the White House, but about getting more people elected at the state and local level. I really wanted to get involved in electoral politics at the national level. I had gotten involved on a small scale in 1982, but not in any capacity to affect the process. Ann Lewis, the political director of the Democratic National Committee, met me at the DNC headquarters on Massachusetts Avenue and encouraged me to volunteer in a couple of congressional campaigns. But that had only whetted my appetite for the larger and higher stakes arena of a presidential campaign.

Mrs. King told me that she didn't think my decision was a good idea but that she didn't think it would do any harm, since I was an organizer. However, she wanted me to reach out to Doris Crenshaw in the Mondale campaign. She said that Reverend Jackson was mostly concerned about Reverend Jackson rather than the movement, and that he wasn't going to reach out to many of his colleagues across the country. It took me a long time to understand the full meaning of her advice about Reverend Jackson, but at that time I saw his presidential run as the next phase of the struggle for genuine civil rights, and if Jackson was the vehicle, I was going to get on board.

There was talk of Congressmen Charlie Rangel and John Conyers running, and Mayor Maynard Jackson and others, but it was just talk. Jackson kept his own counsel and reached out to a small number of people, like Jack O'Dell, Howard University professor Ron Walters and D.C. mayor Marion Barry. He wanted to make history and he wanted to jump out there before anyone else changed his or her mind. He had an impeccable sense of timing and he understood how to get before a story and then become the story. Reverend Jackson was brilliant in terms of politics and he was a master of manipulation when it came to the media. And of all the civil rights leaders, I found him to be the most bold and visionary. He really wanted to push the envelope farther than the other leaders. Reverend Jackson was at the time the best at mobilization and politics, and he understood the marriage between electoral politics and grassroots progressive movements. I struggled with the decision even after I had made it, but I didn't really see it as taking sides, although others did. So there I was again, on the ground floor, ready for battle but with no time to prepare. Yet this was what I wanted. I had written in my diary that I wanted to run a presidential campaign, and what better way to start my career in presidential politics than by going with Reverend Jackson.

I made calls to all my personal political heroes. Dr. Lowery was upset. Ben Hooks was nonchalant, saying he didn't care one way or the other, and I could hear him grinning on the phone. I didn't call Andy Young. Walter Fauntroy understood; he was neutral but supportive. Both the NAACP and the National Urban League had announced their opposition to a potential Jackson candidacy. Mayors Coleman Young of Detroit and Tom Bradley of Los Angeles were also opposed. This was going to be tough. I felt it in my stomach. All the key Black leaders were going with Walter Mondale. Although Gary Hart and others were running, the Black community had begun to coalesce around Mondale. This did not stop Jackson from calling every leader in his black phone book, and he found some Hispanic and Native American leaders, like Tony Bonilla and Julie Henderson, who would come on board the campaign and attend the announcement.

Reverend Jackson made his formal announcement on November 4, 1983, at the Washington Convention Center. Anita Bonds, Marshall Brown and I did not have a lot of time to put the event together. We called Lawrence Guyot, June Johnson and my old friends A. C. Byrd and Steve Miller to all pitch in to build a crowd in less than forty-eight hours. Reverend Jackson was good at giving last-minute orders to build huge crowds, so we learned to pass out leaflets at area churches, call ministers to make announcements, hit the airwaves and put up posters near the event. That day the place was packed. Everyone in D.C. politics and some folks from across the country came to show their support and witness history. After some preliminary speakers, Jesse Jackson took to the podium and gave a two-hour speech attacking Reagan, Republicans, corporations and the Democratic Party. I was standing near the door collecting names and giving out bumper stickers. I was excited. The press showed up in great numbers. We had six TV cameras, and I knew Reverend Jackson would be pleased with the huge turnout and the press coverage.

Tyrone Crider and I were among the youngest people involved in the campaign and were told to take over the political operation, with Tyrone coordinating the ministers and me working the progressive organizations and civil rights leaders. Preston Love was the deputy campaign manager, Barbara Williams-Skinner was the operations person and Anita Bonds was the field director. I served also as the

Rainbow Coalition director until Sheila Collins and Carolyn Kazden were hired. My friend Thomas Atkins, who had helped me with
the various marches, served as volunteer coordinator. Thomas was
from Richmond and I often called upon him to travel with me down
South, especially when I had to drive overnight by myself.

ARNOLD PINKNEY, an African-American businessman from
Shaker Heights, Ohio, was brought on board to serve as campaign
manager. Sylvia Branch was the scheduler. Emma Chappell, an
African-American businesswoman from Philadelphia, was treasurer,
and Linda Moody was our compliance director. The rest of the staff
and volunteers did odd jobs, but for the most part the campaign felt
more like a movement. Mr. Pinkney tried to bring some discipline to
the operation and told us that because of our late start, we had to
help Reverend Jackson get on the ballot and qualify for matching
funds. I decided to put together a team to help the campaign get on
the ballot in key states. Anita assigned me to the South, where I had
the most contacts. Before I got on the road, she told me to sit down
with Mr. Pinkney to discuss a salary. I was so naive. I had no idea
what to ask for so I told him that $750 a month would cover my bills.
Later on I learned that others on staff were making anywhere from
$20,000 to $50,000 annually, but I only asked for enough to pay my
rent and keep me going, and that's what the campaign paid me for
working over eighteen hours a day, seven days a week. Jesse had us in
church every Sunday and often throughout the week.

Before the primaries even began Reverend asked me to take the
lead role in capitalizing on the tremendous number of contacts I had
made during my years of organizing, to facilitate some prominent
endorsements from women's groups and others and then to focus on
getting out the vote. We immediately turned to the march coordinators and made them Reverend Jackson contacts. I had my hands full
when I began reaching out to the women's organizations. Judy Goldsmith, NOW's president, and Mary Jean Collins, vice president for
action, sat down with me to go over the endorsement process. They
told me to contact the national board and local chapters. Judy told
me privately to get Jackson to "update" his position on reproductive

rights—abortion was a taboo subject with most civil rights leaders. When it came to race, they were liberal. But when the subject changed to gay rights or abortion rights, they were either mum or dismissive. Here I was, a twenty-three-year-old Black Catholic girl who had always taken the Church's position on these issues, talking to Baptist ministers about abortion rights. I did not know where to begin, so I reached out to Jean for advice. My mom had nine kids. As we were growing up, she taught us to respect our bodies and to take care of our health, but we never discussed abortion. When I called home that night to ask her about abortion, she cut me off. "Donna, I am not going there" was all I got out of her before she hung up the phone. I could make neither heads nor tails out of Reverend Jackson's position and I could not find Eleanor, who was traveling.

In my diary I wrote that this was so distressing. I had no clue about Reverend's position or how to discuss the topic with him. I decided to call Reverend Jackson's wife, Jackie Jackson, who was one of my best friends and someone I admired as being honest and truthful. She told me not to be discouraged and that I could call Reverend Willie Barrow or Dr. Mary Frances Berry. Reverend Barrow said she was "not working on women's issues for the campaign." I then placed a call to Dr. Berry, who gave me the best lecture of my life on the meaning of controlling my own body. I was back in action and on the phone telling NOW's board members that Jackson was indeed "pro-choice." We picked up a couple of board members after pledging to name a woman running mate, but the Mondale team had enlisted more than half the board and all of the major state chapters. We were going down in defeat. Many of the board members confirmed to me privately that they did not take our bid seriously and that Jackson had no chance of winning the nomination. I was disappointed, but I felt we were doing just fine reaching out to various constituencies only one month into the race.

I was asked to help raise money, which I did by traveling with Jackson to help generate matching funds. Reverend was a tireless traveler. Once you got on the road with him, you could stay for days without getting back home for a change of underwear. Reverend Jackson had a wide network of preachers pitch in to get his name on the ballot and raise matching funds. Fund-raising was as easy as going to a church with Reverend Jackson and passing the hat after his long, uplifting performance. He taught us the elements of a great speech: "start low, go slow, rise high, strike fire and sit your butt down." Reverend would pass the hat, asking five people to raise their hands for freedom, and we would go over and get a hundred dollars from those five people, sometimes in cash, which we later converted to money orders. And then he would ask who wanted to be in the game but not on the field for freedom and justice, and then he would get fifty dollars from those people. We raised money the old-fashioned way. We had people raise their hands, stand up and say they wanted to help us keep the dream alive. And we did voter registration at every campaign stop by asking all the unregistered people to raise their hands and come forward. After a brief prayer, Reverend told us to get their names and addresses or we could just fill out the forms right there in church.

I did the early organizing in the states. I had to learn all about the party's rules and delegate selection process. This was the first time someone was reaching out to Black leaders and activists to take their seats at the table and go to the convention with a platform or agenda. Soon, though, Reverend Jackson began complaining about the rules of the Democratic Party and how they were stacked against us. In some states it was winner take all. In others, you had to reach a tremendous threshold in order to get delegates, and because he started late we needed more time to get on the ballot. It was always exciting, fun and demanding working for Reverend Jackson. We were not afraid to challenge the status quo or to walk into a state party meeting and ask for a place on the agenda. Reverend would call the office and say with only a day's notice, "I'm heading up to New York, can you get up there and organize a rally? Call Basil Paterson, Dave Dinkins, Herb Daughtry, Bill Lynch, Ed Lewis and Reverend Wyatt Tee Walker to pull together an event." We were expected to know all of these leaders, including the church people. If you were on the Jackson campaign you had to know everybody or pretend that you did.

Jesse Jackson kept one of the biggest black phone books I ever saw. He didn't have a regular phone book. It was more like the Black Pages. It was a big black notebook with hundreds of pages and phone numbers for every key leader in the world. I once saw a phone number in the book for Yasir Arafat and an address for Winnie Mandela. My job was to let the key people in every city know that Jackson was coming to town and to inform the press. But I never had more than forty-eight hours to organize a key event.

Whenever they needed anyone to organize I was assigned the key states. The first state I organized was Georgia, and we beat Walter Mondale in three congressional districts. Then I was sent to Louisiana, my home state, which of course we won. We won the Virginia caucuses and in Alabama we came in second. Our motto was "Our Time Has Come." Despite the pass-the-hat effort, we had no money, so we reached out directly to the people. When Jackson arrived in a city, he would draw big crowds, especially on campus. Our little motorcade would cross over those tracks and Jackson would get out of his car, work the line, give a mini–press conference and go inside and talk to the leaders. In every city we had to organize a meeting before the event so Jackson could give out marching orders. After the meeting, the music would start (yes, we always had music) and the crowd would come alive. Some prominent minister or local political leader would heap praise on Jackson and then Reverend would take the stage. He began his sermons on the struggle to get the vote and who died for that right. He would then remind us of the challenges ahead and why voting would help us to protect and expand our freedom. The speech ended with a call to conscience to register and vote or give money—sometimes both. The campaign gave me everything I had ever wanted to learn about organizing masses of people. We had an infrastructure, a good message and a daily dose of uplifting sermons. I never grew tired or bored listening to Reverend Jackson's speeches. I was completely won over by his energy, zeal, enthusiasm, brilliance and charm.

We were doing better than people expected because, while we didn't have a lot of resources, we had the people. Jackson told us we had a "poor campaign with a rich message." It was a crusade. The Mondale campaign was top-heavy with consultants and an array of talented people, like Doris from Alabama, who came out of the civil rights movement. She was one of my mentors, like James Orange of Atlanta, who had taught me how to organize. Mondale had money, resources, the support of organized labor, a large staff, but Reverend Jackson's campaign had people—Black, White and other people of color—excited about politics. We started to generate a buzz in some progressive circles, especially in the peace movement. Jackson condemned Reagan's Star Wars program as a huge military buildup. Thus, we began to pick up folks like Steve Cobble, a white organizer with ties to labor, to help us make inroads into the Progressive community. Because Jackson wanted to build a national Rainbow Coalition, made up of environmentalists, labor leaders, Hispanics, gays and lesbians and peace and justice folks, he encouraged me to allow Caroline Kazden and Sheila Collins to begin organizing White women. Armando Gutierrez and his sister Gloria were supposed to focus on the Hispanic vote. Alexis Herman and Ron Brown, who were serving as unpaid advisers, gave us lots of advice about how to get more involved in the Democratic Party apparatus. Many of us were outsiders and had no idea about the party's rules or nominating process.

Yet despite the excitement that Reverend Jackson was generating in many parts of the country, we couldn't crack the Democratic establishment in terms of key support. I grew frustrated that so many in the civil rights community failed to take the campaign seriously. I told the *Washington Post,* "This is very disappointing because Reverend Jackson represents the activist tradition. . . ." I told the *New York Times* that "the charge that Reverend was 'unelectable,' which was the excuse many were giving for not endorsing him, was simply wrong. We believe Jesse's just as electable as Mondale." I spoke to them on the record. And when the National Organization for Women failed to support us, we began to call them "THEN." We just kept organizing and trying to make a difference. When I was home that Christmas, Jean organized the entire family to come over to see me. They were so proud of me and what I had accomplished with the King holiday and the marches. I was just glad to be home to eat a normal Christmas meal of filé gumbo, jambalaya, stuffed bell peppers with shrimp, dirty rice and bread pudding. Over dinner I went around the table and asked the adults "Are you registered to vote?" Many of them said yes.

We began the year in many of the early states, including Iowa and New Hampshire. Reverend qualified for matching funds and he received Secret Service protection. Throughout that period, Jackson received death threats and I was less than happy to be on the road with him, so I traveled a great deal with Mrs. Jackson. She began to generate huge crowds and people liked her. Then in February all hell broke loose. On February 22, 1984, the *Washington Post* reported in an article by Milton Coleman, a Black reporter, that Reverend Jackson had called Jews "hymies" and New York "Hymietown." This was a tough one. Initially Reverend Jackson denied that he had made the remarks. Many of us working for him asked him point-blank when he came into the office about it, and he told us it was a smear campaign. Arnold Pinkney had called us to the headquarters at Twentieth and M to discuss the furor, and Jackson walked in during our staff meeting. He told us to keep our eyes on the prize. We believed him. We had no reason not to. Florence Tate, our press secretary, was saying that the media was blowing this out of proportion. I believed everything I was being told. I was a foot soldier in the movement. There was no reason to go against the leader of the movement when he denied such a charge. Because I was close to so many Jewish people who had been active in the movement, like Joseph Rauh, Hyman Bookbinder, Rabbi Saperstein and all the others from the March on Washington, I was asked to call them and tell them that Reverend Jackson had not made the remarks.

In my phone calls, I told them that I trusted Reverend Jackson because he had never lied to me before. This was a huge dilemma because the Jewish community was a big part of our base. It became a real mess, with allegations that Louis Farrakhan had threatened the life of Milton Coleman, and Black journalists criticizing Farrakhan for implying that Black journalists who criticized Black leaders were traitors to their race. This mess was getting out of hand. In the middle of my first major presidential campaign, the Black-Jewish tension was erupting again and I did not want it to escalate out of control. I knew I had to handle it again. I considered the dispute like a family feud. But with Farrakhan's statements and some residual impact from the march, our campaign was beginning to lose its focus and go flat. Something had to give. I leaned on Mrs. Jackson to see what she knew. She was in the dark, too. Finally, Jackson admitted that he had made the ethnic slurs. He told Frank Watkins, his longtime communications adviser and press secretary, to prepare remarks for delivery in New Hampshire, and on one of the morning news shows he said, "Even if I lose the election, I must maintain my integrity, that's what's important to me."

What about my integrity and the integrity of the staff? I wrote in my diary. We lied for Jesse Jackson. I was outraged. How could he set us up to tell people he did not make the remark when he in fact had? I had to do something. Mr. Pinkney wasn't talking, nor were Preston Love, Jack, Frank or Florence. We were left to ponder all of this by ourselves. We had no guidance on the next step. The clock was running out and we knew it. I made a personal decision that I could no longer work for Reverend Jackson if he could not tell his staff and inner circle the truth. I was tired of learning things in the newspaper and confronting him later for an explanation. I was ready for some answers. I wanted it to be over with soon if it meant Jackson being pulled off his message.

In spite of all this, as we got closer to the convention, it was clear that Jackson had achieved much that he had set out to do. He had expanded the number of people who could see themselves as part of the civil rights and progressive struggle. He created a coalition of conscience, bringing together White women, Hispanics, environmentalists, peace activists, gays, lesbians and organized labor, saying to them all that they were part of the movement. We estimate that we registered over three million new Black voters as a part of his campaign and increased the number of local candidates running for office. But when you try to do that in a political context, you have to run almost a flawless campaign, and we weren't capable of doing that.

As the campaign wound down, we were cutting back on office staff and Jackson was up front about the amount of debt we were facing. He asked everyone to take a 20 percent pay cut, which for me meant that I'd end up with next to nothing. He said that we had to get to the Democratic National Convention in San Francisco in the most economical way. He wanted to end on a high note and that meant having a role at the convention. He named C. Delores Tucker, chair of the Arrangements Committee, to help coordinate our activities at the convention. I was assigned to help with floor operations and to get our three hundred plus delegates information on a daily basis. Over four thousand delegates would be attending, representing the Mondale, Hart and Jackson campaigns. I was very excited to fly out to California to take part in this event. Reverend Jackson had a suite at the Hyatt Hotel. Most of the staff stayed in some dump around the corner. When I arrived, I checked in with Reverend, who told me to find Mr. Pinkney. I had another assignment. When I caught up with Pinkney a couple of hours later in our trailer at the Moscone Center, he asked me if I could help round up 350 delegates from the Mondale campaign to sign a petition to place Reverend Jackson's name in nomination. I told him, "Of course." He had given me less than twenty-four hours. I immediately ran over to the St. Francis Hotel to ask for help from Doris Crenshaw, Mondale's director of African-American outreach and a key civil rights organizer.

By our estimates in the campaign, Jackson had won 21 percent of the popular vote in the primaries. Yet, we went to the convention with only 9 percent of the delegates. The rules were a barrier to our progress and we wanted them to change. Doris didn't hesitate to help us because the last thing the Mondale folks wanted was a fight on their hands at the convention. We got our signatures and I ran back to the hotel before the deadline to get Jackson's signature. When I knocked on his door, Mrs. Jackson answered. She always greeted me warmly and I told her that I had all the signatures. She pointed toward the bathroom and told me Reverend was shaving. I walked in on him in his bathrobe and told him to sign the papers. He said, "What for?" I took a deep breath and said, "It's for you to address the convention." He thanked me and I went running back to the Moscone Center to file on behalf of the Jackson campaign.

The convention hall was huge. I stood there on the floor with my rainbow-colored vest and hat and took it all in. I heard that Barbara Jordan, who had recently resigned from Congress, was there and

I went running to the Texas delegation. I just missed her. Next, I ran to the New York delegation to meet another hero—Shirley Chisholm. Ms. Chisholm was a petite Black woman who ran for president when I was in high school. The Soul Sisters Club had endorsed her bid. I just wanted to meet her. When I got to the area where the New Yorkers were sitting, I saw Bella Abzug holding court. Bella was wearing a dark suit and a wide-brim hat—one of her signature items. She was one of my feminist heroes, along with women like Gloria Steinem, whom I was working with on the board of advisers of Voters for Choice. (During the Jackson campaign, I became actively involved in the pro-choice movement.) Ms. Chisholm was standing next to Maxine Waters, then a state representative in California and the Jackson's campaign convention coordinator. I tried to make eye contact with the two of them. Maxine told me to come over and she introduced me to Ms. Chisholm. I told Ms. Chisholm that I had read her book, *Unbought and Unbossed.* She gave me a strong handshake and told me to visit her suite later. I was so excited! Governor Mario Cuomo of New York, who was to give the keynote speech, walked past us with his security detail in tow and waved at Ms. Chisholm. Right then, I thought to myself, I should get their autographs, but I was too busy listening to the great speeches and working the crowd.

I went back over to the trailer to talk to Anita, who was working on delegate tracking. We were afraid the Mondale folks would pick off some of our delegates, so the campaign kept Lisa Levine, Thomas and me on the floor talking to people, especially the elected leaders. Soon we got enough delegates to get Reverend Jackson a chance to speak before the convention during prime time. The speech itself was classic Jesse Jackson—biblical, political and all-around inspiring. Because Reverend Jackson had dared to make the run without the support of the civil rights establishment, and because of the Hymietown scandal and the undeniable achievements of the campaign, there was enormous anticipation as to what he would say. He began his speech reminding the convention that his constituency was "the desperate, the damned, the disinherited and the despised. They are restless and seek relief. They've voted in record numbers. They have invested faith, hope and trust that they have in us. The Democratic Party must send them a signal that we care. I pledge my best not to let them down." And he proclaimed near the end of the address that "Our time has come. No grave can hold our body down. Our time has come. No lie can live forever. Our time has come. We must leave the racial battleground and come to the economic common ground and moral higher ground. America, our time has come." It was a powerful speech and everyone was pleased with it. People openly wept as he spoke and he was given a rousing ovation as he brought his entire family—Mrs. Jackson, Santita, Little Jackie, Yusef, Jesse Jr. and Jonathan—onto the stage with him.

I felt that my time had come as well. I was so proud because I knew that I had made the right choice to work with Jesse Jackson. I had had to break with Mrs. King and her wing of the movement, but everybody could see that a new chapter in Black politics had begun. They would soon follow and bring others into the electoral arena, including Martin Luther King III. Not only did I feel vindicated, but I finally had something to stand on. I had a major presidential campaign under my belt. No matter how much the party had tried to marginalize us, nobody could deny how we had energized national politics. And now I was part of the major leagues. Paul Tully, who was active in the Mondale campaign, Gina Glantz, Doris Crenshaw and all the other major-league strategists in the Democratic Party and Ann Lewis all approached me that night after Jackson spoke and asked if I would consider working for Walter Mondale.

This was all heady stuff for me, but my personal victory was overshadowed by another and more negative political trend affecting Black women. Ms. Chisholm, C. Delores Tucker, Mary Frances Berry, Eleanor Holmes Norton, Addie Wyatt, Maxine Waters and Reverend Willie Barrow had met privately during the primaries and the convention to discuss the disrespect being shown to Black women by the Democratic establishment. They talked about the fact that Mondale had floated the names of Barbara Mikulski, Dianne Feinstein and Geraldine Ferraro, a three-term New York congresswoman, who eventually became the nominee, to be Mondale's running mate, but no Black woman was mentioned. I was torn between working for the

Mondale campaign and working with these women to create the National Political Congress of Black Women. I met with the group in San Francisco during the convention. Shirley Chisholm convened several meetings where we decided that we would form this national organization devoted to electing Black women and making sure that Black women had a seat at the table. We decided that never again would Black women be excluded from the political process.

Meanwhile, Gina Glantz, who was Walter Mondale's deputy campaign manager and the director of field operations, called me and said, "Look, when you get back to Washington, let's sit down and talk about your future." This lifted my spirits. I had somewhere to go. Another decision to make, perhaps another break and a new opportunity.

When I got back to D.C., Gina and I met at the Mondale headquarters on Wisconsin Avenue and it turned out that I was the first person from the Jackson camp that the Mondale campaign wanted to hire. After all, I was the kid who went out and beat them in many of the Southern congressional districts. They offered me $2,000 a month, which was fine with me. I'd have a real salary and could pay off some of my debts. I would work with Nikki Heidepriem, a lawyer from South Dakota who later became one of my best friends. Paul Tully also told me that he wanted me to do women's outreach as well as help with the Ferraro campaign because of the rift that had developed between White and Black women over the selection of Geraldine Ferraro. So once again I had to make another big decision, this time about leaving Reverend Jackson. I felt as torn as when I left Coretta Scott King's camp.

Despite the Hymietown issue, I was still Reverend Jackson's number one runner. And I wanted him to be proud of the fact that I was leaving to go work with Walter Mondale. But Ernie Green, the civil rights hero and one of the Little Rock Nine (who integrated the public schools in Little Rock, Arkansas), warned me that Reverend Jackson would not take kindly to me making such a decision, cutting my own deal without involving him in the negotiations. At the convention, Jackson decided that he wanted Ernie and Yolanda Caraway to go over to the Mondale campaign. He told me to stick with him because I was an organizer. But this was an opportunity for me to work with the party's nominee and to move up in the party. I'd be working with the former vice president of the United States. This was the highest calling you could receive in national politics. And I also thought that for Reverend Jackson this would have been personally gratifying because he had groomed, trained and taught me so much.

The conversation that I had hoped would be a fond send-off instead became a showdown. It took place right outside the Mondale campaign headquarters as I was leaving and Jackson was coming in to meet with Jim Johnson, the campaign chairman, and Bob Beckel, the campaign manager. Someone must have told Jackson about the offer from the Mondale camp, because he asked me if I had made my decision and I said, "Yes, I'm going to work with Walter Mondale." Reverend is a tough person to look in the eye. He's tall and he had become a major influence in my life. Without missing a beat, he looked at me and said, "You'll be like a branch without a tree."

"A branch without a tree?" I asked him, puzzled.

"You will no longer be rooted in the movement if you work for Mondale."

"But this is what you trained us for, trained me for, to run a mainstream campaign, and now that's what I'm ready to do."

I argued that there were so many other young people coming up through the ranks of the movement, people he was mentoring as he had mentored me, who could take my place. I tried to get him to tell me why he didn't want me to work with the Mondale campaign but he wouldn't say anything more and he turned and walked into the building. His words completely destroyed my spirit. The next day I asked Arnold Pinkney to try to help me smooth my relations with Jackson. I didn't know what he had told the Mondale people about me. When he didn't want you to go somewhere, well, no one wanted to go up against him.

Jackson complained that the Mondale campaign was "cherry picking" his team. I was nervous. Would Jackson torpedo my job? Would he put the word out on me and tell everyone that I had betrayed him? I went to praying almost immediately to calm my nerves and to find ways to talk to him about my decision. I reached out to Eleanor, who told me to stand my ground. I wanted affirmation so I called Mrs. Jackson and she told me I should "not forget the people." Yes, the people, I thought. This was not just about Reverend Jackson; it was about the people who caught the early bus like my mom and her friends. The people who worked two and three jobs to make ends meet like my dad. I did not owe Jesse Jackson as much as I owed my people. Those were the roots, I believed, that would keep me grounded in national politics.

Many people in the Mondale campaign were fed up with Reverend Jackson and simply wanted him to go away. He kept hammering at issues like divestment from South Africa, abolishing rules that had the effect of keeping the number of African-American delegates very low and second primaries or run-off elections. Reverend Jackson talked to Ron Brown, Vernon Jordan and Ron Walters, then a professor at Howard University, about proposing a fairness commission to examine the delegate issue. He wasn't about to stop his campaign. He was still organizing, but I wanted to help Mondale get rid of Ronald Reagan. In my diary, I wrote "Jackson could not wait until the election was over to get the Rainbow movement back in gear."

Reverend and I did not heal our rift for another several months. I was quite bitter. I had worked for him for peanuts, and yet he refused to stand by me. He had supported Yolanda Caraway and Ernie Green in working for Mondale and what irked me was that they had not worked full time on the Reverend's campaign as I had. As senior advisers to Reverend Jackson, they became his liaisons to the Mondale campaign. Their job was to negotiate whether or not he would campaign on behalf of the candidate, if he needed to do additional voter registration on behalf of the party. Jackson never stopped campaigning. Campaigns were like the movement—and the movement didn't have a deadline. The election wasn't the end of the movement. The election was just the beginning of another phase of the movement.

I got real close to Doris, Gayle Perkins, George Daley and Charles Atkins, who were all with Walter Mondale. They became part of my extended political family. And I kept in touch with Mrs.

Jackson, who didn't seem to hold my decision against me. I heard that she had said of my decision, "Well, she does have to eat." She was always someone who would slip me $50 or $100 to make sure that I could eat and stay on the road. Mrs. Jackson once told me that I needed to update my wardrobe, which I had never cared about. But I did now, because I was traveling with her.

Jesse Jackson was my mentor. He was my champion. He taught us we could do anything with faith. He often told us, "Suffering breeds character and character breeds faith." In the end, Reverend Jackson would say, "Our faith will never disappoint us." He taught me the value of relationships and how to build coalition. Jackson would lecture us to never surrender or give up. When we would grow tired and weary of registering new voters or talking up his candidacy, he would reach over and pick up one of the Bibles he carried and read us Scripture. His favorite, like one of Grandma's, was Psalm 30, "Weeping may endure for a night, but joy cometh in the morning." Our joy was now in electoral politics. Jackson taught us to dare to win. I did not want to give up the struggle or the fight to empower the disenfranchised poor people, women and minorities in the political process. I made the decision to move forward to keep the rainbow movement alive in the Mondale campaign. Our time had finally come.

CHAPTER SEVEN

THE MELTING POT

Many Cajun and Creole dishes combine a great variety of sauces into a singular mixture. Most dishes include a vast array of seasonings and spices, including chili pepper, salt, cumin, oregano, garlic, cayenne pepper, black pepper, parsley, onion, bay leaves and thyme. Of course, if that's not enough, you can always add some Tabasco sauce, too. Like those ingredients, I entered the Mondale campaign as someone on the periphery of national politics, but would soon get mixed into the entire brew.

I HAD LEFT Jesse Jackson's campaign behind, but ironically, on the Mondale campaign, my job was deputy field director working with Gina Glantz. I was assigned to outreach for the Jackson delegates and supporters and to help our vice presidential nominee, Congresswoman Geraldine Ferraro. I made several trips on behalf of Ferraro including the October 21 trip to Harlem, where she had her first rally at the Adam Clayton Powell Building on 125th Street. Gordon Gant and I organized that rally and then I traveled down South to try to help Mondale shore up his support in Louisiana, Georgia and other Southern states.

Working on the Mondale campaign I became one of the "players" within the Democratic Party. It was an opportunity to be on the same playing field with other young grassroots organizers like Tom Cosgrove, Steve Rosenthal, Michael Whouley, Teresa Vilmain, Tad Devine, Elaine Kamarck, Tom Donilon, Mike Ford, Joe Trippi, Doug Sosnik, Steve Elmendorf and Julie Gibson. These people were state directors, and they were the best in the party. They were all young,

twentysomething go-getters I had heard about as the future strategists in the Democratic Party. We were all up-and-coming. Some of
them had worked on Ted Kennedy's campaign in 1980. This was my
first opportunity to go head to head with the people I would later call
my peers in the political profession.

I found that in this profession, with the exception of Charles
Duncan, George Daley, Charles Atkins, Doris Crenshaw and myself,
there were only two or three African Americans at every stage of the
game. And there were hardly any women or Hispanics. The more
deeply involved I got as an operative, the more White and male the
landscape became. There were a few women—Gina Glantz, Alice
Travis, Wendy Sherman, Katie Whelan, Pat Eltman, Marcia Hale,
Susan Brophy and Susan Estrich, who later became manager of the
Dukakis campaign—but overall it was a very small universe of people.
It was like an exclusive club and I had become a member. If I'd stayed
with the Jackson family I would never have had the chance to com-
pete with the more experienced White operatives and become a
"Democratic strategist."

I didn't want anybody putting "Black" in front of my name when
they saw me. I wanted them to put "Democratic." I wanted to be a
Democratic strategist. I didn't want to be just a Black grassroots organizer. I had to shed the movement background a little bit to reach
the next level in the political arena. For me it was always about making it to the next level. It was about never staying in one place. I had
been on a path since childhood to realize a dream that I had shared
with only the pages of my diary for fear that my dream of running a
presidential campaign one day would be ridiculed.

Nikki Heidepriem was the director of women's outreach and I
was supposed to be her deputy along with doing the fieldwork. In addition, I worked with Doris Crenshaw on outreach to the African-
American community. Nikki had an office on the main floor at the
campaign headquarters. I found that my desk was outside her office.
I asked her if she expected me to sit outside her office as if I were her
secretary. She said no. I said fine. The next day when she came in
I had put my desk and my chair in her office. I didn't want anyone to
mistake me for her secretary. I wasn't secretarial material. I don't take

orders from anybody, just directions. Tell me where you want to go and I will help you get there, but I would rather quit than take orders.

They understood that. I had to take the number 30 bus from Pennsylvania Avenue in southeast Washington all the way up to Wisconsin Avenue and back at night. I was catching the bus while they were riding to work in their cars. They were eating expensive lunches while I was bringing my lunch in a brown paper bag. I had a head on my shoulders, no doubt. Reverend Jackson would tell us that our ego was gasoline for our ambition, and I used my ego and everything that he had taught us. I put it all into practice. I think I carried Jackson's water better than anybody that he assigned to work for Mondale.

I came to greatly admire Paul Tully, Mondale's political director and a veteran Democratic strategist. Imagine me being in a room with someone who had worked on all these campaigns going back to Bobby Kennedy's day. It helped that he was dating Nikki at the time. That's the other thing I learned about political campaigns. They were notorious for sex and relationships. I didn't have a personal relationship during my work on the campaigns. I never wanted my business discussed around the table like everybody else's business. There was a soap opera quality about campaigns that I didn't like at all. I wanted to get my job done so I could go home and not be bothered with all the crap. Nikki lived near me on Capitol Hill at Eleventh and D Street, S.E. Paul was indeed a charmer. Nikki constantly talked about him in the office. Paul was invaluable to our efforts. I listened. I also listened to Nikki reach out to women leaders to discuss the Mondale campaign, especially her calls to Congresswoman Barbara Mikulski (D-Md.), who was one of our national co-chairs.

Paul was short on conversation. He was always on the phone. When I first met him, I said to myself, "Oh my God, he drinks and he smokes. What could be the big deal with him?" But Nikki told me about Paul's life and career. Every day when I came into the office Nikki had another story to tell me about Paul. "Tully," as she called him, "has a big heart. He worked for Bobby Kennedy. He understands targeting and organizing." Nikki encouraged me to finally get up the courage to talk with him. After my first week on the job, I finally decided that I needed to get to know Paul. I wanted to know why he was considered so brilliant, so smart. Why did people think he was the best thing since sliced bread? So Nikki pulled me into Paul's office and from that day forward, I had a mentor, the person I needed in order for me to reach my goal. I was clearly nervous. Finally, Tully said, "So you know how to organize?" I just nodded my head. The man was staring straight into my eyes.

The first thing Paul taught me is that message drives politics. When he told me this I looked at him and asked, "What's a message?" No one had taught me what a message was. Paul told me that we had to look at polling and decide how best to position Mondale on both domestic and international issues. Having a strong message could help Mondale define his candidacy. Next, our mailing and media campaigns would focus on just a few issues to move undecided voters into the Mondale camp. This was exciting. Tully shared polling information and some campaign sound bites with me and asked my reaction. They didn't sound like what we did on the Jackson campaign. "Come Alive on May Five." "Punch eight before it's too late." With Jackson, those themes got us through election after election. But for Tully and the Mondale campaign, we didn't just have themes or slogans, we had a message. Mondale wanted to draw a sharp contrast between himself and Reagan. He focused on the administration's neglect of working families and argued against the ballooning budget deficit.

Paul was the one person I didn't mind being a gofer for. Being his gofer meant making sure that he had a pack or two of Marlboro cigarettes. When he drank in the evening, I would booze it up with him like the best of them. I'd spend hours in Paul's office and he would tell me everything about polling, targeting, organizing, what the Democratic performance in a particular district was and what precincts you should target based on performance. We discussed base vote, voter contact programs and how to expand the electorate. Paul was a wealth of information—a walking political encyclopedia. I was one of his beneficiaries.

UNTIL I MET PAUL, I had based my political strategizing on where people lived, where they shopped, where they worked, where they played and where they prayed. My organizing was never based on statistical factors like how a congressional district had voted in the last six presidential campaigns. Paul taught me the strategy of targeting and how you got the numbers you needed on election day. He taught me there was a correlation between the number of people you needed to turn out on a particular day and Democratic performance in those districts, so that you knew exactly the people that had to be targeted with messaging—meaning phones, mail and door-to-door contact.

I'd always known *how* to organize; Paul Tully taught me the *science* of organizing. There were grids you could put together to create a model of how to win the presidency. Over the course of the three months that I worked for Walter Mondale, Paul Tully nurtured me. I would never go back to being that little kid from Kenner, Louisiana, who just organized. I was on my way to becoming a strategist. I understood the connection between message and politics and communication. I knew gross rating points, how many points you needed on TV and what market to reach and how many voters and what precincts. I missed Reverend Jackson and the movement, but I was happy to be exposed to everything I was learning.

Yet there's something about the movement that's just so wonderful and unpredictable. The Mondale campaign was predictable—you knew what you were going to do every five minutes, and it was boring. It was like watching paint dry. In the Jackson campaign, every day was different, every hour chaotic and every minute a challenge.

You didn't know where Jackson was going the next day. You didn't know where you were going either. You didn't know what Jackson was going to say, you didn't know what church he was going to hang out in for three hours. Because I missed the spontaneous, almost combustible energy of the movement but needed the mainstream campaign I was now a part of, I kept a foot in both camps. Jackson taught me that everyone needed a base to start from and a base to come home to. I never wanted to stray far from my base in the Black community. It was a source of energy and pride.

Ted Mondale, the vice president's son, introduced me to his dad after a labor rally. Vice President Mondale was warm and talkative. He had a yellow pad in his hand and was writing something down when Ted walked in the holding room with me. "Dad, this is Donna

Brazile," he said. "She worked for Reverend Jackson and is now help-ing us out in various states." Vice President Mondale looked up and greeted me with a nice firm handshake. "Welcome, thanks for all your help," he said to me. I nodded—I didn't really know what to say. I had too much on my plate, with many Jackson supporters still sitting on the fence and reluctant to switch alliances. All I wanted was to win and beat Ronald Reagan.

That was easier said than done. In October 1984, I was assigned to go to Woodbridge, New Jersey, before I went to New York. I was told that Doug Sosnik, who was running the campaign there, was having trouble getting Mayor Ken Gibson of Newark and Reverend Reginald Jackson and some other statewide leaders on board for Mondale. There were problems in Newark and I had to go see what they were up to and if I could help out.

I called one of my friends, Councilman Donald Tucker, to meet me at the train station. We decided to go to a little club in Newark for dinner. Once we got there and got settled in a booth, he gave me a briefing on the political situation. Newark, like Detroit, did not take kindly to outsiders coming in and telling the locals what to do. Tucker told me that the Mondale folks were arrogant and abrasive and someone needed to get them out of the state before all hell broke loose. Andy Young had recently made a statement about "smart-ass White boys who don't know what they were doing" trying to run the political show. Well, when Tucker told me the news, I said, "I hope you're not going to kill me because I'm the messenger. Besides, I am on my way to New York, I'm just stopping over and I don't have any-thing to do with running New Jersey." The truth is, I knew from Tully that the campaign was trying to work on a formula as to how much money each state would receive for the Get-Out-the-Vote (GOTV) operations. I was not in that loop and did not want to take responsibility for passing out money that I did not have. The only money that was passed on to me was known as "campaign drafts" for a specific purpose, not street money. That night I was scared. Never before had anyone threatened to ruin my career over street money, but I was told, before I went to Woodbridge, to explain to Doug that the locals wanted their cash.

For years, the Black community relied on the party to underwrite the cost of campaigning in Black neighborhoods. "Street money" was given to organizers, elected leaders and community activists to help them get out the Black vote. Unless the candidate or the local party provided these resources—normally in the form of cash—activity would grind to a halt.

When Tucker took me over to the headquarters in Newark, I looked around the room and said a quick prayer. When I looked up, I had to get it off my chest, so I said, "I don't know what they promised you, but they're going to keep their promise because we want to win New Jersey." Some of the problems in New Jersey also sprang from the fact that African-American support for Mondale was largely symbolic. It wasn't deep, and although Jackson endorsed Mondale, the marriage had not taken place. It was still in the making. Reverend Jackson went to Minnesota and met with Mondale for hours. Later he said he would embrace the campaign for Mondale. But I knew Jesse Jackson. Jackson was not about to give his undivided support to Walter Mondale because he was still bitter and he didn't like the fact that he got the popular vote in many congressional districts but hardly any delegates. So when I got this major threat from Black folks that they were going "to kill the White boys," I called Tully and Gina and told them, "Next time you send money, you better send it directly to Mayor Gibson's political team, because they're not getting their money and people are not going to come out to vote. I don't want to have anything to do with brokering cash payments in New Jersey."

Mondale's defeat was painful. We thought Reagan was beatable because of the huge budget deficits and the massive number of Americans out of work. Mondale had built a strong base of support among labor unions, civil rights organizations and women's groups. We waged a fierce uphill battle against Reagan. We went after him daily, but in the end, he was too strong and popular with Middle America. Mondale was defeated in a landslide, winning only the District of Columbia and his home state of Minnesota, securing only 13 electoral votes to Reagan's 525. My first major presidential campaign at the national level went down in flames. It's hard to describe losing when you believe there is a slight chance people will wake up and vote their pocketbooks instead of their hearts. We threw everything at Reagan, but the Teflon was hard to penetrate. When it came to deflecting criticism or shifting blame, Reagan was a natural.

We had worked very, very hard. The American people had totally bought into Reagan's vision of America and his personality. As much as we thought Reagan was not up to speed, that he was an actor without a script, that he didn't know which side the sun would come up on, we couldn't beat him. That was a very hard reality to face.

Reagan was the king of optimism. In our campaign we kept saying that Reagan was cutting the social safety net, that he cared for the rich, but Reagan's vision was one of unity, bringing America together, of America being militarily strong, defeating the communist threat and remaining independent. He told people America was soaring and shining despite the fact that America was unemployed, the deficit was growing and America was despised by her traditional allies. By Democrats rallying around what I considered a negative message, we only attracted those who were angry and not those who wanted to be optimistic. And the optimists always win.

After the Mondale campaign I spent a couple of months at home. The move from Kenner into a house in New Orleans was tough on the whole family, and I think it was toughest on my mom. She went into a mild depression. During the campaign I had managed to get home every time I had an opportunity. If I was within a three- or four-hour drive I went home. I saw Jean give up. She missed her friends in Kenner. She was broken spiritually but would not talk much about it, not express bitterness for losing her home and her good friends. Yet it was clear to me and to my other siblings that she was profoundly hurt.

The house we rented was in mid-city, right off of Tulane Avenue and South Jefferson Davis Parkway. It was in a working-class integrated neighborhood on the bus line. That was important because nobody had a car. It was a nice neighborhood and our neighbors eventually started visiting us. The saddest part, though, was that the Brazile side of the family, whom I had come to love so much, had betrayed us. It was hard to visit them; I didn't trust them anymore.

Heading to Korea, here
is my father, Lionel,
in 1950.

My mother, Jean,
at Southern University
in Baton Rouge.

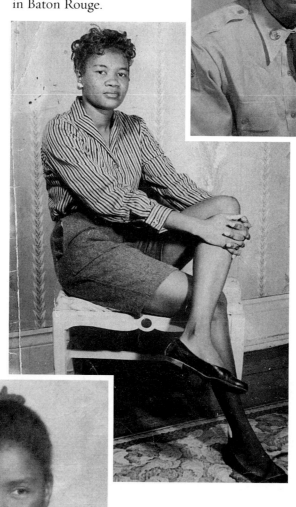

Say cheese. Here I am
in my official third-grade
class photo.

I got my first taste of state-wide politics at Girls State,
organizing behind the scenes. I'm at the back, right.

Here I am after a press conference on Capitol Hill, with (*from left*)
David Marks and Nancy Cross, also of the United States Student
Association, and former congressman Peter Peyser (D-N.Y.).

Standing for jobs, peace and freedom at the Lincoln Memorial for
the twentieth anniversary of the March on Washington in August 1983.
I helped turn out more than 300,000 people at the event.

In 1982, Congressman Walter Fauntroy (at the podium) along with
Coretta Scott King announced the twentieth anniversary of the historic
1963 March on Washington.

In the field with the Gephardt for
President campaign in 1988.

Holding down the fort on a trip to
Kenya in 1992 as we prepared
to travel to Somalia.

As President Wilson looks on, here I am meeting
with President Clinton, Vice President Gore, Minyon Moore,
Franklin Raines and Eleanor Holmes Norton at the White House
in 1997 as we tried to solve the District's budget crisis.

At the 1998 White House Christmas Party
with President Clinton soon after he was impeached
by the House of Representatives.

On the campaign trail with Al Gore, briefing him
on a plane ride to Georgia in December 1999.

On the stump, revving up the crowd for my candidate in 2000. Meeting people on the campaign trail is one of my favorite parts of politics.

My family was very proud when I introduced them to Vice President Gore on a trip home to Kenner, Louisiana, in 2000.

Addressing my party at the DNC
after the 2000 election, when I became
chair of the Voting Rights Institute.

An election postmortem with the campaign managers at Harvard.
(*From left*) Moderator Maxine Isaacs; Bush's general strategist, Karl Rove;
Bradley campaign manager, Gina Glantz;
McCain campaign manager, Rick Davis; me;
and Theresa D'Amato, Ralph Nader campaign manager.

They could not look us in the eyes. Jean's family, especially her mama, did everything to make us comfortable in our new surroundings, but it was never quite the same. My family had a difficult transition from living in a small town to living in a big city. In Kenner, we could sleep with the windows open. In New Orleans, they were kept shut. My brothers and sisters had a difficult time making new friends.

My sister Sheila also became very depressed during this period and had to drop out of college temporarily. Sheila was always the strong one. My younger siblings—Teddy Man, Chet, Lisa, Demetria, Kevin, Zeola—were having a tough time adjusting to the city. We were not city people. Kenner was small and everyone knew one another. When we ran out of food or supplies, someone could lend us a couple of dollars or Mr. Joe would let us borrow until payday. New Orleans wasn't very hospitable. We were raised in the open fields. Now we felt as if we were in an open pit with everyone fending for themselves.

I had Sheila come to Washington after she left school. Jean thought the change of scenery would be good to recharge her batteries. Sheila is a wonderful painter and, like Lionel, can draw just about anything. I gave her money to visit the museums. I tried to get her involved in some of the things I was doing in Washington, but she didn't like politics. Nobody in the family liked politics but me. Some of my siblings decided to drop out of college to help out. Jean called to urge me to motivate the rest of them to stay. Eventually they would all finish college, but we didn't know that at that time. Jean's family really stepped up to the plate and helped us adjust to our new surroundings.

Lionel got sick. He was such a strong man who never stayed home from work. The children didn't know it at the time, but he had been diagnosed with prostate cancer. After the Mondale campaign, I wanted to go home to recuperate. My family needed me; I wanted to help them heal. State legislator Mary Landrieu, a good friend who allowed me to intern in her office when I was in college, hired me to do some local projects. I visited LSU and talked with Rene Nesbitt, one of my resident counselors, and others about going to graduate school or law school. I went to visit Ernest Morial, the first African-American mayor of New Orleans, for advice on what I could do at home. They all put together little political projects for me so I could take care of my family, make some money and decide what I was going to do next with my life.

I wasn't ready to sign on to anybody's campaign for the next congressional, senatorial or presidential election. My family was my glue. It was the only thing I lived for outside of politics. I had nothing else. I felt that until I got them back together, and got my mom refocused, things would be tough. And they were.

When I returned to Washington in February of 1985, I met with Shirley Chisholm and took a job as executive director of the National Political Congress of Black Women (NPCBW), the group that came together in the aftermath of Mondale's selection of Geraldine Ferraro as his running mate. Shirley Chisholm, C. Delores Tucker, the former secretary of state from the Commonwealth of Pennsylvania and the chair of the DNC Black Caucus, Reverend Willie T. Barrow, Gloria Toote, Bernice Fletcher, Mary Frances Berry, Eleanor Holmes Norton, Shelia High King and Mary Terrell spearheaded the organization.

The NPCBW was founded to help recruit more women of color to seek elective office. Our mission was to help train and educate Black women at the federal, state and local levels about the importance of public service improving the lives and conditions of those in the Black community. From a strategic point of view, Black women were more active than Black men in politics. However, when the decisions were made on who would run for office, Black women were often overlooked. NPCBW worked to change the status of Black women in politics. It was logical for me to support this nonpartisan organization.

Shirley Chisholm served as the first president. She set the tone for our mission when she said at our first board meeting, "When are Black women going to realize that God helps those who help themselves? We're going to have to realize we can no longer be timid or reluctant. We were appendages in San Francisco trying to get our little piece of input. We can have input. We have to form our own organization. I'm sixty years old and I'm at the end of my rope trying not to upset Black men . . . not to upset White women."

We had offices at 2025 Pennsylvania Avenue, N.W., near the campus of George Washington University. And we had a bare-bones budget. They barely paid me, but once again it didn't matter. The money never made a difference. What mattered most was I was still able to keep in touch with all the people I had met across the country, and I started chapters nationwide that encouraged Black women to get involved in politics, to run for office, to help them raise money. I was using my experience working in politics to empower African-American women. We helped Mabel "Able Mabel" Thomas run for office in Georgia. We encouraged Julia Carson in Indiana, Gloria Lawlah in Maryland, and Maxine Waters in California, who were also prominent in the Jackson campaign, to run for state senate or for Congress. Even when we were refused, we did not give up.

I worked for the National Political Congress of Black Women for almost two years helping to build a nationwide database of donors and activists. Although I loved the work, I left the organization unceremoniously. As executive director I had met women like Madeleine Albright, Hillary Rodham Clinton, Nadine Hack, Judy Lichtman, Ellie Smeal, Nancy Rubin, Gloria Steinem, Ellen Malcolm and Kristina Kiehl—well-connected women who really wanted to help Black women become more involved in the political process. And they wanted to give us money to make this possible. They wanted to help NPCBW recruit Black women to run for state legislatures and Congress. Once I got connected in this circle of women I was able to raise $20,000 from a donor who wanted to remain anonymous. I knew the representative of the donor but the donor did not want his or her identity revealed. At a board meeting, C. Delores Tucker pressed me to reveal the source of the money and I refused. In fact, during the meeting I banged my fist on the conference table and said, "Hell no, I'm not giving you the name of the person who contributed this money." Then C. Delores Tucker said, "I think Donna's going to have to leave if she won't tell us her source." And I said, "I quit," all the while pounding the table, insisting that I wouldn't reveal the source of the money.

It boiled down to a fight between the old women and the young women on the board. Lezli Baskerville, Shelia High King and Mary Terrell stood up with me. Reverend Willie Barrow and Addie Wyatt were sitting next to me. Reverend Barrow did not take sides. She said, "Let us pray." Barrow is chairwoman emeritus of Operation

PUSH, and whenever Black people got into a conflict and it was about to break out into cursing, Reverend Barrow always wanted us to pray. But I shouted, "I'm not praying right now. This is principle and I will always be a principled politician." So I quit and the person who helped me get the $20,000 hired me as a consultant for another worthwhile project.

I wanted to learn more about race relations and the status of women in politics. Ann Lewis and Irene Natividad, a Filippino-American woman who was part of the National Women's Political Caucus, invited me to join a national delegation of women from the United States on a trip to Bonn. Germany was fascinating. I had a couple of friends in Berlin—Alton Lathrop and his friend Jürgen—who invited me to come up from Bonn and spend some time with them. Alton was a Black man who loved jazz. He was a dancer and had performed with the Dance Theatre of Harlem. During one of its European tours, he met someone and fell in love and the next thing we knew, he was living in Germany. I stayed with them for two weeks and used that time to visit East Germany. After all those years of reading about communism and the Berlin Wall, I took time on one of my trips to cross over at Checkpoint Charlie.

When I came home, I was ready to work on another campaign, but the midterm elections were almost a year away. I needed to find work. Shortly afterward, Gina Glantz, with whom I had worked on the Mondale campaign, told me about Hands Across America. During the Thanksgiving holiday, I spent time working with Ron Pollack and others on the Thanksgiving Action on Poverty. We organized events in five cities to educate the public about the growing problem of hunger and homelessness in America. The report we issued discussed how the Reagan administration was ignoring the 33 million Americans, 14 percent of the population, who were living below the poverty line. The *Washington Post* and wire services picked up our report, but it was largely ignored by Congress and the Reagan administration. I had decided to leave electoral politics and focus on the movement again. This work was rewarding and I enjoyed working with the Children's Defense Fund and other grassroots organizations that focused on children and poverty.

Hands Across America was a project designed to create a hand-to-hand, coast-to-coast human chain to raise money and awareness to fight hunger and homelessness in America. I served as the local D.C. coordinator for the event, which took place on May 25, 1986. My job was to identify tens of thousands of Americans in the metropolitan Washington area to connect with citizens in Maryland and Virginia. I went back to my friends for help. Gwen Benson Walker, Thomas Atkins and Julie Gibson all signed up. We got some free office space from a local real estate mogul, Oliver Carr, right next to the White House at 1730 Pennsylvania Avenue, and John Hechinger, a prominent Democratic donor and leader, gave me office space in Northeast D.C. near Hechinger Mall.

Hunger and I have been on a first-name basis and homelessness was right around the corner, so this was a project that was easy for me to be a part of. We wanted to run the human chain through the White House but we were told that we couldn't. I sent a letter to the White House. No response. We appealed to Maureen Reagan, who informed us that no one at the White House knew about the invitation to participate. Ken Kragen, one of the national co-chairs, told me that the letter had been sent. I called the White House Public Liaison office and told them that we wanted to allow little homeless children to stand on the White House grounds. The next day, we were told that the children would be allowed to stand with the president at the White House. I was glad. The human chain would not be broken. In the end President Reagan, Nancy Reagan, Maureen and several members of his staff were part of the Hands Across America human chain, holding hands with two little homeless children.

The climax of the event came at 3:00 PM that day when 5 million people joined hands along a 4,152-mile route that looped through sixteen states. The line stretched from Battery Park in New York to Queen Mary's dock in Long Beach, California. For fifteen minutes, the participants, who had paid fifteen to thirty-five dollars apiece to take part, clasped hands and sang. Coretta Scott King and Reverend Billy Graham were among the participants in the D.C. chain. But Mitch Snyder of the Center for Creative Nonviolence (CCNV) held a protest in Lafayette Park across the street from the White House during the event. Mitch and his homeless men clasped hands and chanted "What About Tomorrow? What About Tonight?" They were criticizing what they saw as Reagan's hypocrisy, participating in the event yet doing little for the homeless. I welcomed the president's participation. I disagreed with his policies, but I felt that he was just another participant. I also felt that the demonstration ruined the spirit of the day. The president wrote a "very substantial" personal check to Hands Across America the next day.

After Hands Across America, I went over to the Democratic National Committee (DNC) to help out with the 1986 senatorial and congressional campaigns. Once again, I was assigned to the South and I made it home to Louisiana to help Jim Nichols and Norma Jane Sabiston on the Breaux for Senate campaign. John won, as did a lot of other Democrats that year. Democrats took control of the Senate with the help of a large, energetic Black turnout. Once again, I got the political bug. I was ready to transition back to electoral politics.

At the beginning of 1987, as I did at the start of every year, I wrote in my diary what I hoped to learn that year. I knew the campaigns I wanted to work on. Nothing was left to chance. I didn't plot my social life. I only plotted my political life, and I knew where I wanted to get to and how. My social life consisted of hanging out with my family in Louisiana or with my friends Al, Pam, Thomas and Barbara back in Washington. They kept me sane. If I wanted to go out, I just called Thomas, who was always eager to hang out with me. We got into a lot of trouble driving around D.C. looking for bargains and a good meal. When I tired of Thomas and my apartment buddies, I went over to visit Eleanor and her husband, Ed, a New Yorker. They loved politics, and I could also pick up some tidbits from Eleanor, who was always working on some project.

I knew that I wanted to work with Mary Landrieu, who was first elected to office at the age of twenty-three. After seven years as a state representative she was ready to run statewide and came up to Washington for a visit. When Mary came to town, she always called to see if I needed some red beans or that famous Louisiana coffee with chicory. Mary and I sat down to dinner at the Hyatt Regency Hotel on Capitol Hill and she laid out her plans to run for state treasurer. Mary was a good friend. I knew she wanted to be the first female governor of Louisiana. Hell, I wanted to be the first Black woman governor of Louisiana. I was very close to the Landrieu family. Moon Landrieu, her dad, was the last White mayor of the city of New Orleans before Blacks took over. He was very liberal and had worked in the Carter administration as secretary of housing and urban development. Mary had kept me in the Louisiana political loop when I was off working on both the Jackson and Mondale campaigns. It was time to go home again to work on a statewide race. I was ready to manage a campaign. She offered me the job of campaign manager. I accepted.

So in the spring of 1987 I was back home spending time with Jean and helping Mary. Her campaign headquarters was right across Comiskey Park, near my house. I could walk back and forth, which was good because I wanted to keep an eye on my mom. Jean was suffering from diabetes and she continued to do things her way. Once, when I asked her why she was buying white bread that was on sale three loaves for a dollar when she knew she wasn't supposed to eat white bread, she shrugged and said, "That's why I toast it." You couldn't tell Jean anything. My mom always said you had to die of something, so she wanted to live her life in a way that suited her.

Mary took an early lead in the race for state treasurer. She was thirty-two and I was twenty-seven. We were both Catholic from large families. She was ambitious and so was I. Mary understood that women could take their seats at the table, and I wanted to have a hand in that process. We put together a good team across the state. I visited all the major cities—Shreveport, Monroe, Alexandria, Lafayette and Lake Charles—to encourage Black leaders to endorse Mary. The campaign was on course and Mary was winning statewide. I knew she would not have a problem winning the seat. It was time for me to get back on the national campaign trail. I began to receive phone calls from the presidential candidates. After months of being home, reconnecting with friends and family, I was ready to get back to reaching one of my goals—putting a Democrat in the White House. Politics was in my blood and I was ready to once again do what I knew I did best—organize at the grassroots level.

CHAPTER EIGHT

SMOTHERED CHICKEN

After college, I tried to give up meat. But one day, I came home and Jean was smothering chicken. The chicken is cut up, seasoned and pounded into thin pieces, then browned in a mixture that can include wine, chicken stock, onions, garlic, butter and many spices, and is served over rice. I, too, was finally seasoned enough in national politics to earn a seat at the table and garner the respect of the Democratic establishment.

THE FIRST PRESIDENTIAL CANDIDATE to contact me was Paul Simon, followed by the campaigns of Al Gore, Mike Dukakis and Dick Gephardt. Reverend Jackson summoned me in April to come and talk to him in Memphis for a Southern summit. I drove six hours from New Orleans in bad thunderstorms to meet with him. Everybody else came to me when they visited Louisiana, but I had to drive to see Reverend Jackson in person. He hadn't decided if he was going to run, and he asked me to hold off on my decision until he made his. I told him I would. That meeting with Jackson was important for me. It was crucial for me to be able to look at him face-to-face and tell him that I was shopping around for another candidate. I wanted Reverend Jackson to know I might be working for someone else's presidential bid.

Ron Daniels, one of Jackson's chief strategists, and Emma Chappell, the campaign's treasurer in 1984 and a businesswoman from Philadelphia, forwarded some reading material on the goals of the Jackson 1988 bid. The Reverend was on the cover of both *Time* and *Newsweek*. He was a hot candidate. During that long drive up from the Bayou through the Mississippi Delta, as I passed stretches of cotton and soybean fields, I had a feeling of nostalgia. Although things did not end as well as I had hoped in 1984, the Jackson campaign was succeeding in its goals of registering new voters and bringing in a new generation of Black political leaders. Jackson, in the intervening years, was instrumental in helping the Democratic party win back the U.S. Senate. Still, I had my own personal and political goals that year. In my diary, I wrote that it was time for me to step up to the plate and demonstrate my skills in organizing beyond African-American voters. I was also ready to assume a management position in a campaign. But Jackson deserved to hear it from me. So I kept my foot steady on the accelerator driving toward Memphis at sixty miles an hour.

When I arrived at the meeting site, Jackson was sitting in the front row next to Reverend Samuel "Billy" Kyles and Reverend Wyatt Tee Walker. Jackson had called on me to attend a meeting with representatives of the National Rainbow Coalition. Once again, I saw that the usual players would be involved: Mayors Barry and Hatcher, Percy Sutton and Ron Daniels. C. Delores Tucker was on her way, as were others from Washington. I spent the entire day listening to speeches and discussions on why Jesse should run again, the difficulty of raising money and how to target states and congressional districts that we carried in 1984. I presented some of my findings on the growth of the Black electorate in those states, mainly in the South. Jackson interrupted the session and asked everyone to say a prayer for the mission ahead. I prayed for faith and strength for what would follow. When I left, it was after dark. During the six-hour drive back to New Orleans I thought long and hard about my next move. Should I go back to Jackson, or was it time to move on? What role would I fill in the 1988 Jackson campaign? Would Jackson take my advice on strategy? What would I learn by playing in an entirely new ball game? In the end, I chose to work with Dick Gephardt.

My old friend Gillis Long, with whom I had worked back in the early eighties as an intern on Capitol Hill, had highly recommended Gephardt. At the ripe old age of twenty-eight, I was ready to transition from organizing Southerners, women and African Americans to putting in place a national grassroots field program. And as I looked at the long list of candidates, I knew I wanted to work for a moderate Southerner. People don't think of Missouri, Gephardt's home state, as Southern, but look on the map. I was really torn between Gore and Gephardt. Everybody wanted me to be their director of Black outreach. But I had no interest in only running Black people's business anymore. Gephardt wanted me to play a more strategic role.

Dick was attending a fund-raiser in Louisiana while en route to Los Angeles for the Hollywood Women's Political Caucus. The caucus was Barbra Streisand's baby, and she was having a meet-and-greet organized by Marge Tabankin. Gephardt asked me if I would fly with him to California, after which the campaign would fly me back home. When I had met Dukakis and the other candidates, it had been at various campaign-type events. The meetings were always hurried and I never got a really good feel for the individual. Personally, I had to like the candidate and get to know him before making a commitment to support his candidacy. And now here I was, sitting on an airplane next to Dick Gephardt. He was a six-term congressman, part of the House leadership and up-and-coming. He was a Watergate baby and had been an alderman (St. Louis City councilman) before his election to Congress.

So flying coach on this long plane ride, we sat next to each other. Gephardt looked at me and asked me what I thought about trade. I knew everything about slavery, the civil rights movement, African-American history, domestic issues, sports, current events and pop culture. But trade? "You mean like trade with Mexico, Japan and Europe?" I asked. He nodded and said yes. I told him that I didn't know a lot about trade but I knew about jobs, health care and organizing union workers.

We talked about trade and foreign policy. We talked about everything except what candidates talked to me about all the time—being Black. Gephardt was talking to me on a whole different level—foreign policy, international issues. I told him about my trips to the Soviet Union, Europe and Africa and what I had learned there. We talked about our families. Dick was a Baptist. I was Catholic. He loved his mom. I loved my mom. He had one sibling. I had eight. He had three children. I had none. And when he told me his wife's name was Jane, I cracked up. Dick and Jane. He wanted me to meet his mom and wife soon. They could, if needed, fill me in with more detail about his background.

We had the most comfortable conversation. It was like I had known him all my life. This was a man from Milquetoast, Missouri, and we sat on that plane for hours talking about everything under the sun. The next day Bill Carrick, who was the campaign manager, called and made me an offer to be deputy campaign manager and national field director at a $36,000 annual salary. This was the title that would put me on the next rung up the political ladder. I was overjoyed. When I got back to Kenner I told Jean that I was going to work on Gephardt's presidential campaign, and that this would probably be my last. She didn't have to worry. I felt that the rank of deputy campaign manager was as high as I was going to go in politics. I was pretty sure that I had reached the glass ceiling and that nobody was ever going to make me a presidential campaign manager.

There are so many "isms" in national politics: ageism, racism, regionalism, sexism. I knew that I was fast becoming one of the best grassroots organizers in the country. I had won more states and congressional districts than most male organizers. But despite all that, I couldn't see a path for me to actually realize my dream of becoming a presidential campaign manager. There were no role models for what I wanted to do and be. Everybody was still coming up through the ranks or dropping out. Ron Brown had not yet been named DNC chair. Susan Estrich was still working her way up the ladder. Politics is a billion-dollar industry, probably $3 billion now, with the amount of money the Bush-Cheney campaign is pouring into the system. And big-money industries don't usually have women or minorities in positions of authority or power.

I had talked to Paul Tully and Gina Glantz about the Gephardt offer, and they gave me sound advice that I used in the final negotiations. I told the Gephardt people that during the primary campaign, if there were any major decisions to be made, I had to be at the table helping to make them. Whenever you're excluded from the table you can't be responsible for the outcome. They agreed and then I asked for $42,000, timely reimbursement of my expenses and health insurance. They agreed to that as well. I wanted full hiring authority in key states, including Iowa and New Hampshire. Bill told me some decisions were still under negotiation, but I would have significant input. Carrick, a South Carolina native, was eager to complete the deal. We shook hands. I was ready to move back into my old apartment in Washington, D.C. Barbara and Al watched over my stuff when I was away on a campaign or visiting my family.

The 1988 campaign season hadn't really started yet—we were still in the preprimary phase where candidates hire seasoned veterans and raise money. Gephardt was doing both. Bob Shrum, a key operative in the 1980 Ted Kennedy campaign, and his partner David Doak, were hired as media consultants. Ed Reilly, out of Boston, was hired to do the polling. Carrick hired Joe Trippi and Paul Begala to fill out the management team. Dick also wanted his congressional campaign manager, Joyce Aboussie, to play a key role, and Debra Johns (now Hayes) was going to work on media strategy from his leadership office. Debra was a young Black communications guru who was one of the first Blacks to hold that position on Capitol Hill. Jackie Forte, a Black New Orleans native, was hired to serve as our comptroller. More Blacks and women were being called on daily. The next hurdle was to tell Reverend Jackson. I waited until I got back to Washington and settled into my apartment to check in with members of the Black Caucus and the leaders of the civil rights organizations.

When I arrived back on Capitol Hill, Al and Barbara welcomed me home with a delicious home-cooked meal of smothered chicken, dirty rice, collard greens and corn bread. After dinner, I called Mrs. Jackson to see what kind of mood Reverend Jackson was in. I wanted to catch him coming off a trip, when he was exhausted. That's the only time you could have a decent conversation. He had to be really fatigued. So I called and told him, "I just wanted to let you know that I am going to work with Dick Gephardt; it's going to be in the newspaper tomorrow." I was ready to hang up and then he sputtered out the words, "Back up, back up, you're going to work for an asterisk over me? I can't believe you're going to leave me for some unknown member of Congress." He used some profanity. Boy, he was pissed. Once again I reminded Jackson that this was the kind of opportunity he had trained me for. I even used his own "I am somebody" speech on him, but it had no effect. When I hung up the phone I knew he still considered me a traitor, but this time it didn't matter so much. I was prepared to move on and establish my own credentials as a political strategist.

Working with the Gephardt campaign, I was twenty-eight and my neck was on the line. For the first time I was in Paul Tully's seat. Immediately I had to hire a field team. Steve Murphy was assigned to work in Iowa. I wanted my friend Julie Gibson, who had worked with me on the Mondale campaign and Hands Across America, to serve as his deputy. Next, in New Hampshire, Mark Longabaugh was hired. Mark was from Ohio, so I asked my friend Dan Calegari, who had worked for Gary Hart, to be my eyes and ears up in the Granite State. Then I went out and recruited every twentysomething I could find—students fresh out of college or young people willing to take a year off work to be on a presidential campaign. My first hire was a redhead name Andrea La Rue. She was my anchor for the regional desk system that I wanted to set up to monitor the states—it was key to establishing strong teams in the states. I hired two young African Americans fresh out of college in South Carolina, Maurice Daniels and Kerry Pearson, and three more young White kids—Richard Sullivan, Donnie Fowler Jr. and Randall Rainer. Maurice worked for Dick Gephardt in the 2004 Democratic primary. He was also Gore's political director when he was vice president. And now Kerry is a big muckety-muck in the District of Columbia and a successful businessman. Andrea worked for Tom Daschle and is now a partner in a consultant firm. Donnie became my national field director when I was hired to manage the Gore campaign and briefly ran General Wesley Clark's 2004 presidential campaign. Richard is one of the party's leading fund-raisers, and Randall is always making news in the business world. These were all my kids. I wanted to start the way Paul Tully had. He trained me to bring in young people. And because I knew there were not enough Black people in the business, I started hiring lots of them.

In the end we had as many Black people as did Reverend Jackson's campaign, because I refused to allow us to have fewer. By the time the primary season got under way in 1988, I was really proud of what Jackson was doing—registering more voters, winning more congressional districts and picking up additional delegates. We put on a good fight, but I knew that if Gephardt lost the Southern primaries we would be out. Reverend Jackson, however, was going all the way to the convention. I wasn't on his team but I was rooting for his supporters.

The first presidential campaign hurdle is Iowa, and it was a huge shock to my system in terms of the weather and the culture. I went from organizing in the Deep South to organizing in Iowa and New Hampshire. At times, Debra and I, who often traveled with Dick, were the only Blacks in the room. We would give each other that look. One night in New Hampshire, Debra and I purchased a bottle of red wine and just sat up and cried as we went over the horrors of campaign life: long hours, constant stress, low pay and time away from your family. Gephardt would always lift our spirits and tell us we were doing a great job. I wanted to work for Gephardt to have the experience of organizing Democrats across the board. I found out my experience with Jackson was a net plus, as White voters required the same kind of information as Black voters, the same kind of activity as Black people and the same amount of resources as Blacks. There was hardly any difference. Both communities required information about the candidate and some voter contact.

The weather was a real challenge. Growing up in New Orleans, I never experienced subzero weather. One time I ended up in Sioux Falls, South Dakota. I'd gotten lost traveling to Fort Dodge, which is in western Iowa. Oh, it was so scary. I kept singing to myself going across Route 20 to keep from falling asleep. And I couldn't get back to Des Moines because they had a bad snowstorm. I had two choices: go to Omaha, Nebraska, or go up to South Dakota. I chose South Dakota because I had never been there, and I wanted to see what it was like. I drove four more hours because the snow was heading across the plains, and I was trying to get to a hotel before dark. I was switching back and forth between radio stations, desperately trying to find some music I could sing to. I didn't hear any Black music or see any Black people for hours. All I saw were abandoned cornfields. I was scared out of my mind. But then I asked myself, had I driven so far north only to become afraid of everything white: the snow and the people? There were just plains but they were so vast, so big and intimidating.

Nightfall came and I was going to call Randall Cunningham, our state director in South Dakota, to find me a nice warm place to stay. But I was too scared to get out of the car, so I pressed on with a bag of potato chips, Doublemint gum and several cans of Coca-Cola to keep me going. I finally made it. When I did, people stared at me as if I just arrived from another planet. I finally got in touch with Randall, who told me how to get to a nearby Holiday Inn. When I arrived, he found me some of the best fried chicken and potato salad. It may have been South Dakota, but the food was hot and delicious. After a good night's rest, I was back on the road to Des Moines, ready to organize. Debra and I shared an apartment in downtown Des Moines. I could not believe the weather. I begged Debra, a West Virginia native, to keep the window shut and the heater up as high as we could take it.

Dick won the Iowa caucuses, but we did not get a major bounce off the victory. I deployed many of my troops to New Hampshire and to Super Tuesday states. The rest of us drove back to Washington in a rented van. I told the kids to sleep, and I drove nonstop all the way from Des Moines to Pittsburgh. Back then, I hated airplanes and I could drive for hours nonstop. The other reason I drove was because Carrick told me the campaign was running out of money. I did not understand. My parents may have been poor, but they could manage with what little money we had. When Carrick told me that he would not pay the kids before the holiday, I challenged him to go downstairs so I could whip his ass. I could not get over what he said. These kids were being paid $600 a month plus health insurance, and some of them could not go without pay, even for a few days. I went downstairs to confront Bill. He explained the situation about our finances. I told him to cut the consultant fees. Carrick shrugged his shoulder, but sent word that the kids would get paid. I was furious for days.

The Dukakis campaign, on the other hand, not only had money, they had more expertise on the ground. Paul had put together his team early. With Jack Corrigan, Charlie Baker and Michael Whouley in charge of the field operations, the Dukakis team was all muscle. In the end, they whipped us. With characteristic humility, Gephardt bowed out of the campaign at the end of March 1988, saying at a press conference that he had "no alibis" for losing. "I didn't get enough votes."

When the campaign folded there was the opportunity for me to return to Reverend Jackson's campaign and I considered it. That was my natural home. But when I talked with Reverend about that possibility I was rebuffed. He had just won the Michigan caucuses and we were both staying at the Pontchartrain Hotel in Detroit. He was very testy during the meeting, and told me that he didn't need me to work with him through the convention in Atlanta. I kept remembering his prediction that without him I would always be a branch without a tree. I had to find my roots elsewhere, but I did send some of my kids over to help Jackson complete the primaries. I wanted them to have a different experience and I knew Reverend would allow them to grow in their understanding of the movement and electoral politics.

Then, on April 16, I got a call from Jack and Charlie. They wanted me to come aboard the Dukakis campaign as the deputy field director. I would go from being the deputy national campaign manager and national field director to working as a deputy field director. I had to take a demotion in title, but I got a hike in salary. I told the Dukakis campaign that I wouldn't move to Boston without $45,000—and I got it.

I was working in the Dukakis campaign headquarters on the eighth floor at 105 Chauncey Street, and Susan Estrich was the campaign manager. She had succeeded John Sasso, the first campaign manager, who got in some trouble. A woman was finally elevated to campaign manager. She became the first female manager of a major presidential campaign. And I thought, all right, the glass ceiling has been broken. I was very happy for Susan, and I was glad to be working with her. I wanted to see her succeed. I was part of her inner circle. *Ms.* magazine even did a profile of all the Dukakis women.

Susan was surrounded by White males—Paul Brountas, Chuck Campion, Jack Corrigan and Charlie Baker. They made all the major decisions. One decision they made early on was to put the "senior" staff on the ninth floor and the junior campaign staff, the interns and the volunteers on the eighth floor. I was out of town traveling with Dukakis when the decision was made and when I returned I was told that my office was on the eighth floor even though I was part of the campaign leadership. This slight brought back memories of how I'd had to set Nikki straight about my desk not being outside her office, as though I was her secretary on the Mondale campaign.

In addition, I was still more than a little traumatized by what I had experienced of race relations in Boston: I had managed the brutal winter in South Dakota and Iowa, but nothing prepared me for the racism of Boston. It took me weeks to find an apartment while I lived with my friend Ellen Kurz. Ellen had been with Dukakis for months and was settled in the campaign. I got so many rejections for apartments that I had to ask Ellen, who was White, to get an apartment for me. I wanted to live close to the campaign headquarters in downtown Boston, and Ellen found me an apartment on Tremont Street, within walking distance. It was lovely, with a balcony that gave me a great view of Boston Common and the city. Ellen filled out the apartment application and paid the deposit and first month's rent. When I moved in, the landlord asked me who I was. I told him that I was the tenant and Ellen was helping me to move in. I had read about the school busing conflicts and the racial tensions, but there was a level of just pure hostility and disdain of Blacks in Boston that I had not experienced even in the Deep South.

Now, though I was supposed to be in the inner circle of the campaign, I was relegated to an office on the floor with the junior staff. It was just too much. Nobody on the senior staff thought at all about how the office assignments looked. Essentially, all the minorities were on the eighth floor and all the Whites on the ninth floor. It looked like segregation. It looked like apartheid. But I was the only one to see it.

As they say, "Hell hath no fury." I bided my time and I waited until the end of the day. I went to the ninth floor and picked out an office. There was a conference room across from the campaign offices, and that night when everyone had left (I was always the last to leave, at around 10:00 PM), I went into the conference room and I got Wanda Williams, Susan Rice, Janice Thurmond and two volunteers to help me rearrange the room. Well, word got out, and Joe Warren, who was Dukakis's best Black friend and adviser, and Paul Parks called me to ask what was happening. I told them "I just want to tell you what I'm doing in case they fire me." Joe asked, "Why are you doing it so soon?" I told him what had happened in my absence. He told me to do what I had to do. I did. The room was transformed into the Sojourner Truth, Harriet Tubman, Ida B. Wells Room—also known as the "colored girls room—we shall not be moved." Joe had my back. He planned to speak to Dukakis. I was grateful, but I had more I needed to get off my chest.

I also told Joe about an event that happened a few days earlier, when one of the networks had come in to profile the campaign while Chris Edley, Dukakis's issues director and now the dean of Boalt Hall, U.C. Berkeley's law school, wasn't in the office. I was asked if I would sit in on the interview as part of the "face of the Dukakis team." I took my seat around the table across from Susan, Corrigan, Baker and others. Luckily, that day I had on red lipstick and was wearing something nice. As the camera was rolling I said, "It's so good to be around this table. After all, I find it amazing that I'm now a token in this campaign, after coming from an operation that had so many Blacks in senior-level positions. I'm here for window dressing." I was bruised from the racism I'd had to deal with in the city and frankly, back then, if I thought it, I said it. I had no filter.

They couldn't handle me. They couldn't button me up. Susan was furious with me. That night we went out for drinks and she asked me to work with her. She was a vodka girl, and for that evening I was, too. Susan was very, very smart. She was Harvard-educated, a lawyer, the whole nine yards. She could, at times, be insulting, condescending and patronizing. I told her, "Susan, if you treat me like dirt you should expect me to throw dirt back at you." I was angry about her attitude. I had been promised that despite my title I would be a major player in the campaign. And I had ended up flying all over the country with Dukakis just so he could avoid having an all-White campaign.

"I'm window dressing here," I told her. "I was window dressing this morning. When you make the major decisions, I'm not in the room. If you let me make decisions, the first one I would make would be to bring more Black people in here so you wouldn't have to deal with my big mouth." Susan agreed to hire more Blacks, but it would have to wait until after the convention and that would be my project. She also promised that I would be kept in the loop.

My concern about Dukakis was that he needed to start reaching out to the Black community much earlier than he wanted to. There was a lot of indecision among Blacks about Dukakis. Black voters and leaders knew he was Reverend Jackson's competitor in the race for the presidency. He was a good Democrat, but that wasn't enough to get people excited about him. I also knew that as important as the Black vote was, it alone would not win any state except Washington, D.C., which was fighting for statehood. I didn't spend all my time on the Dukakis campaign protesting, but sometimes it seemed like it. They brought in Debra Johns to help with media and to travel on the campaign press plane. I started calling up members of the Black Caucus to come on board, and Ron Brown began to make some inquiries on our behalf.

When the choice of Lloyd Bentsen was made for the vice presidential running mate, Paul Brountas, who was the campaign chair, was responsible for calling Reverend Jackson, and Susan was supposed to call Ron Brown to tell him who Dukakis had chosen. In addition, I was supposed to inform many of the civil rights leaders. Of all those planned phone calls, the call to Reverend Jackson was the most important because of the role he would play in turning out the Black vote for the Democratic nominee. But in fact, many inside the Dukakis campaign hated having to call Reverend Jackson. They hated acknowledging how much they needed his skills, and how they really couldn't get the Black vote without him. But I called Reverend Willie Barrow and told her that I was sure the call to Reverend Jackson would be coming soon. Reverend Jackson was in Cleveland, changing planes, but there was a way to get in touch with him: They could have paged him, or sent a staffer to the airport to meet him. Well, the call wasn't made, and two hours after I spoke with Reverend Barrow, Reverend Jackson was on the national news upset that he had been snubbed, not consulted on the choice of Bentsen. I didn't speak to the staff for a whole week over that one. During the convention you would have thought I worked for Jesse Jackson again. I was so embarrassed by the arrogance of the Dukakis folks.

After Dukakis got the Democratic nomination for president, the tension in the office remained pretty high. As much as I hated to fly, I chose to travel around the country with Dukakis rather than work out of the Boston headquarters. There was so much isolation between his original staffers and all the newcomers in the campaign. As determined as I was to help him defeat George H. W. Bush, I couldn't take it. By this time I had become very strong in my convictions. Before the Dukakis campaign, I sought the approval of others before I stood up for my beliefs. There had been an incident before the convention when we went to Philadelphia, Mississippi, the place where the three civil rights workers Chaney, Goodman and Schwerner were killed in 1964. Susan announced at a meeting that all that week we were going to talk about education. I said, "You can talk about education all week until the day we go to Philadelphia, Mississippi. But on that day we're going to have to acknowledge what happened there, and Dukakis is going to have to give a profound statement on civil rights." But it was as if I were talking to the wall. They just didn't get it. They had started inviting me to the message meetings and allowing me to write talking points, and my role was evolving. But I had little impact before or after the convention.

So we're on the plane to Philadelphia, Mississippi, and I'm writing Dukakis's notes. I give him what I have. He looks at it, sees it's about civil rights and says, "We're talking about education." It was a hot day in the Delta. Upon arrival, I looked around the plane for Debra. I wanted to huddle before we went to the event. Debra was getting on the press bus with Michael Frisby of the *Boston Globe,* Ken Cooper of Knight-Ridder, Michelle Martin of the *Wall Street Journal* and Kevin Merida of the *Washington Post*—all Black—along with others. And at one point Sam Donaldson, veteran newsman with ABC, came up to my seat and told me that word had filtered back about what I was trying to do. Sam looked at me and said, "Don't fight anymore. I see what you're trying to do." But I told Sam, "I have to do this. It's not about me. It's about Fannie Lou Hamer, and Medgar Evers, and I'll be damned if we're not going to mention what happened in Philadelphia, Mississippi." I was ready to resign but Sam told me not to quit. All the Black reporters on the plane winked at me or gave me a knowing look that said, "Hang in there. We got your back."

Well, that night on the evening news, Sam Donaldson put a foot up the campaign's behind. He said we went to Philadelphia, Mississippi, and we ignored twenty-five years of struggle and history and that once again this showed Dukakis's insensitivity to the African-American community. It was the worst moment of press coverage the campaign had had. And that's when I realized that I didn't have to fight this battle by myself. I had help. It was at that point that I stopped fighting. I'd go to the meetings, give my advice and walk out. In a way the Reverend Jackson in me came out. And then, there was the matter of pride.

George Herbert Walker Bush had an incredible strategist as his campaign manager, Lee Atwater. Atwater was from South Carolina, and he had cut his political teeth during the Nixon campaigns. He was a young, brash Republican and he wasn't afraid to, as he said, "take a little bark off of Dukakis." It did not take long for the general election season to heat up. Willie Horton was a Black inmate at a prison in Massachusetts who had been furloughed, and while free, he kidnapped a woman and her husband and raped the woman while her husband was forced to watch. During the campaign, Dukakis was made over and over again to answer for that. Atwater had only mentioned Horton's name once. It was enough to turn my stomach.

Atwater made the statement during the campaign that by the time the election was over, the American people would think Willie

Horton was Mike Dukakis's running mate. This, of course, was an appeal based on racial fear among Whites. There were other debacles, as well, like the charge that Dukakis was "a card-carrying member of the American Civil Liberties Union," which the Bush team made seem like a communist front. But nothing hurt the Dukakis campaign as much as the racial smears and the fear of tackling them head-on. The campaign held back and thought the media would defend it and attack Bush. It was wrong.

Race is the third rail of American politics. You're not supposed to bring it up in any kind of discussion in a campaign. Once you inject race into the discussion you can't keep it from festering in other areas. So the Dukakis campaign thought the best strategy was to ignore the blatantly racial overtones of the Bush campaign.

Whenever Republicans go down in the polls, they unleash the most horrific personal attacks on a candidate. They don't go after visible issues, they go after the candidate on wedge issues that are below the radar—busing, welfare, abortion, gay rights, guns, religion, affirmative action, the Confederate flag. The mail they send to their primary constituents basically says that the "Democrats will take away your guns, Democrats are going to allow those kids to attend your schools, and Democrats don't want to preserve your heritage." They conduct push-polls designed to smear the Democratic candidate's character. Sometimes they mail it out under the signature of the candidate, the Republican Party or its well-financed allies, and sometimes they don't, but either way it has the same effect. It's racial intimidation that whips a huge chunk of the electorate into an angry, hostile bloc of voters.

The Dukakis campaign was really tough, and I'm not one who believes that if you're in the gutter you can get out by letting everyone throw dirt on you. You get out by taking the dirt off and throwing some of it back at your attackers. The fall campaign was rough-and-tumble all the way. Poll after poll showed the race tightening. Dukakis was up after the Atlanta convention, and Bush took the lead after the Republican convention in New Orleans. I spent most of my time on the road signing up new supporters and helping state leaders put together their GOTV operations. From time to time I would get back on the plane with Dukakis or check in with Tully to see if I had my head on right.

The first debate was held in Winston-Salem, North Carolina, on September 25. I went along to coordinate surrogates for the post-debate spin. I got to meet Ann Richards, then state treasurer and later governor of Texas. Another governor was on the roster to defend the campaign that night, Bill Clinton of Arkansas. Susan Brophy and Marcia Hale introduced me to him and I was impressed with his deep knowledge of the issues. It was during that debate at UCLA that CNN anchor Bernard Shaw asked whether Dukakis would favor the death penalty for the killer if his wife were raped and murdered. I heard Dukakis's answer and my jaw just dropped. He sat on that stage and uttered words no rational person could support, speaking in very general terms about his opposition to the death penalty. After that debate, the campaign sputtered.

The Bush team was on a roll, picking up a key endorsement from the Teamsters Union. Back on the plane, I did my job, talking up the campaign, even if it was faltering. My anger subsided. I was worn out from constant travel. I wanted to get back home to see my family. I had no personal life on the campaign trail. After a long and exhausting trip to Missouri, I started hearing rumors coming off the press bus. The *Washington Post,* according to several sources on the press bus, was about to print a major story on Vice President Bush's private life. The *Post* denied it was going to print anything of the sort. Without attribution, I picked the story up and gave it new life.

When we started out in New Haven, Connecticut, Dukakis had been told that if he was seen with Black people during the day on the campaign trail, his campaign would be weakened. It would turn off White people—as if Whites weren't turned off already. By October, I wasn't aware of it consciously but I was ready to explode. I'd had enough of the skirmishes and the battles, all of them in some way related to lack of respect for me and arrogance, indifference and the profound misunderstanding of Black people. These had been Reverend Jackson's motives for running for president in the first place— to keep us from being taken for granted. So I went to the back of the bus to brief the press on the day's itinerary. I told them that we would be doing a town rally in Hartford, a walk-through in Little Italy and then the Al Smith dinner at the Waldorf-Astoria Hotel in New York.

What the reporters really wanted to know was when Dukakis was going to Harlem. They wanted to know if he was going to even campaign in Harlem. I said, "Of course he's going to campaign in Harlem. We're just looking for the appropriate venue, the appropriate day." I was trying to fudge it. I really didn't know our schedule or future campaign plans. No one was sharing information with us on the plane. But the questions kept coming: Will he campaign during the daytime down there in New York? How come he's not campaigning in the Black community during the day? I kept looking at these reporters. Many of them were my friends—at least I wanted to believe they liked me.

So I said, "Let me just say this. If you guys want to ask all these questions, why don't you ask George Bush if he intends to take Barbara to the White House?" It just came straight out. And the reporters shouted back at me, "What did you say?" I was in it now and didn't know how to stop. I just saw myself back at T. H. Harris, standing in the hot sun being pelted with eggs. "You know, they talk about family values, they talk about all these family issues, but tonight on CBS News, no one is going to report that George Bush has a mistress and her initials are J.F." I was sick and tired of the reporters asking me about Dukakis and Black people, so I threw them something that I thought would change the subject.

The reporters looked shocked. They started circling around me as if to take a long look at me for the last time. Mike Frisby spoke up first. "Donna, are you on or off the record?" I thought for a moment about my comments and I knew they went overboard. Deep inside, I wanted to take back the words. But I looked at him and said, "I am on the record, but I am not speaking for the campaign." Debra looked at me as if to say, "Girl, you're in deep shit."

Well, on the bus on the way to New York City, I cleansed myself. I had spent years defending the Democratic Party and months defending Michael Dukakis, but my soul felt so corroded. I spent two and a half hours on that bus releasing it all. I gave my version of the "sermon on the mount" and the reporters wrote down my every word. I talked about how racially insensitive the Dukakis campaign was, how intolerant America was. I talked about the complicity of racism in the Bush campaign and the Republican Party and how nobody wanted to talk about this. I talked about how the Party establishment had snubbed Jesse Jackson. I got it all out. It flowed like a river. An hour more, and I would have called for reparations. This was my epiphany—a solemn moment of truth coming out in vile language. In hindsight, I should have shut up. But I was too angry to stop.

I continued to talk about the code words in American politics— taxes, crime, welfare and affirmative action. The reporters were absolutely stunned and kept asking me, "Donna, is there any of this you want us to keep off the record? Do you want this on background?" They were trying to help me, trying to save my butt. There was NPR's Linda Wertheimer, CNN's Wolf Blitzer, John King of AP, and all the Black reporters, everybody. They all liked me for being straightforward and because I was honest with them. They didn't really want it to hit the wire. But I shrugged and said, "Print it."

BY THE TIME WE GOT to the Waldorf-Astoria my tirade and my comments about Bush and his mistress had made the news. At 5:15 PM, Susan Estrich was on the phone in the staff room calling from Boston. "Young lady," she screamed, "what do you think you're doing?"

"Well, Susan, I was just telling the truth."

"What do you mean?"

"Well, the rumors about Bush have been all over the press bus and the news. The stock market fell forty-three points today and Dan Rather was going to put it out. The rumor was already there. What are you so upset about? Are you upset about the Willie Horton part or the racism? Are you upset about the code words or are you upset because I called the vice president an adulterer? Just what are you upset about?"

"Don't you dare step on our message," she said. Susan was upset. I could hear it in her voice.

"What do you want me to do," I said. "If you want me to resign then write the press release."

She wrote the release within fifteen minutes and I asked Debra to read it to me. I was sick to my stomach. Part of me wanted to fight back. I called Minyon Moore, who was back in the colored girls' room, to ask about the mood of the campaign. She told me the staff was with me but I was in serious trouble. I thanked Minyon and told her to call Jesse Jackson. I was about to be fired.

Debra, who was with me during all this, was telling me, "Donna, you know if you go down, we all go down with you."

"If we must die, let us nobly die," I chuckled, bitterly quoting the famous Claude McKay poem.

"Right," Debra assured me.

It was October 21 at 5:30 PM, a beautiful fall day, when I was fired. It happened at the plush Waldorf-Astoria Hotel in New York City. Dukakis was really upset with me. He did not wish to see me again. Then I got a call from Kitty Dukakis. She told me to keep my head up high; they had a good friend who lived on Fifth Avenue now. I tell people, "If you're going to get fired, get fired at the Waldorf and then get invited to a Fifth Avenue apartment for a drink." Ruthie Goldmuntz was going to buy me Chinese food and invite me over to rest. Debra volunteered to go with me. We ran out the back door, like servants, down the hall and out the entrance and grabbed a cab. When I got there, Ms. Ruthie gave me a hug and told me to settle down and get myself together. They were afraid that I had more to say to the press. I was finished talking, but I knew I had to call home before the press got to Jean.

The Reverend had warned me that I would one day be a branch without a tree, and that's how I felt—utterly rootless, and tired. I needed his advice, too. So I went to Ms. Ruthie's bedroom to sob and call the Reverend. Debra fixed me a cocktail, and I started dialing home.

The press release that Susan had written was humble and apologetic and it attributed the following mea culpa to me: "Today I made certain comments which I deeply regret. I believe too strongly in the importance of electing Mike Dukakis and Lloyd Bentsen to allow myself to become an issue in the campaign. Because the time is short, and the issues are important, I have decided to leave the campaign. I wish Mike Dukakis and Lloyd Bentsen the best in the final weeks of the campaign."

All my life the one thing that had motivated me more than any other was the desire to make my family proud. So I knew they would be upset. Before I dialed the numbers, I said a little prayer to St. Jude. I was worried about their reaction.

When my mom answered the phone I just blurted it out. "Jean, I got fired today. I quit my job and I got fired." Never before had anyone in the family gotten fired.

"Well, which one is it, did you quit or get fired?" she asked me quietly.

"It was pretty much both."

"What did you do?"

This was the first time that I had ever broken down on a campaign. And my mom wasn't used to me breaking down, but I couldn't stop the tears. I cried the proverbial river.

"Donna, what did you do?" she insisted, more concerned. She could tell by my emotions that anything I might tell her that I had done, it wasn't that bad.

"I called the vice president of the United States a racist, a liar and a whore," I said. And then I explained that I'd told all the reporters how racist and vicious the Bush campaign was and about the exclusion and the insensitivity of the Dukakis campaign.

"That's what you did?"

"Uh huh," I whimpered.

"Well, that's not so bad. Come on home." I couldn't believe Jean. She was still proud of me, I was still her child.

Then I got up the nerve to call Reverend Jackson and he told me straight out, "I got your back." I was shocked. His response moved me. I was so surprised. I thought Jackson would still be upset with me. He, too, was fed up with the Dukakis campaign and the Democratic Party. That was the point at which I decided never again to go against the Reverend. I had learned a valuable lesson of faith and loyalty.

In the days that followed, Lloyd Bentsen, Alan Cranston and Ted Kennedy all called me and offered me their support. It was interesting the way the press spun my remarks. The charge about Bush's mistress was soft-pedaled, although it had been in the rumor mill for weeks, and everybody was expecting it to break as a major news story. But it was the charges of racism that made the headlines.

Everybody was calling me. Vernon and Ann Jordan called me when I got back to D.C. and took me out to an expensive Sunday afternoon lunch. Eleanor Holmes Norton called. Debra Johns spent that weekend with me helping me transition back to Washington. Minyon was calling to tell me that what I'd done was an act of courage. The campaign was roaring back. I never got any calls from inside the party, and I can understand that. They wanted to distance themselves from what I had said. Dukakis even called George Bush and apologized for what I had said. On one of the Sunday morning shows Lloyd Bentsen even said that the Republican tactics on Willie Horton were below the belt, and he spoke out. He and his wife, B.A., were very good people and I respected them very much. I think he wanted to say even more but he was told not to talk about it.

I had thought I was a pariah, like I was walking around with shit on my shoes. The day after the story broke my dad went to work. He was a janitor at a local high school and he carried that morning's *Times-Picayune* to work with him because I had made the front page. I'd gotten fired but he was still proud of me. Dutch Morial defended me and so did Lindy Boggs. Louisiana people always hold on to their own.

Still, I never disavowed my support of Michael Dukakis. I wanted the Democrats to win, and I wanted Dukakis to provide jobs and health care to millions of unemployed Americans. When the election was over, Dukakis finished with one of the lowest voter turnouts for any Democratic candidate.

Bush whipped us. In the end, it was no contest. The Republicans ran a low-down, nasty campaign and got away with it because Dukakis was slow to respond to attacks on his character and his views on social issues. As I sat in my apartment on election night watching the returns, it reminded me of the 1980 and 1984 elections, when

Reagan won by a landslide. Just as then, the Democrats did not have a real game plan. We had the initial lead in the polls because Democrats outnumbered Republicans when it came to registered voters, but we Democrats never worked that political edge to our advantage. The Republicans found ways to exploit our weaknesses. They found ways to beat us at our own game and, in the process, put Democrats on the defensive. They never hesitated to hit below the belt, hide their right hand and knock us down with internal distractions on race, gender, sexuality or moral permissiveness.

CHAPTER NINE

BROWN GRAVY (ROUX)

Roux, a critical part of many Cajun dishes, is thick as any brown gravy. Roux requires time, meticulous attention and patience, something I learned from my mother. Roux is the glue that binds most Cajun food, much like my mother held our family together throughout her life. Her legacy was her wit, grace and love. Her devotion to her children made us all want to stick together.

THE DUKAKIS CAMPAIGN left me literally flat on my back. Not only was I physically exhausted, I was mentally tired and spiritually drained. My feet even hurt. But, most of all, I was politically wounded and ashamed.

As I sat on my couch back in Washington after the election looking for a miracle, I realized nothing was happening. Occasionally, I would get a phone call from one of my campaign kids to see if I was still breathing. I was still pissed off and upset with myself for losing it on the campaign trail. I had lost it! I knew I was done. My political career was over. Overnight I went from a promising up-and-coming political operative to a has-been.

Still, I was under thirty and, for some reason, I still had some fight in me. I had promised never to abandon poor people, working families, women and minorities. But with the public firing, what could I do? Who would hire me? I was so worried that I went back to St. Joseph's Catholic Church to speak with Monsignor Murphy, an old-fashioned Irish priest. The monsignor was also a closet Democrat. I knew he would offer me some advice and help to console me.

Sitting in his office at the Rectory, he looked at me and asked if I had any contrition. Of course, I did. I wanted to cry, but I held my tears back. Finally, after a deep breath and strong swallow, I told him, "Yes, I'm sorry for my actions in the Dukakis campaign because I let my people down." He nodded, I looked over at the crucifix and asked for a blessing. Monsignor, who always had a sense of humor, told me to get out of politics for a while and start living my life. Why not, I thought to myself. Grandma told me that when you fall down, dust yourself off and get back up. I wanted to get back in, but I didn't have a clue as to how to begin my career again. Walking out of the Rectory with Monsignor, I agreed to volunteer at the church and make soup for the homeless. He walked me out through the backyard to the gate and gave me a pat on the back. We said good-bye and I pulled a cap over my head and slowly walked back to my apartment.

All I could think about was my career in politics. For ten long years I had sacrificed everything to get a seat at the table. I took little money, traveled in bad cars, ate cold pizza, slept on floors, and flew on prop planes all to reach my goal. Here I was at the height of my game—broke, busted and disgusted with myself. This was a good time to get out of Washington to recharge my batteries, make a little money on the side to pay off my campaign-related debt and check in with my family. I thought long and hard about my next move. Monsignor Murphy was right, it was time to get a real job and make some money.

THE HOLIDAYS WERE APPROACHING and I needed a good home-cooked meal. It was time to go back home.

My mother had not been well for some time, and since my grandmother's death I had powerful premonitions of when people would physically leave us. Jean's health had deteriorated and she wasn't feeling well. My mother was an active woman who always watched her "figure" and health. Lionel was home recuperating from prostate surgery—Jean had stopped working during the summer to take care of him and now she herself was getting sick. Sheila told me that Jean was barely eating anything and she looked tired. When I called home, she told me not to worry. But, I did. Dr. Kaplan, Jean's doctor, told my sisters that Jean needed to rest and take it easy. Her blood pressure was high and she just appeared to be tired. The last thing I needed was to have something happen to Jean. On my baby sister Zeola's birthday, they rushed Jean to Charity Hospital. She was having difficulty breathing and they thought it was a heart attack. Cheryl called and caught me while I was unpacking the rest of my boxes from Boston. The doctors told us that she would get better after some rest. As I began unpacking I kept saying to myself, "Jean never took time to rest. She worked all her life, rarely took vacations and her body was tired." I cried so hard that I thought my head would burst wide open.

The doctors kept her for further tests and observation. They wanted Jean to rest. Jean kept on working from her hospital bed. On election day, Jean called from the hospital and told me to go and vote, as if I needed to be told. Here she was, in the hospital with tubes stuck inside her arms giving orders to her children to vote. I wanted to go home, but she told me to finish up my work in D.C. and come home over the weekend. Before I could make it to New Orleans, my mom died.

I had talked to her the day before, on November 18. She wanted me to send Janika, her first grandchild, a birthday gift and to check on Sheila and Teddy Man to make sure they were paying her bills at home. I also spoke with my sister Lisa who was there in the hospital with her, along with her mama and sister Gwen. Lisa said that Jean was weak. She was coughing up fluid that was in her lungs and had taken a sudden turn for the worse. She had been scheduled to leave the hospital and she seemed to be doing much better, but then the doctors said they needed to keep her to see if they could drain the fluid from her lungs.

I had already made plans to go home, but then on Saturday, November 19, at 2:10 that afternoon, I was giving a speech downtown to a women's conference that my good friend Nikki had organized. Everyone was trying to help me get back on my feet. Nikki had kept in touch and was someone I could always count on to help. She knew I wasn't working and could use the money. I'd get $1,000 for talking about politics in Washington and that was the only reason I was hanging around the city. I'd use the money to help my family pay some of their bills. And Nikki told me that after the speech I could catch a flight home. Later I found out that my plane was late so I went home and while I was sitting in my apartment I just suddenly felt low, it was like something hit me. A gentle wind, light like a feather, blew across my face. I grew alarmed and looked down on the floor. There was no energy in my body and I was feeling despair.

I called home and no one picked up. Someone is always home in my family. I knew something was wrong. I was feeling the same things I had felt just before Grandma died. I had even dreamed about my grandma the night before. She was sitting in her rocking chair and smiling at Jean and me. This was a sign of departure. It was my time to say good-bye to Jean and to tell her how much I loved her. I needed a hug and in my dream she kissed me on the forehead. I smelled roses and I knew in my heart that I had to call the hospital and check on Jean. When I called, one of Jean's doctors told me that she was slipping in and out of a coma. I knew Jean was about to pass away. I could feel it. I called all my siblings and told them that they needed to get to the hospital because Jean didn't have much longer. I called my mother's brothers, Uncle Johnny and Uncle Nat, in New York. I called everybody just to let them know. And around 7:00 that night my sister Cheryl called and said that Jean had passed. I went into my bedroom, turned off all the lights, lit a candle and prayed. I wanted God to know how much I loved my mother. I wanted the angels to take her home. Jean was more than just my mother; she was my best friend in the world.

My friends Al and Barbara took me to the airport at 6:00 the next morning. It was a cold wintry day in Washington. On the way to the airport, my favorite radio station, WHUR, was playing Mahalia Jackson singing "Precious Lord." I started to cry all over again. I knew I had to be strong. Hell, I was always strong, but this time I wasn't in the mood to be the tough one. I had just lost the most important person in my world. Sitting in National Airport, I was in too much pain. I felt horrible, especially after the dream, that I had not gotten back to see Jean before she passed. I was so upset, but Jean kept urging me to complete my work in D.C. and help get the vote out for Dukakis. This time I listened.

When I prayed at night, I always asked that nothing would happen to my mother. I simply wouldn't want to live if something happened to her. For the first time, I wasn't scared to fly. I just got on board, took my seat, and continued my crying. When I landed, Marc and his sister Elise from across the street were there with my sister Demetria to drive me home. Teddy Man was standing on the front porch looking over at the children playing basketball in the park. Sheila was sitting on one of the chairs Jean often sat on in the evenings. Cheryl, Chet, Lisa, Zeola and Kevin were all inside sitting in the living room. Demetria was walking in behind me, crying. Lionel was in his room with the door closed. I hugged every one of them—something we Braziles rarely did. We never showed our emotion for fear that someone would take it as a sign of weakness. I heard noise coming from the back room. It was Janika walking up and down the hall in Jean's slippers. I felt an instant pain in my chest. This was hard, but I knew I had to break the silence. "When," I asked, "should we bury Jean?" No one answered me. I kept talking about the burial. "Where should we send her body?" "Jackson Funeral Home," Cheryl said. But Lisa was stirred up. She started to talk about Jean's death.

We all agreed. There would be no autopsy. We didn't believe in doctors cutting on bodies after they were dead. We wanted to prepare for the funeral. Jean was just fifty-two years old and the official death certificate said that she died of a heart attack, with a blood clot in her lungs. Dr. Kaplan also told us she had emphysema. But we believe she died of exhaustion. When Jean left the Hilberts, she went to work for the Wren family on weekends and would help her mama with the catering business with her sister Gwen and cousins. She never stopped working and expected all of us to do the same. She would tell us that we would all die of something one day. And we would owe someone when we died. We never paid much attention to her discussions about death. But when she told Sheila that her body felt drained, and that she couldn't go any further, we began to worry. And I think she knew in her heart that the end was near for her.

Because I am a woman of strong faith, I have come to believe that my dismissal from the Dukakis campaign was God's way of telling me to check on my mom. In the midst of a campaign you couldn't catch up with me. But when I got fired I had to slow down. Earlier in the fall my mom had seemed fine. She wanted to meet Mike Dukakis—a first, since she never cared much for politics. After the rally in the French Quarter, Jean and Janika met Dukakis and got back on the bus and went home. Later that night, she had hugged me for doing such a good job at the rally. I was totally shocked. The only times of affection usually came in the mornings when she combed my hair and rubbed my shoulders. She would then take a swipe from her lips and clean my eyes before allowing me to run out of the house. I admired Jean so much for her grace and wisdom. After Grandma's death, we grew very close. She was my confidante.

Sitting in the living room with my siblings, I learned that Jean had cashed in her insurance policies, had paid off all her bills, had given away most of her clothes and told some family members that she knew she was going to die. When we went through her things we recalled how she never wanted to buy anything for herself. She was always about her children. We had to beg her to buy things for herself. She had worked so hard all her life. And primarily, she had worked to support her family. Back in August, she had told me that she would have to help my sister Lisa raise her daughter Janika, her first grandchild. Lisa was moving into an apartment with a new male friend. Jean didn't approve of that situation so she wanted Janika to live with her. They would send Janika to Catholic school. My mom was doing for Janika what my grandmother did for me. She was teaching Janika the basics of life—faith, family and friends.

The night before the funeral many of the family's old friends from Kenner came to the viewing. It was like a reunion of sorts. Jean had died five years after the move and her death brought everyone back together. During all this, Lionel was still recovering from cancer and I didn't know what to do for him. I was trying to deal with my mother's death and my father's illness and it was too much. I simply prayed to God not to take Lionel, too. I couldn't handle losing my job, my mother and my father all at once.

The funeral was held at St. Joan of Arc Catholic Church. I made up the program and I put in the Twenty-third Psalm and the Scripture from the book of John 14:1, "Let not your heart be troubled," because they were Jean's favorites. Family members sat, I spent most of the funeral outside the church; I couldn't deal with it. Mrs. Hilbert, whom my mom had worked for all those years, came. I guess she wanted to pay her respects. We did not invite them, but they walked in and took a seat in the back of the church, behind the family.

The Hilberts had paid Jean a hundred dollars a week for working forty hours plus, for raising their kids, with no health insurance, no Social Security. I was not too happy to see them. My mom died in Charity Hospital because she had no insurance, no benefits from a life of hard work. I knew I had to contain my disappointment so I just looked away when I saw Mrs. Hilbert and her husband nearing the church. But my sister Lisa wasn't so polite. She stood up in her pew when they entered the church and said loudly, "Well, look who's showing up."

And my mom's brother-in-law Flint Hawthorne came with his mother, who was wearing this loud, yellow dress, and I thought to myself, if anybody's going to wake my mom up from the dead, it's going to be this woman. It became a typical New Orleans funeral with laughter and liquor flowing outside the church (liquor that everybody brought in their pockets, pocketbooks or underneath their dresses). Uncle Nat and I were outside drinking Scotch, and Uncle Floyd would come out and we'd drink some wine. Jean was a partier and it felt as if we were honoring her spirit. We even poured a glass of Sir Malcolm, her favorite Scotch, and left it outside of the church. I knew she was nearby, I felt her presence.

Years earlier, I had purchased a burial plot that would hold two people. There was a plot for Jean and one for Lionel. I was trying to be economical. So at the gravesite Jean was buried in her plot. Nobody else in the family knew that I had purchased two plots and my siblings accused me of once again trying to micromanage the family. That gave me reason to pause and I started thinking that with Jean's death it really was time for me to allow my brothers and sisters to grow up. I would make a resolution to allow them to control their own lives, get in debt when they wanted to and date whoever they pleased. I would give up control once and for all. I would stay out of their business and allow them to do as they pleased. It was tough, but

I needed to get my own life in order. My excuse was always that with a big family, somebody's got to be in charge. Well, no more. Of course that promise lasted about twenty-four hours. I went right back to running things because Thanksgiving was the next day, the day after we buried Jean.

So Jean was dead and Lionel was sick. Lionel is a great cook but he was in no shape to cook that year. So the question was who was going to make Thanksgiving dinner? Who was going to stir in Jean's pots? Her pots were sacred and she didn't allow just anybody to use them. There was her black skillet. There was her gumbo pot. There were her frying pans and cast-iron skillets. Every pot, pan and skillet had a certain seasoning. If you wanted to cook popcorn you had to use the popcorn pot, not her skillet, or she'd kill you. You could only fry chicken in her frying pan, you couldn't even fry bacon in it. One tradition we had was that we not only cooked Thanksgiving dinner for ourselves, we cooked for all those who had no place to go on that day—extended family, cousins and neighbors. So on a typical Thanksgiving, Jean would cook for thirty or more people. People came because she was a great cook. She would start early and we'd have baked chicken, fried chicken, smothered chicken, turkey, Creole gumbo, dirty rice, eggplant, white rice, collard greens, fried okra, stuffed bell peppers, macaroni and cheese, corn bread, rolls, sweet potato pie, pecan pie, apple pie, muffins and cake.

In answer to the question about who was going to cook, I designated myself. But I was also the tomboy of the family. I wasn't the cook. When I asked Sheila and Cheryl to help, they said flat out that they were not going to go in the kitchen and mess with Jean's pots. So it was all on me. After the burial, I went to Schwegmann's, where we stocked up on groceries once a month. Schwegmann's was where the poor people shopped, and you didn't buy groceries there, you "made" them. As I walked the aisles, I asked myself "What would Mom cook?" It was almost like her spirit was guiding me down the aisles to the things to buy—celery, green onions, garlic, fresh okra, parsley, red and green peppers. I knew Jean's spirit was in me when I reached for the macaroni and cheese that was on sale, three for a dollar. That was Jean all the way, how to save a penny.

Now, I had left home at seventeen. I wasn't a cook. Over the years, she had given me her recipes and had treated them as if I needed top-secret clearance prior to getting them. But I simply knew what she would have bought. When I got home Lionel looked at the groceries and asked me if Jean had left a list. I knew how big the turkey had to be—twenty-two pounds or over, because her turkey pan was not for a small turkey. My mom liked to put two pounds of shrimp in her gumbo and she liked to take the heads off and use that as stock—you'd boil them first with bay leaves. I knew I had to clean the crabs just the way she liked them and the way she liked to break them up. As Lionel and Teddy Man watched me cook, my dad shook his head and said, "She left you a list." "No, Lionel, I swear, she's been talking to me all day." He understood.

I was drinking a glass of wine to steady my nerves and convince myself I could do this. All my siblings had abandoned the kitchen like it was the scene of a crime. Nobody believed that the tomboy would be able to pull this off. While they were upstairs in the *bouvetroire* consoling one another, crying, I prepared a Thanksgiving dinner that would have made Jean proud. My sister Lisa finally came down to help and pretty soon we had everything cut up and ready in the refrigerator.

My head was tight, but I got up at 4:00 the next morning. I had slept on the floor in the *bouvetroire* and I felt a kick. I looked up and swore that I was seeing a ghost. I thought Jean's ghost had come to haunt me and I needed to stop drinking wine. But it was Janika. She had put on my momma's slippers, padded down the hall to where I was and kicked me gently. When I woke up Janika said, "Mama gets up right now to put the turkey in the oven."

"Janika, please give me one more hour. Auntie Donna had a little bit too much to drink."

"You have to get up now so the turkey will be ready in time and you can take it off the stove and make the gumbo."

This was Jean talking to me, ensuring that the dinner was a success, telling me through Janika what I needed to do. Sometimes I'd call home when I was homesick or had a craving for some of Jean's cooking and I'd ask her how to stuff a pepper, or something like that, but I never asked her how to bake a turkey or a ham or how to cook seafood gumbo. That day I had to make my first pot of gumbo—gumbo takes six hours.* Everybody knows how to make soup, but gumbo is not soup. Gumbo is a layered process where you start off by using shrimp heads to make the stock and then you add your bay leaf, and once that comes to a boil you scoop out the shrimp heads and the bay leaf and then you put in your crabs, your parsley and your celery and you let it all cook down in this huge pot for another hour.

Meanwhile you add your salt, pepper, Tabasco, all your seasonings, and this gets the house smelling real good. The okra is already chopped up. But you've got to make your roux. You want to turn the stock from being something that looks like red gravy because of the tomato paste you added, to something brown, like the Mississippi River. My mom said the roux always had to look like me or Teddy Man, the two darkest kids. So I looked at my skin and knew what color the roux had to be. I got out some of Jean's cooking grease and got it hot in a skillet and poured a teaspoon of flour in the skillet and it started bubbling really quick; so I knew it was real hot. I then put a cup of flour in and it got a nutty, grainy texture. Then I threw in the onions, the green peppers, the red peppers and the garlic and let it get real, real, dark and then all of a sudden it just started smoothing out. I poured in two cups of water and stirred it and I had my roux.

It was five days after Jean's death and one day after she was in the ground and I was getting enormous help from some unusual sources. There was a fly in the kitchen. One little fly that kept swooping over the stove. I couldn't kill it. None of my brothers and sisters could kill it and it was like it was watching me. So I told everybody the fly was Jean watching over me, making sure I cooked everything just the way she liked it. I didn't have to think. I just cooked like I was possessed. I was cooking in Jean's pots. I was stirring things up. I felt like that day I finally grew up. My uncles opened up the Scotch and asked me

* Please see Jean's Seafood Gumbo recipe on page 317.

if I wanted my "taste." My mom used to get her taste in a little cup and then she'd take a sip and put it in the window. I got my little sip and I put it in the window and said, "Yeah, that's for you, Jean."

The food turned out just right and everybody was shocked. They thought I had taken a cooking class. But I told them that it was my first time cooking a meal this big. Even I was shocked that I had cooked in Jean's pots. Lionel made a shrine to my mom in one room after her death, and although we eventually took most of Jean's things out of the house, we left her pots. We cooked in her pots. That whole day was so symbolic for me. Clearly, I was ready to start all over. I was ready to step into Jean's courageous shoes, to take my place at the table. Before her death Jean had begun grooming me to step into that role, to take care of the family, to watch over everybody, to make sure everybody understood that we had to stick together. She left me in charge. That's what that Thanksgiving dinner was about.

Jean and I had developed a strong friendship. We would talk on the phone for hours about everything going on in the family. My mother was up on everything. She would tell me everybody's secrets, but I never had to worry about her talking about my personal life. Jean came to visit me once in D.C., to see my apartment, and she met Al and Barbara and she loved them and they loved her.

I would tell my mom about the ups and downs of the campaign trail, but she didn't care about that kind of stuff. She wanted to talk about her sisters and brothers. She wanted to talk about their lives and their problems. She was everybody's confidante. Everyone put their deeply held close-to-the-chest secrets in my mom's hands. My mom was a counselor, an adviser, a strategic planner, and before she died she shared a lot of her wisdom about living. Jean always preached the same exact sermon: "Take care of your body because when it's tired, you are going to feel it." I was extremely tired of fighting for inclusion in the political process and for respect.

I stayed in Kenner until the end of the year and came back to D.C. in January. After Grandma died, I had Jean to lean on for comfort and support. But now with Jean gone, I felt as if I had no one. I didn't know what to do with my life. I was doing consulting work here and there. Mayor Marion Barry offered me a job, but I declined.

I wasn't ready to work for the mayor or local government. I received some calls from Capitol Hill, including Dick Gephardt, who wanted to keep in touch and check on the status of my health. Dick was a major freak about health care and would often call me to remind me to exercise. But I just kept waiting for someone inside the Democratic Party to call now that Ron Brown had taken over the DNC. Nothing happened. One day I got a lucky break. Senator Alan Cranston of California wanted to recommend me to serve as a consultant to the Forum Institute. They needed someone who knew the Deep South to work on a redistricting project and the impact on the Democratic Party. Cranston said they would pay me five thousand dollars a month for that. That was more than I ever made before as salary. I needed the money to help pay Janika's tuition. Alan Cranston was a neighbor, a good old-fashioned Democrat, and he saved me.

Rob Stein was at the Forum Institute. Rob was very close to Paul Tully and Ron Brown. After a couple of weeks of doing research, I figured it out. Ron was putting me to work, but I wasn't working directly for him at the DNC. He told me to stay in touch with Paul and Alexis Herman, my good friend from Mobile, Alabama. The project was exciting. On my first trip to Atlanta, I sat down with my friend Bobby Kahn, who was executive director of the Georgia Democratic Party. He urged me to call state representatives Tyrone Brooks and Billy McKinney to see if they were cutting deals with Republicans to create majority-minority districts. I was more familiar with Tyrone Brooks and arranged a meeting with him the next day.

The Black lawmakers across the South were up to something. I knew as much because back in Louisiana, Avery Alexander and Bill Jefferson told me that things were gonna change next time. I didn't understand the politics, but the Republicans were offering Blacks an opportunity to serve in Congress—something the Democratic Party had denied us. Tyrone told me that he was planning on voting on a new plan put forward with the help of the Republicans. Georgia, he believed, would be able to elect more than one African American. The plan passed. My report was finished. At the end of it, I knew no one paid attention to my warning. The Democratic Party was in trouble down in Dixie. They needed it, but the leaders refused to address racism within our party. Ron tried to get their attention and he was somewhat successful.

But the Party did not act fast. In April, Mitch Snyder, who had started the Community for Creative Non-Violence back in the 1970s, called and asked me to work with him on organizing a big march on the growing problem of homelessness in America. Mitch was a deeply passionate, committed and caring individual. I told him I would give him an answer when I came back to D.C. after a visit home for Easter. I still felt that political work was my calling, but I was unmoved by his request. I was still searching for the best way to keep going. I didn't want to give up on politics. I asked my sister Cheryl for her advice about Mitch's offer. In some ways I felt illegitimate in terms of my work. Cheryl worked for AIG, a big insurance corporation, and my other siblings seemed to have legitimate jobs, the kind that didn't only last the run of a campaign. I told Cheryl about Mitch, that he was a big homeless advocate and that he wanted me to work on organizing the march out of the homeless shelter he ran on Second and D—the Federal City Shelter. I didn't get much support on the home front. Everyone expected me to grow up after Jean's death, to put politics and activism aside and get a regular job, and here I had found another cause instead of a real job. Over Easter dinner of baked ham, string beans, potato salad, stuffed peppers and smothered chicken in a strong roux, we went back and forth over my job prospects. Cheryl was adamant; it was time for me to grow up. I felt equally strong in my personal convictions that my political life was not over. I was not done with organizing. I left home disappointed in my family.

Initially, I told Mitch that I had to get a real job. I needed health insurance, I had enough campaigns under my belt and I was burned out from the Dukakis campaign. I told him I didn't want to march anymore; I told him anything to avoid saying yes. The next night, however, I had a nightmare about my own family's struggle to keep our house, and how we had been homeless for a spell. I woke up knowing I had to say yes. I wondered if this was God's test to see if I could keep the faith, if I was really true in my calling to help people, a calling I had heard since I was a child.

Mitch had this tremendous gaze; it was the gaze of a person truly on fire with conviction and yet there was sadness in his eyes, too. He was gentle, yet tough and determined that the march would revive the Poor People's Campaign that Dr. King had led in the last months of his life. Mitch was ecstatic that I agreed to work with him and said that he would work on fund-raising while I organized the march. To my surprise I found that working in the shelter, being thrown, in a sense, to the bottom, was my therapy; it was a powerful form of rehabilitation for me. The CCNV was headquartered in an old federal government office building, not far from the Capitol. I would walk from my house past the Capitol, past the Supreme Court, to the shelter each day. It was a huge shelter that housed over a thousand men and women. But mostly it was a sea of Black men with broken spirits who called the shelter their home.

The march was being planned for Saturday, October 7, 1989, and my job was to put together a national coalition in support of the march; the theme was ending homelessness in America and building affordable housing around the country. Homelessness had been the legacy of the Reagan and Bush years. It just exploded and in D.C., during the winter months, maybe a dozen or more people died on the streets because they had no place to go. I told Mitch how much my rent was. It had gone up to $400 a month and he said he would cover my monthly expenses, and I ate most of my meals at the shelter. As long as my rent was paid, and the young people working for me were paid, I was satisfied.

This was the most unusual march I had ever worked on because in a shelter there's no structure, no organization. You are working with homeless people and so I dealt with a lot of angry people who were convinced that the world hated them. I was not only dealing with their broken spirits but with my own as well. It was tough to bring organization to the shelter, but there was Mitch and his partner, Carol Fennelly, who helped me heal my wounds.

Mitch was deeply involved in D.C. politics. He was always pressing the buttons of local officials, Marion Barry in particular. People either loved Mitch or hated him. I knew that I ran the risk of people responding to me with the same mixed attitude they had toward Mitch. Right before a City Council session on the annual budget, Mitch would announce one of his hunger strikes or would organize some of the homeless to fill the chambers to show the City Council he was serious. Mitch and Carol were always staging hunger strikes to bring attention to the plight of the homeless and they felt the city was doing too little to solve the homeless problem. In fact, Mitch was on a hunger strike during the organizing of the march. I would go up to his room to give a report. Mitch was weak, but he made the fundraising calls and spent hours talking about the state of the world. We became close. I had a lot of respect for Mitch and Carol.

For my part, I tried to bring the homeless movement into the mainstream. I worked with Barry Zigas of the National Low Income Housing Coalition, the local NAACP, civil rights groups, housing groups and every shelter in D.C. We formed a group called Housing Now, which was the name of the national coalition that brought together about a hundred different groups, all supporting the goals of the march. I was in charge of a staff of 25 paid workers and 275 volunteers.

This was the year in which I reconnected with my spirituality. I was growing up, developing my own language of the spirit, of what I wanted for myself. It was hard work, but it was fulfilling and I felt a strong sense of gratification because it gave me a chance to give back.

I roamed around the shelter talking to the men and women who called it home and I learned about their lives and how they had come to be homeless. Most of them wanted jobs: they wanted to work. The shelter offered poetry and drama classes. I read my own poetry in some of the classes. It was a place where nobody pointed a finger at you and asked why you were there. I was surrounded every day by hundreds of people who were often my age but looked twenty or thirty years older because of what drugs, alcohol, poverty and homelessness had done to them. The system had beaten them down. There were so many Vietnam veterans in the shelter, people who had served their country. They were my heroes. And they told me their stories. It got so everybody knew me and I was okay because I was working with Mitch.

There was a deep spirit of connectedness among the people. They really cared about one another. Over the years many of the residents had died, and because they'd been separated or exiled from their families or ashamed to let their families know how they were living, no one would come to claim their bodies. Mitch would have these people cremated and place their ashes in little vases all over the shelter. Mitch would write their name and the date they died on the vase. All this was so humbling for me. I call this my period of penance. When I look back at the Dukakis campaign, at my mother's death, I feel like I was having a wilderness experience, one designed to heal and revive my soul so I could continue my life's work.

I had recovered from all the damaging things I had done in my political work and this was my way of apologizing to God and recommitting myself to the struggle. It used to just blow my mind looking at those vases with the ashes of people no one had been able to claim. Mitch was racked by his own demons and a year after the march he committed suicide inside the shelter.

Mitch was a fighter, but there were some things he could not handle, including losing Carol, who had left to start a new life. Mitch left such an amazing legacy of giving life and hope to others. He made it easy for people to live in the shelter. Mitch took care of all their needs. He got them clothes. He met their medical needs. The second floor of the shelter was the AIDS ward. That part of the shelter was filled with the first wave of Black people with AIDS who weren't serviced much by the Whitman Walker Clinic in those days. We didn't call it the AIDS ward but that's what it was. Mitch encouraged people to go out and look for jobs, even a temporary job. He also had people come in and train the men and women, give them skills they could use on the job market. The shelter was really a movement, not just a building. Mitch was on a crusade to fix the world, he was a dreamer and maybe that's why he took his own life.

One of the most unforgettable people I met at the shelter was Big John, a tall, stocky White guy whom every Black person at the shelter just loved. He had a tremendous heart. He was in charge of driving around the city and picking up homeless people off the streets, from grates or lying in the streets sick. He had a truck and he would pick them up and bring them to the shelter. He died a few months after the march when his pancreas failed. I was there when he stopped breathing. For weeks I tried desperately to find his family. I couldn't. So Mitch took his ashes and put them over the fireplace near the big window at the shelter where they would always be kept warm.

I started going back to church again and during confession Father Murphy at St. Joseph's would tell me to stop making things up. But I would tell him that I knew I had sinned and that I felt that my mother died because I had not paid enough attention to her health. And I still felt terribly guilty about the Dukakis campaign and all the trouble I caused. I even asked Father Murphy to help me reach President Bush so I could apologize to him and Mrs. Bush. I just wanted to start fresh with a clean slate and heart. Father Murphy counseled me to get back on the campaign trail. It was the only way to recover from the last campaign. I agreed.

Harold, Darryl, Jerry and the people at the shelter were all fighters. They helped me get back into my fighting spirit. Two days before the march, we had a lobby date. We went to Capitol Hill and lobbied the members of Congress for legislation to help the homeless and to restore budget cuts to the Department of Housing and Urban Development (HUD). Everything was going well until I realized that the homeless men and women who were lobbying didn't have any money, and so I decided that at noon they would go to the cafeteria in the basement of the Rayburn or Longworth building and demand a free lunch. And that's exactly what they did, all three thousand of them. These were homeless people from all over the country. Once they started eating they forgot all about lobbying. There was a cafeteria, and there was food and that became their gathering place. I had to call friends and ask them to send over $100, $500 to pay for their meals. They even went back for seconds. I had to call Capitol Police Chief Albrecht and explain to him what was going on and not to make any arrests. A small delegation of the march committee met on Friday morning with HUD secretary Jack Kemp, who was very sympathetic to our cause. Congressman Rangel helped arrange the meeting. After the lobby day, there was a vigil the night before the march.

There were all kinds of logistical problems I had never encountered in a march before because of the constituency we were dealing with. You can't mail homeless people information in advance; you can't call them at home on the phone. Bernard Demczuk, Julie Gibson and Bob Bosch, friends from my campaign days, all came on board to give the march a professional feel. Other friends inside the Democratic Party came to my rescue and volunteered to help with logistics and communications. The march brought over 200,000 people to the city in the largest housing demonstration since the sixties. I reached back to my friends from the civil rights movement for help and support and got Stevie Wonder to perform. Mitch had Cher reach out to Tracy Chapman and Los Lobos to perform. Reverend Jackson, Coretta Scott King, Walter Fauntroy, Mayor Barry and Ohio governor Richard Celeste all spoke. The homeless were so pleased. I was overjoyed.

I had no way of knowing it, but those months working at CCNV gave me a bird's-eye view of local D.C. issues and politics, and it paved the way for my next cause, which landed me in the midst of D.C. politics. After years of running back and forth to Louisiana to work on local campaigns, I made a decision to go local. Looking for a candidate to back wasn't hard. I knew everyone on the council and school board. Walter Fauntroy's seat was safe, but I thought it was time to get involved in the D.C. mayoral race. Then everything went up in smoke.

Marion Barry, a hero in the civil rights movement and a fellow Southerner, was arrested at a downtown hotel smoking crack cocaine.

CHAPTER TEN

CRABMEAT LAFITTE

*People in Southern Louisiana are fond of their crab dishes. We put crab in
our gumbo and stuff it in our fish and peppers. I clawed my way back up the
political ladder after my painful defeats in the eighties and, like most Democrats, I was determined to achieve better fortunes in the nineties.*

AS SOON AS I HEARD the news about Mayor Barry, I called
Eleanor Holmes Norton. She wasn't home. I tried her at Georgetown Law School. She wasn't there. I needed to talk with Eleanor
about what was happening to Marion. The city was buzzing about
the mayor and how he finally got caught. I knew Eleanor would know
something.

Eleanor Holmes Norton was also one of my closest friends, and
our friendship had so many different levels. She was always urging
me to go to law school, or at least graduate school. She was smart and
savvy. I admired her life story: a young girl who attended the segregated schools of Washington, D.C., and went on to champion civil
rights and civil liberties. Eleanor worked side by side with people like
Fannie Lou Hamer; she knew Medgar Evers, Malcolm X, Thurgood
Marshall, Maya Angelou, Dorothy Height and other civil rights icons
I grew up admiring and worshiping. Eleanor was my springboard
and I was very close to her family, her mother, Ms. Vela, and her sisters Portia and Nellie. When I was in D.C., if I wasn't hanging out
with my neighbors Al, Thomas or Barbara, I was with Eleanor, Ed
and their children, Johnny and Katherine. They became my second
family.

❀ ❀ ❀

IN THE AFTERMATH of Marion Barry's arrest at 8:00 PM on January 18, 1990, at the Vista International Hotel in downtown Washington, it was clear that Washington residents were ready for a change in leadership and direction. Two days after his arrest, I spent time defending his record of public service and trying to encourage citizens not to rush to judgment until all the facts were on the table. Like Eleanor, Marion Barry was a veteran of the civil rights movement and one of the lead organizers of the Student Non-Violent Coordinating Committee (SNCC). He was in his third term as mayor after defeating Republican Carol Schwartz in 1986. But his days seemed over. The FBI videotape of Barry smoking crack in a rendezvous with Rasheeda Moore, one of his longtime friends, was all over the news. This time Barry's legendary Teflon would start coming off in the heat. Mayor Barry was going down fast.

IT TOOK SOME TIME after Barry checked himself into a residential treatment facility in Florida before he announced that he wasn't going to run for mayor again. Walter Fauntroy made plans to discuss Black politics in the city and convened top leaders to evaluate the future. With Barry on the sidelines and about to go to jail, it was clear to me that Walter wanted to assume control of Black politics in the District. A week later, Fauntroy announced his intention to step down as D.C.'s nonvoting congressional delegate in order to enter the race for mayor. He made the announcement at a strategy meeting attended by Bill Lucy, Shelia High King, Bob Johnson, Clifton Smith, Lezli Baskerville, Delano Lewis, and his longtime aide Wayne King. I just sat and listened. After the meeting I called Eleanor at home and gave her a minute-by-minute rundown of the meeting. When I finished, I told her that she should run for congressional delegate to fill Walter Fauntroy's seat.

Eleanor practically cussed me out, telling me how good her life was teaching at Georgetown, writing essays, columns and op-eds and lecturing on college campuses across America. Her basic response was "go to hell," but knowing Eleanor like I did, I knew that meant "tell me more." So my next step was to write a memo outlining just how she could win. In drafting my documents, I knew I had to be specific. Eleanor wasn't a typical politician. She would not understand words like "targeting," "message" and "tracking." I called Ivanhoe Donaldson, Dorie Ladner, Reggie Williams, Lawrence Guyot, June Johnson and Courtland Cox, who had worked in the Barry administration but were some of Eleanor's SNCC buddies. They all agreed it was a great idea. Next, I reached out to Vernon Jordan, Marian Wright Edelman and Christine Philpot, Eleanor's classmates at Yale Law School and powerful Black lawyers who would provide some insights. My memo was complete and a few days later, I met with Eleanor and her husband on a Saturday afternoon at their home. They were excited by the prospect.

I told Eleanor that any opposition would be token at best, that she would bring in the civil rights and women's communities and that she would be able to raise money nationally because of her high profile. As the human rights commissioner for the city of New York, the chair of the Equal Employment Opportunity Commission and a respected and gifted thinker, Eleanor, I felt, would be an ideal delegate to Congress. This was the year of change. A year to reform the District government and image in the wake of the scandal that Barry had created.

At that time—1990—D.C. was over 65 percent Black and 80 percent Democratic. I knew that Eleanor had a natural appeal in a progressive city. My calculation was simple. Stay out of the mayoral race. Focus on winning Wards 4, 5, 6, 7 and 8. At the time, those Wards had substantial Black populations. I knew Eleanor could also generate support in Ward 2 because she had been an early champion of gay and lesbian civil rights. She grew up in Ward 1 and her mother resided in 4. Wards 5, 7 and 8 were competitive in a large field of Black candidates, but I was reassured by some of my early calls that Eleanor could garner some important endorsements. This left Ward 3—west of Rock Creek Park and the city's most affluent. I knew from phone calls that one of our opponents, Councilwoman Betty Ann Kane, was extremely popular in the ward, but I asked Betty King, a close Barry adviser, and former councilwoman Polly Shackleton to make inroads to see if Eleanor had a chance. Next, I called Colby King, Dorothy Gilliam and Courtland Malloy of the *Washington Post* to get their input and advice on the mood of the city. Colby was a gifted writer and a former Hill staffer who had worked on voting rights and home rule back in the 1970s. His advice was rock solid: Eleanor was nationally known, but the "people at the [local] barber shops and beauty parlors did not know her." He was right. For all of Eleanor's honors and achievements, she had to campaign as a local girl with roots in the city.

Once Eleanor committed to the race I reached out to my community contacts—Mary Preston, Lawrence Thomas, Philip Pannell, Lozzie York, Josie Meeks, Loree Murray and Richard Rausch. I called Josh Williams, head of the Metro Washington chapter of the AFL-CIO. They were all ecstatic. Eleanor's former seventh-grade teacher, Bill Simons, president of the city's largest teachers' union, was calling up other friends in the labor movement to get behind Eleanor. Ron Richardson of the Hotel Workers Union was on board. Phil Pfeaster was ready to get the Teamsters on board. The essentials were done. We were ready, but Eleanor still had to discuss this with her family.

I told Eleanor that all we needed was an announcement date and location. The money was coming in and she needed to file with the Federal Elections Commission (FEC). I even talked privately to Effi Barry, the mayor's wife, about how Marion would feel about a run for Congress by Eleanor. Ivanhoe had told me that Marion would give his blessing, but I wanted to hear it from Effi. She agreed with Ivanhoe's assessment. Marion Barry was a man disgraced at that point, but I knew that despite his personal problems he was one of the most gifted politicians around. He remained extremely popular in key sections of the Black community whose support we needed. So even though nobody wanted to be anywhere near Barry or get his blessing on anything, it mattered to me what he thought.

I wanted Eleanor to announce her run to Mark Plotkin, a local political analyst. She wanted me to hold off on telling Mark until after another conversation with Ed. Although Ed initially thought the idea of Eleanor running for Congress was interesting, he soon got cold feet. Eleanor suspected as much and put off talking to Ed further until she was committed to running herself.

Ed Norton was the former chair of the D.C. Election Board and a very well connected lawyer in the city. As it turns out, Ed ran into Mark, who told him that he had heard a lot of noise about Eleanor running for Congress. Now Ed knew for sure. When Eleanor came back to D.C. from a trip to Detroit, they had a huge argument. Ed thought he had convinced Eleanor to drop the idea and that she had told me that, but I had successfully convinced Eleanor that she was the best possible representative for the city. She had to run. And I wanted to manage her campaign.

ELEANOR MADE HER ANNOUNCEMENT the first week in May at her old elementary school, Bruce Elementary, and we even had Bernice Reagon of Sweet Honey in the Rock, a powerful vocal group and Eleanor's friends, in attendance. All her old classmates from Dunbar High School showed up. We filled part of Georgia Avenue with people from all eight wards and folks who had served with Eleanor in the Carter administration. I wanted to localize Eleanor, to have the people at her announcement testify that she was a native Washingtonian. The polls we had conducted a few weeks earlier confirmed that while Eleanor had a very high national profile she did not have a local presence. So we stressed that she was a fourth-generation Washingtonian and that what she had done in the civil rights, women's and poor people movements had helped the citizens of Washington, D.C. I was Eleanor's campaign manager, strategist, consultant and adviser.

In the primary election, Eleanor had several opponents: at-large city council member Betty Ann Kane; Donald Temple, an up-and-coming African-American lawyer; Barbara Lett Simmons, a D.C. statehood activist and former school board member; Joe Yeldell, a major player in the Barry administration with whom I had worked on all those demonstrations; and Sterling Tucker, former chair of the D.C. City Council. I knew that in the debates, Eleanor could beat them all without batting an eye.

Eleanor was leading in the polls by a slim margin going into the last week. We had built our campaign around creating an image of her as a champion (complete with big Afro) of both civil rights and the city's plight on Capitol Hill. The District of Columbia had been granted home rule and limited self-government back in 1972. With home rule we could finally elect our own mayor and local officials. We even won the right to vote for president of the United States. Congress, however, retained final oversight over the local budget and legislation approved by our city council and the mayor. We called it taxation without representation because the position Eleanor was running for did not come with full voting rights. During the campaign, Eleanor stressed her national connections, and the need to renew the drive for full statehood and voting rights for District residents.

We did not make any references to Walter Fauntroy in our campaign ads and mailings, we focused instead on Eleanor's bio and how she could usher in a whole new era of representation for the city. The election was to take place on Tuesday, September 11, 1990, and the week before election day was going well. David Axelrod, our media consultant, had sent us a bio spot tracing Eleanor's roots from the segregated classroom all the way to serving in the Carter administration. Then on Friday, September 7, at around 5:30 PM I got a call from Mike Abramowitz, a reporter at the *Washington Post*. He wanted to know if I knew about Eleanor's tax filings over the past couple of years. I told him that I did. He asked me what the status was. Without a moment's hesitation I said, "Paid in full."

"Are you sure?" he asked me.

"Well, I asked Ed several months ago because I know that's one of the standard questions a candidate for public office is always asked and Ed told me the family taxes had been paid in full."

"Well, I have a form here that says her local taxes haven't been paid in the last ten years."

I freaked out and asked Mike to just hold on a minute while I tracked Ed down at work. I knew that Ed took care of the finances. I called Ed at work and told him about the call and asked him what was going on. He told me that he would be home in thirty minutes and for me to meet him there and we would talk. He never said yes, no or maybe. As I was leaving the office to go meet Ed, I told Gwen McKinney, who was our press person, that the story was going to run pretty soon on the wires and that I would have a response, so hold down the fort.

But before I could even walk out the door, it had hit the local news, and the press had found Eleanor. I was at Eleanor's house. Ed walked in just as Eleanor called the house and asked, "What the hell is going on?" Before I could say a word she said, "Put Ed on the phone." I handed the phone to Ed and I just heard him say, "Uh huh, uh huh," and then he said, "Well, Eleanor, *I've been trying to tell you.*" Then he raised his voice and at that point I sank down into the living room sofa and just said "Oooooh." While Ed went upstairs to get all the tax papers, I sat downstairs waiting for Eleanor to come home.

Ed came down with both the local and federal tax forms and I looked at the pile of papers. I knew I wasn't an accountant but I also knew that before we could say anything to the press we had to know what was what—which taxes had been filed and paid and which hadn't. By this time there were two reporters, Sam Ford of Channel 7 and Bruce Johnson of Channel 9, outside the house waiting for Eleanor. Tom Sherwood of Channel 4 was on his way. Bill Strickland of Channel 9 caught Eleanor on the way home. When Eleanor finally got home she looked at Ed. If looks could kill he would've been dead on the spot. I was trying to be the mediator, telling Eleanor that Ed was getting everything together, that we had an answer for the press, and Eleanor looked at me and told me to shut the hell up and she told Ed that he had a lot of explaining to do.

To his credit, Ed remained calm. When we went over all the paperwork we found that Ed had not filed a couple of D.C. taxes and there were various fines and penalties due. Some years he had paid quarterly estimated taxes to the District but didn't file the actual form, and so he owed on the actual filing of the taxes and back penalties and interest to the tune of $15,000 to $20,000. I had enough to talk with a reporter, but I decided to hold any statement until we talked to an accountant. I knew all this was way above my pay grade and my friendship, so I put in a call to Alexis Herman. She was over at the DNC serving as Ron Brown's chief of staff and she was somebody who could fix things when they needed fixing. I am a fixer now, but back then I had no experience in situations like the one we were facing. Alexis gave me the name of an accounting firm, Thompson & Bazilo, and I called Jeffrey Thompson and asked him to come over right away. Alexis was on her way as well. We put out a pretty ambiguous release that said the Nortons' federal taxes had been paid but the local taxes were in bad shape.

Jeff, an accountant with a Caribbean accent, talked fast, while Ralph, his partner, sat taking notes, reviewing Ed's materials and listening. We decided to just write a check, no matter what the amount was, to the District government so we could say that the delinquent taxes and penalties and fines had been paid.

I left Eleanor's house around two in the morning and once I got home I couldn't sleep. I stayed up all night calling as many of Eleanor's friends as I could. We had to do a press conference the next day and I knew that she had to be flanked at that conference by her civil rights supporter friends, all the people who had initially endorsed her. At 9:00 AM I went to Eleanor's and found her in bed in a fetal position, depressed and not wanting to get out of bed. I could tell that neither she nor Ed had slept. I told Eleanor that we had to have a press conference. She went into a monologue about how her life, her career, everything was ruined. I told her that there were people depending on her, who believed in her. "You're still going to win this election despite what happened. Look, you're going to have to explain that you had no idea that the taxes were not paid. Ed has taken full responsibility for what happened. We'll find a way to make it all work out, but you've got to get out of this bed."

My pleas had no effect and I had to call Dr. Dorothy Height, president of the National Council of Negro Women, and ask her to talk to Eleanor. Betty Shabazz, Malcolm X's widow and Eleanor's personal friend, was on the road campaigning for us in the predominantly Black neighborhoods east of the river. I called Ron Brown, Gloria Steinem and Coretta Scott King and asked them to call Eleanor and urge her on. I called everybody Eleanor respected, like Charlayne Hunter-Gault and Vernon Jordan. Eleanor didn't realize how big this was. Already the word on the street was that, once again, a Black leader was being taken out by the establishment. There were rumors that Betty Ann Kane or somebody else in District government leaked the information to the *Washington Post*. We didn't know who, but we knew somebody had leaked the tax forms.

We held the press conference at Freedom Plaza and everybody showed up. Dick Gregory called and asked what he could do. After the press conference Eleanor would not take any questions because we had put out a statement. Alexis taught me that when you have a major crisis in a campaign, you release everything you have and say that's it and button up. When I'd get calls from the press I'd say, "I gave you everything we have. It's paid in full. It's done." And the *Washington Post,* which had earlier endorsed Eleanor, went after her almost as though what happened was a personal betrayal. They didn't let up. They informed the local voters of Eleanor's shortfalls. For eight weeks in a row, with harsh editorials and negative press coverage, we went swimming upstream for support.

We were literally down to the wire with seventy-two hours left before the primary election. We deployed every surrogate to churches to remind people Eleanor was in a fight for her life, and we got attacked on all fronts. The hate calls started pouring in from all over the city. Some of the staffers were crying. D.C. councilmember Jim Nathanson, who had not supported any of the candidates, called on Eleanor to withdraw, saying that the failure to file taxes was not just "disabling, it's disqualifying." Jim was defeated years later and replaced by a woman. The Black community was enraged over his suggestion. We knew we had to get back on the offense. With the smell of blood in the air, our opponents began to circle. It made Eleanor angry. The old civil rights warrior was about to return to the campaign trail.

Eleanor started receiving flowers from friends across the country who wanted her to stay the course. This buoyed her spirits. She began making phone calls to friends. I told her to call people like Mary Preston who would defend her to the bitter end. Eleanor moved forward to make her calls. Many of our supporters told us not to give up. Ed was there in the background helping out as well. He urged citizens not to punish her. He told reporters that it was his fault. He was quoted on the day of the election as telling reporters, "I am the one who's the villain in this." Many people accepted his statement that he was solely responsible for failing to tell Eleanor that their taxes were not filed on time.

Then Gwen McKinney, a great media strategist, came up with the idea of Eleanor sitting down for a one-on-one interview with Renee Poussaint, an anchor at Channel 7, as a way to tell the public how hurt she was by what had happened, how disappointed she was in Ed. How this had hurt her marriage. This was a very low point for Eleanor and she wanted the public to know that at no time had she set out to deceive anyone. The worst part of it all was that when Ed pulled out the paperwork, we saw that just as Eleanor had told everyone, she signed off on the forms but Ed had not filed them. So we did the one-on-one with Renee and by Monday we were being denounced as injecting race into the campaign because of the visits to Black churches. Eleanor's daughter Katherine has Down syndrome. The media accused the campaign of exploiting Eleanor's daughter because Katherine was at the rally along with the rest of her family, her mother, her sisters and Ed.

In the midst of all this, Cathy Hughes, the owner of WOL-AM, the popular Black talk radio station, went on the air on Sunday night and had a heart-to-heart talk with her listeners about the uphill battle Eleanor was now facing. Cathy was an entrepreneur, a community activist, and her station's slogan was "Information Is Power." WOL was considered the voice of the people in the city. Cathy had been one of Eleanor's most vocal supporters, and her opponents demanded equal time. She said in essence, "I'll take you on in support of my candidate." Well, Joe Yeldell and Betty Ann Kane took the bait and Cathy Hughes blasted them on the air, just blasted them. She played a key role in minimizing our opposition and that allowed us to get back on our campaign message of championing D.C. voting rights before election day.

I learned from this crisis that when you're in trouble and your opposition has more money and the local media is killing you that you fight back with another strategy. I called up our key supporters and told them to call the talk radio shows on WTOP, WAMU, WHUR and the gospel stations to jam the lines with calls of support for Eleanor. Everybody called in to encourage Eleanor to keep on run-

ning. David Wilmont, Pauline Schneider, Maudine Cooper, Joyce
Ladner and Beverly Perry—friends from the Washington business
and political establishment—all came over to volunteer. This was going to be a street fight to the bitter end.

ON ELECTION DAY, Eleanor worked her behind off. We got her
up at 5:00 AM and she was at the major bus stops, the busy Metro
stops before anybody else. I had to get two or three replacement
drivers before the afternoon shift because Eleanor wanted to go all
over the city. The fight energized her. This was important because
people needed to see her getting down and dirty with the best of
them. And she did. This became a political crusade and Eleanor was
our leader. She was manic; she wanted to just win and get this over
with. I asked Reverend Jackson and Dick Gregory to get on sound
trucks in the racially mixed Wards 4 and 5. Calvin Rolark, publisher
of the *Washington Informer* and a longtime civil rights activist, was going
to work Ward 8. Dick Gregory was in Wards 6 and 7. Ron Brown was
raising money to help me pay our workers. We were cooking with
grease. Eleanor worked up to the time the polls closed. She called the
office and told me to meet her at the Washington Court Hotel where
we had planned to celebrate our victory. Eleanor wanted to hear what
was happening. I wanted to rally our troops.

Eleanor learned how to be a strong politician during her first
campaign. She knows how to keep in touch with her grassroots supporters; she knows how to keep in touch with the people. She will
never forget those early campaign supporters. They were the people
who got her in despite everything the *Washington Post* was throwing at
her. This was a campaign unlike any I had ever experienced.
Louisiana politics is often described as brutal, but D.C. political leaders took it to another level. I learned grace under fire. Eleanor was
like a surrogate mother to me. An attack on Eleanor was an attack on
me. I decided not to flinch. I decided to find me some mud and
throw it back on everyone coming after Eleanor. If our opponents
were willing to take us on, I was ready to destroy them before they
could strike again. D.C. was my kind of town.

❊   ❊   ❊

AS THE VOTES CAME IN, it was apparent that we lost the morning box, the voters who go to the polls from 7:00 AM to noon. Whites, seniors, white-collar workers vote in the morning and Blacks, young people and blue-collar workers vote in the evening. So I called Marion Barry, Dick Gregory and Jesse Jackson and I asked them to go back into the neighborhoods, to go into every place where Black folks congregated and get them to the polls. I got my folks back on WOL and other radio stations. I had them calling in to the stations saying that Betty Ann Kane was leading. That was all we had to say.

Renee Poussaint came by the headquarters and asked how our candidate was doing and I told her that Eleanor was very optimistic, very upbeat. I couldn't tell the truth, that Eleanor was in bed with the covers over her head, angry because it looked like she was losing, even though she had quit her job at Georgetown and all the corporate boards. I smiled and told Renee, "The tide's going to turn." And it did. We won the evening box and the primary election. Eleanor won 36 percent of the vote and her nearest opponent won 32 percent. We won. That night we celebrated. I knew that the next morning I had to work to pull Eleanor's multiracial coalition back together. We lost every precinct in Ward 3. Eleanor was devastated. I told her we could win them back.

WHEN THE GENERAL ELECTION geared up we had lost virtually all our support west of Rock Creek Park and Georgetown. We went from having 50 to 60 percent of the White vote to less than 10 percent. Our money dried up. In the general election Eleanor ran against Harry Singleton, a Black Republican who had been endorsed by the Republican National Committee. He was a friend of Supreme Court Justice Clarence Thomas and all of a sudden the *Washington Post* started championing this know-nothing man from nowhere. At first no one took Singleton's candidacy seriously. He did not garner any serious endorsements and I knew that the District's Democratic base would turn out in our favor. Sharon Pratt Dixon, a former businesswoman, had beaten Walter Fauntroy in the mayoral primary and had token Republican opposition. So I knew the focus would be on Eleanor and it was time to get down to business with Democratic voters. We asked the DNC to help us raise money. Eleanor reached out to the *Washington Post* to make amends and to see if she could answer some of the weekly editorials.

I urged Eleanor to speak directly to the people and so we gave exclusive interviews to the *Washington Afro,* the *Washington Informer,* the *Capitol Spotlight,* and of course we had WOL. This meant that Eleanor didn't have a filter. She could speak directly to the Black community. This was our base and I could not afford to take their votes for granted, but I was worried about Ward 3 and the loss of White support.

Before the tax mess, Eleanor had raised close to $400,000 from all over the country, from feminists, the pro-choice groups, gays and lesbians and suddenly it all just dried up. We were so broke that I called Ron and Alexis over at the DNC and I told them they had to send us some staff and some new donors because we had nothing. We went to members of the Congressional Black Caucus and we asked for a thousand dollars, and Charlie Rangel and John Conyers sent us some money. Gephardt sent a contribution. Steny Hoyer from Maryland promised to help. Labor continued to stand by Eleanor. I would never forget the AFL-CIO's support. Nor would Eleanor. By this point the race was neck and neck. Singleton was closing in on us because of the strong support he was getting in Ward 3. Finally, we got a break.

It came out in the press that Singleton had experimented with marijuana in college and there were allegations of spousal abuse in his divorce proceedings. He denied the abuse but not the pot. He was put on the defense. This was our chance to remind voters about Eleanor's roots in the civil rights movement. In the end voters had to choose between two scarred candidates, but we had an advantage. We got our vote in the largely Democratic wards. We had a high Black turnout and that offset the White defections.

Eleanor walked into office with a 72 percent negative approval rating. So when people tell me about how politicians have 58 percent approval or disapproval, I say well, my ex-boss won with 72 percent disapproval. I ask them, "Have you ever had seven out of ten people disapprove of you and you still won the election?" We won by sheer voter turnout. We made it a movement, and of course I was uniquely qualified to run that kind of campaign.

DURING THE WEEKS OF TRANSITION, when Eleanor was paying her campaign debts and closing the campaign office, I was unsure what I wanted to do next. I thought of making a break from Eleanor and allowing her to hire Charlotte Hayes, a lawyer she was grooming, to work on her staff. But the *Post* ran an editorial predicting that Eleanor would be a complete failure on Capitol Hill, and because she was my best friend, I took those words personally. I wanted to help Eleanor prove her critics wrong. So I went to work for Eleanor and I set up her office. Within six months of taking office, Eleanor's poll ratings had gone from 72 percent disapproval to 50 percent approval. She worked tirelessly. Our motto was where two or more are gathered we would be among them. She went to every community meeting. She outshone Sharon Pratt Kelly, who had been elected mayor.

Eleanor had tremendous contacts on Capitol Hill and members of Congress respected her intellect and her loyalty to her constituents. She arrived with the attitude that she was D.C.'s representative and she took on every fight. Instead of going on the Judiciary Committee like Barbara Jordan, Eleanor decided to get on the Transportation Committee. She also wanted Post Office and Civil Service to be able to fight for government workers. Of course, as the nonvoting delegate, she was assigned to the District Committee. Meanwhile, I spent time interviewing staff. Eleanor wanted experienced people. So I hired Cedric Hendricks to oversee Eleanor's legislative shop. Cedric and I had worked with Congressman Conyers during the time we were lobbying to make Dr. King's birthday a federal holiday. Next, I hired René Redwood to handle Eleanor's District and Constituent Service Office. René had helped out with polling during the campaign and knew Eleanor's supporters. Julia Hudson, a recent graduate from Spellman and a native Washingtonian, was hired to handle the front desk and interns. Cartwright Moore, Thomas Atkins and another old friend, Gwen Benson Walker, who all worked on the campaign, came on board to help Eleanor establish her congressional office.

Our first chore was to help the mayor win an increase in the city's annual federal payment. Although Democrats were in control of the House, George H. W. Bush was in the White House. We spent time cultivating our Republican friends on the Hill and reaching out to people we knew inside the Bush administration. Eleanor fought to get the District more money and to keep extraneous matters off the D.C. appropriation. And we were aggressive in terms of constituent service. By the end of 1991, the *Washington Post* ran an editorial apologizing for predicting that Eleanor would not succeed. They had to admit that she was doing a great job fighting to increase the District's annual payment, as well as her focus on local projects. As her chief of staff and press secretary, I felt vindicated. I had told Colby and Bob Asher, another member of the *Washington Post*'s editorial board, that Eleanor was going to help improve the District's budget process on the Hill.

At the end of 1991, as the presidential season was about to start, I told Eleanor that I had to get my campaign fix. Eleanor understood me as only my grandmother and mother understood me. She knew that there were simply certain things I had to be able to do and one of those things was to get into the political fray on a regular basis. She asked me what I wanted to do. I told her there was a little march I needed to organize, and so she would let me go for two or three weeks to do that. Then I got a call from Mayor Lottie Shackelford of Little Rock on behalf of Bill Clinton. Lottie is currently a vice chair of the Democratic National Committee. Clinton was one of my favorites in the primary field, but I also liked Senator Tom Harkin of Iowa. I was torn. Former Virginia governor Douglas Wilder was also thinking of running. After years of campaign debt and living on the road, I was firmly established in Washington, D.C., and I had a good job that I enjoyed. I couldn't decide and I asked Lottie to hold off until after the D.C. primary, where I could help them out. Then Cathy Hughes offered me the chance to host a live two-hour radio show on Tuesday nights. I jumped at the chance to do the show and used it as a platform to talk about what Eleanor was doing for the city on Capitol Hill as well as national politics.

Things were going well in my life and I felt settled and secure

e Democrats got it right. We managed to mobilize our base and
rsuade swing voters. I got my chance to help Quincy Jones fill the
all from the Lincoln Memorial to the Washington Monument.
e presidential parade featured all kinds of local bands from across
e country. I worked hard to get local talent on stage and got Shaw
ior High on the roster. Rahm Emanuel, the chairman, and Debbie
lhite, the co-chair, of the Inaugural Committee gave me lots of
ibility in pulling the local team together.

Ron Brown was still chairman of the DNC. He encouraged many
s to begin sending in résumés to fill thousands of open positions.
kis went over to work on the transition, along with Vernon Jor-
Deep down inside I wanted to work in the Clinton-Gore ad-
istration, but I could not leave Eleanor. We were a team, a strong
. We had so many goals to achieve and I wasn't ready to work
e the White House. That had never been one of my goals, but I
ed to remain on the "A" list, so I did everything the campaign
of me during the transition. Most everyone in Washington was
ed to get rid of the Republicans.

the weeks after the election, I was giddy, too. We had finally
I was elated. It's hard to get a smile out of me, but I was so
d and excited for the Democratic Party. I called my friends, old
imates and family members across the country to thank them
ning out the vote. Not only would the country have a Demo-
president, but two Democrats from the South had finally won
t there. By focusing on the economy, Clinton demonstrated a
mainstream politics that united many diverse Americans.
or the first time in years, Democratic operatives were in high
. My colleagues and I took advantage of this new surge of in-
nd allowed some of the major fat cats to treat us to fancy
n K Street. Feasting on crab cakes, cole slaw and baked pota-
ad my eyes on helping with the next phase of the campaign.

enough to buy a house. I was making $55,000 a year working for
Eleanor and my lifestyle was so frugal that I had managed to put
aside about $15,000. I thought it was time for me to have a home
and to start thinking about a personal life. My good friend Al died
suddenly from pneumonia. The apartment building where I had
spent all those years organizing and plotting strategy seemed to go
downhill. I wanted a change.

I loved Capitol Hill and I wanted to stay there. My cousin Anne,
Uncle Sporty's daughter, actually found the house I bought. She was
staying with me off and on. She was, along with her brother Jack,
very close to both Jean and Lionel. She had been diagnosed with
breast cancer and they had already removed one breast and the cancer returned in the other breast. She had gotten experimental treatment at Johns Hopkins in Baltimore. Anne would come up from
New Orleans for the weekend to have treatments at the National
Institutes of Health, so I decided it was also time for me to buy a car.
One weekend after a huge winter snowstorm we were driving around
and we saw a yellow house on the Hill. Anne thought it was cute. I
didn't like the color, but I liked the price and location down the
street from the Frederick Douglass home near the U.S. Supreme
Court. The next day I bought it. It was important for me to buy a
house because it symbolized what I had lost as a child, what we had
all lost. The same year that I bought my house I started saving
money to help my siblings buy houses of their own. My sister Cheryl
bought a house on the West Bank in Gretna, Louisiana. Lisa was
preparing to put a down payment on a house, and so were Demetria
and her husband. Chet was still dating and Teddy Man and Sheila
were home with Lionel. It was a good season for us. It took a long
time but we were all sinking roots, growing up, making homes.

And because I was getting more and more settled in my personal
life I had no interest in pulling up stakes and moving to Arkansas
to work for Bill Clinton. Paul Tully was working with the Clintons
and I told him that I was still somewhat upset about the way I was
treated by the Dukakis campaign. I had no intention of moving away
from my friends, but I could help out in Washington and travel off
and on to rally the Black vote. I knew Hillary Rodham Clinton very

well through the Children's Defense Fund. She was on its board and I had done a lot of work for Marian Wright Edelman. I liked Hillary a lot. She was smart and passionate about children's and women's issues.

Neither Reverend Jackson nor Dick Gephardt were running in 1992, so I was free to find a new dance partner. Doug Wilder of Virginia, who was elected in 1989 as the first Black governor since Reconstruction, was making lots of noise about a potential bid and I had a great deal of respect for him. In the end, Eleanor and I decided to help the Clintons, but recommended that the campaign hire Alvin Brown and Sterling Henry to do the day-to-day operations because I didn't want to leave my Hill job. I wanted to become a senior adviser, not a staff person.

I HAD MET BILL CLINTON on September 25, 1988, in Winston-Salem, North Carolina, at Wake Forest University. My first impression of him was mixed. I thought he was smart but too full of himself and overconfident. At the 1988 convention he gave a speech that lasted, it seemed, for three hundred years. At that time, I never thought he would run for a national office. I had no emotional ties to the Clintons but I had a deep emotional tie to the Gores. I liked Al and Tipper. They were my friends and I really enjoyed talking with Tipper. She was wise and warm. We could relate to each other. Al, on the other hand, never let me forget that I went for Gephardt in 1988. So when Gore got on the ticket I told him, "Now that you're on the ticket as the vice presidential running mate, I'm going to quit my job to help you." I wasn't so interested in helping Bill Clinton but I told Gore, "I want it known that you're the reason I want to help get out the Black vote." Craig Smith, the campaign's field director, called me to pull together events with Clinton's senior Black strategists, Carol Willis and Bob Nash. I agreed to work with members of the Black Caucus and to focus on urban politics.

Clinton was an energetic campaigner. He came to Washington often and I did a lot of advance work for those trips. Before the election, in September, I helped pull together a last-minute rally on the Washington Mall during the Black Family Reunion. Clinton made a

cameo appearance and the crowd stormed the sta[ge] look at the potential next president of the Unite[d] called on all his former staffers to hold conferenc[e] nized so many that I realized that no one was payi[ng]

George Herbert Walker Bush was a very pop[ular] had high personal approval ratings after the Gul[f] thought the Democratic Party would make a co[ntender] The team decided that the major focus of the domestic issues, not foreign policy. We had wo[n] was a lot of anxiety about the economic situatio[n] to exploit that, how to take the media focus aw[ay] perceived flaws and put it back on the agenda h[e] all Americans. Clinton also had a very strong included Lottie, Ernie Green, Bob Nash, Rodr[ick] and other Black folks from Arkansas. The [F] record numbers to support the Democratic ti[cket] Republican domination of the White House

Bill Clinton had his faults, and the righ[t] lowed us to forget his shortcomings. But I the team of people around him and the had put together. Tully passed away during back for all of us. He would be greatly miss[ed] Cajun brother James Carville, Mandy G[rove] and Paul Begala had developed a strategy and win on.

Black leaders felt a connection to Bill a piece of the campaign. I wanted to be p[art of the elec]tion. I wanted to fill the Mall again with ica. On November 2, 1992, Bill Clinto[n] vote. Bush had 37 percent and Ross Per[ot] vote. I was with Eleanor and the D.C. the victory on election day. People streets, honking their horns and celeb[rating] Gores hit the stage in downtown Litt[le Rock] ment. After years of weeping, joy ha[d] nally elected. I wrote in my diary, af[ter]

CHAPTER ELEVEN

STUFFED PO' BOYS

New Orleans's favorite and most common sandwich, the po' boy, can be made with everything from fried shrimp to fried oysters to soft-shell crabs. One of the most popular versions features hot sausage or chaurice, as it's called in New Orleans. Louisiana cuisine taught me the importance of variety, and throughout the early nineties, I got to explore many new interests and pursue new professional goals.

BILL CLINTON WAS THE FIRST DEMOCRAT in the White House since 1976, and there was tremendous jubilation across Washington. We had a lot of housecleaning to do because Republicans had controlled the federal government for so many years. We wanted not only to clean house, but also to begin a whole new era of Democratic activism and progressive politics. But Democrats were not ready for Republican reaction to having a Democrat in the White House. Within months of the inauguration, scandal after scandal erupted and it seemed as if everyone around the Clintons were being subpoenaed, investigated or audited by the IRS. The entire Clinton administration was busy playing defense against ferocious and persistent Republican attacks.

Whitewater, Travelgate, Filegate, and other scurrilous charges were designed to intimidate Democrats working to help the newly elected president. The Republicans felt especially emboldened after the president agreed to the appointment of an independent counsel, Kenneth Starr, who immediately started a fishing expedition into the Clintons' private life. Then Vince Foster, deputy counsel to the president, was found dead in Fort Mercy Park in Virginia. Although it was ruled a suicide, the White House had to put out talking points to defend itself against charges that were being circulated on the Internet and radio.

All around the Capitol, many Democrats lived in fear of being too closely associated with the president and his administration. I spent most of my time calling Clinton's senior Black aides to check on them and to encourage everyone to fight on. The attacks were taking a toll on my friends, and I really felt sorry for them, worrying day in and day out if someone was coming after them or their jobs. The Black staffers bonded both on the Hill and inside the administration. We had each other's backs, and I wanted to take the lead in helping to protect and promote as many senior Black aides as well as women to positions of power. After so many bitter experiences inside the party, I decided to keep one foot inside the door and one foot outside to protect myself from being marginalized and excluded. This struggle was bigger than one person—it was about the empowerment of our people, and all of us both inside and outside wanted Bill Clinton to succeed regardless of the composition of his inner circle.

I knew that in order for the party to survive and succeed during the Clinton years, some of us had to stay and watch his back in the streets and on Capitol Hill. I was a strong proponent of women and minorities being in every camp inside and outside the White House. When the president took office on January 20, 1993, Black power was back in vogue. The Clinton-Gore team began reaching out to Black talent to come on board. From Alexis Herman, who was the public liaison at the White House, to Ben Johnson, her right-hand deputy, Clinton placed more power in Black hands than had ever been the case before. Many of them were my friends or colleagues from Capitol Hill or the Jackson campaigns.

Lorraine Miller, a Texan who had worked for Speaker Jim Wright and Speaker Tom Foley, took a job as Clinton's liaison to the House of Representatives. Another sister, Tracy Thornton, who had worked for Senator Wyche Fowler of Georgia, was appointed to serve as Clinton's liaison to the Senate. Thurgood "Goody" Marshall Jr.,

Supreme Court Justice Marshall's son and a close associate of Al Gore, was also part of the Black insurgency; Bob Nash, who had worked with Clinton when he was governor in Arkansas, was inside the personnel department, while Reta Lewis went inside to the political division. Maggie Williams, from the Children's Defense Fund, went to work for Hillary. Meanwhile, back at the DNC, David Wilhelm was appointed chair and my good friend Minyon Moore was detailed to take over Paul Tully's old position as political director. For the first time in my life, I was not only connected to insiders at the White House, but the Clintons gave Eleanor Holmes Norton senatorial courtesy to select U.S. district court judges, U.S. marshals and the U.S. attorney for the District of Columbia. The second wave of Black power was about to spread across America, and we knew it.

Before I could begin my job assisting Eleanor with her new responsibilities and duties, Congressman John Lewis of Georgia, a part of the House leadership, approached me to go to Africa on a congressional fact-finding trip. The Democrats were organizing operation Joint Taskforce, but Republican congressmen Bill Emerson of Missouri and veteran Black lawmaker Donald Payne of New Jersey decided they wanted to participate as well. I thought to myself, How could I go to Africa in the middle of the transition and inauguration? But I wanted to see firsthand the destruction taking place with the beginnings of a civil war in Somalia and the widespread famine in the region. Besides, I wanted to visit the Motherland to see all my "distant relatives" and to prepare myself for a major transition in politics. By traveling with senior members of Congress, I used my trip to deepen my congressional ties and to build my résumé on foreign policy issues. Emerson, a good friend of former congressman Mickey Leland, was one of the last compassionate conservatives in Washington.

The trip was short, five days in all, but we would be flying in first-class accommodations: President Kennedy's old Air Force One, which was luxurious and comfortable. Despite partisan differences, the members of Congress seemed to get along.

On our way to Somalia, we stopped in Ireland to refuel and in Egypt for some high-level diplomatic meetings to discuss the volatile situation in East Africa. The decision was made to give us all bulletproof vests to wear while in Somalia. We broke up into three teams and were strongly encouraged never to split from the delegation. My team consisted of Congressman Emerson and former congressman Eni F. H. Faleomavaega of American Samoa. After a brief stay in Nairobi, Kenya, and a helicopter trip to Mombasa, we traveled on a C-130 transport plane loaded with food and supplies en route to Baidoa, Somalia. Man, for all my youthful enthusiasm and energy, I was just not up to a trip to this region of Africa.

I had known poverty as a child. We were materially poor. We were taught never to waste anything and to share the little we received. But looking at hungry children and adults, sick people lying in the streets, doctors without supplies, and the smell of death as thick as the smoke from burning tree leaves, I immediately felt numb and sick to my stomach. Here I was tens of thousands of miles away from my home in a white Jeep with a Red Cross emblem on the side driving up and down roads watching people literally beg us for food. I held the small wrinkled hands of a woman my own age who weighed less than seventy-five pounds. When she grabbed me to beg for food, I gave her everything in my purse—my American gum, candy and every dollar I had in my purse. I couldn't help but cry.

By the time the truck pulled over for us to meet with various warlords and other tribal leaders, I wanted to go home. I didn't have the stomach for death. I didn't have the stomach to endure the suffering of starving people when I knew how much food Americans throw away every night. I just sat silently as the translator repeated over and over why America should stay out of the fighting. All I could think of was that woman who had grabbed me with her withered hands and stared in my eyes. I knew we had to help them and I didn't mind sharing my feelings with Congressmen Emerson, Lewis and Payne. I knew they cared and would do something about it. When we were finished, I got back to the plane and took my seat for the short ride back to Kenya. On the floor I saw some beans and rice that had fallen from a sack. I looked back at the door, but it had already closed. I took one bean and put it in my purse where my money had been. Over in my seat, with my back turned, I wept openly for my people suffering in Africa. Africa still remains in my heart.

Back home things were coming together for Clinton's inauguration. Quincy Jones, whom I had met during my Hands Across America days, met with me to find out if I could help build a crowd. "Who, me?" I asked the musical genius. "Quincy, I build crowds like you make rhythm, one person or one beat at a time." He seemed to like me. The truth was I really didn't want anyone to break my record for the largest number of people ever assembled on the Mall or at the U.S. Capitol. So I was glad to take on that role during the inauguration. My other job was to be the liaison with the District government for the White House.

By March 23, 1993, Congresswoman Norton, with President Clinton's backing, formed a panel to recommend the appointments for federal positions, among them federal judges, the U.S. Attorney and U.S. Marshal. This decision by Bill Clinton to empower the disenfranchised District residents was greeted very warmly inside the city. Everyone knew Clinton would be a president that Black folks and Black leaders could work with on important national issues. Despite all of the problems and the setbacks of Clinton's first year in office, he managed to keep his promise to make his cabinet look like America.

By 1994 the Republicans had asserted themselves back onto the national stage in a major way. Newt Gingrich had not only organized the Contract With America, which was unveiled in early 1994, but as soon as Bill Clinton got in office, people from places we had never seen political candidates recruited from were being recruited by the Republicans—churches, farms and factories. Clearly the Republicans wanted to punish the Democrats for winning in 1992. Meanwhile the Democrats were so excited about having won back the White House that we forgot the first rule of politics: protect your own. A kind of arrogance had set in at the Democratic Congressional Campaign Committee (DCCC) and the Democratic Senatorial Campaign Committee (DSCC), as well as in the DNC itself.

Minyon called on me to help plot the Democratic strategy for the

1994 political season. This was going to be tough. Minyon was a warrior and veteran campaigner, and she knew how to put together a coordinated campaign in key states. She and I were also close friends, thanks to the Dukakis campaign. Minyon's first day on the Dukakis campaign was in September 1988, just after Jackson released his people. I was on one of my political protests against the top echelons of the Dukakis campaign. Some of the leaders had decided to cut the campaign's Black outreach budget and called the decision to purchase a table for campaign supporters at the annual Congressional Black Caucus Foundation legislative conference a "slush fund." My budget was small. The Dukakis campaign had lingering problems in the Black community. Although I understood the campaign's position, I strongly objected to the characterizations of the funds and decided to stay home until Governor Dukakis restored the funds and apologized. Minyon got caught in the dispute and stood by me. She was, as Grandma would say, "as solid as a rock."

Minyon was also a woman of strong faith and character. So when she called me during the summer of 1994 to help out, I decided to ask Eleanor for some time off. Eleanor objected, but told me I could help out during my free time, which meant after eight at night and on weekends. It didn't matter, I would sneak out of Eleanor's office at 6:00 PM and go over to the DNC and work until almost midnight. Minyon and I were both worried that the party would go down in flames and everyone would blame poor turnout on Black people.

During the 1994 midterms, the Democrats and Clinton administration were in an uphill battle, but the party's highly paid group of pollsters believed that we could survive the right-wing assault on the president. Based on our conversations with key grassroots leaders from across the country, we knew otherwise. I was hearing from my Democratic colleagues on the Hill and from around the country that Republicans were raising unprecedented amounts of cash in their Districts and that they had Republican opponents who had just come out of the woodwork. State Senator Diane Wilkerson from Boston told me that Ted Kennedy had not budgeted any funds for grassroots organizing. With no funds for Get-Out-the-Vote activities, it would be difficult to reach his voters.

Diane was mad that he was spending all of his resources on paid media and we encouraged Diane to hold on—help was on the way. From my perspective on the ground, I could tell that we were going to get wiped out in the congressional elections, but nobody in the party wanted to hear that.

I took on the responsibility for outreach to Black leaders and the Black press. When it came to organizing a political campaign, Jesse Jackson taught us to always solidify and strengthen the base before moving on to other demographic groups. In the case of the Democratic Party, African Americans were the most reliable and consistent group of supporters and I wanted to strengthen this bond. After a few nights over at the DNC working with Minyon and a small band of Black staffers who seemed to be the only folks working late at night, we concluded that state and local party leaders were taking the Black vote for granted. Minyon and I sounded the alarm bells.

We immediately sent word about the situation to the White House. Harold Ickes, deputy chief of staff at the White House, and Craig Smith, Clinton's political director, gave us some time to discuss the situation inside the White House. They solicited our recommendations. Meeting after meeting, conversation after conversation, memo after memo, we got nowhere. In the weeks leading up to the 1994 midterm congressional elections, there were hardly any resources allocated for Black media ads, voter contact programs or rides to the polls. We started calling friends in organized labor to help us out with sending people into the field, dropping targeted mailings and making phone calls. Everybody in the party was thinking, "Hey, there's no problem. We got the White House. Those fools can't muscle up and beat us." Not only did they beat us, they damn near wiped out more than 10 percent of the Democratic Party.

Two days before the election, President Clinton heard of our alarm and agreed to do a round of robo (prerecorded, automated) calls to Black voters, as well as interviews. Hillary Clinton and Al Gore also pitched in to help. One of the things I've always liked about both the Clintons and Gores was their understanding and respect for Black politics. While Minyon focused on the field organizing, I turned to media and put together a press conference featuring many leaders of the civil rights organizations. The purpose was to warn Blacks about GOP tactics to undermine and suppress voter turnout. Clinton did a radio talkathon for one hour with Maya Angelou, Ossie Davis, Cicely Tyson and Kweisi Mfume.

Despite all our last-minute efforts and hard work, Newt Gingrich and the Republican Party took control of Congress for the first time in over forty years. They not only turned out their base in every region of the country, but the Republicans and their allies managed to suppress voter turnout. As a result, a lot of good progressive candidates were defeated. For days, we sat in silence over at the DNC and mourned the loss of key lawmakers. Meanwhile, I had to return to work on Capitol Hill because a huge mess was brewing locally. Marion Barry was back in charge.

Eleanor was still doing exemplary work representing the District on the Hill. She kept her political focus on local projects to aid the city's poor as well as federal projects to help the District government. Still, as White men were expressing their dissatisfaction nationally with the Democratic Party, local Black leaders decided to turn against the Establishment and vote Barry back into office. The combination of a majority White and conservative Congress and a large Black and liberal Democratic federal city was like oil and water. Not only did the two groups distrust each other, they did not like each other. Still, Eleanor did not want to abandon her native city. She made the decision, and I backed her, to try to bring the two sides together. This would prove difficult.

No sooner had the Republicans taken office than they stripped away Eleanor's limited voting rights in the Committee of the Whole, where legislation is considered, amended and improved before final passage. We understood that the Republican-controlled Congress would wield their power to help their own and punish those who disagreed with their conservative agenda. Then we suspected that we had to find a way for them to help the city without fully taking over the day-to-day operations of our local government.

Soon after his inauguration and our pledge to maintain home rule in the District, Marion Barry visited Eleanor's office to confess that the District of Columbia had run out of money. He was afraid that the city was heading into receivership. Eleanor gave him one of those awful "what the hell do you mean" looks. I sat back and watched the fireworks as the mayor explained how the city was hemorrhaging all over the place and he needed help from Congress. We just laughed at the idea of Congress bailing out the nation's capital.

By February 1995, after investment houses had refused to lend the city money, Eleanor consulted with Mayor Barry and the late City Council chairman David Clarke. Then she held a press conference to announce that a Control Board would allow the city to continue to function as necessary. This decision did not go over well with Eleanor's base, who felt she had betrayed them by giving in to the Republicans. But the truth was our backs were up against the wall. The city was insolvent. After years of out-of-control spending, unfunded federal mandates and a dwindling tax base, the city needed a fiscal bailout of our unfunded pension liability, and federal aid to assist local agencies that performed statelike functions.

We worked closely with the late congressman Julian Dixon of California who, as a native Washingtonian, was extremely supportive and helpful in setting up a Federal Control Board. Eleanor also had to work with Congressman Pete Stark, who served as the chair of the city's Authorizing Committee on the Hill. She also dealt with Stark's counterpart, Congressman Tom Davis of Virginia. Unfortunately for us, Ron Dellums, one of the principal architects of D.C. home rule, and Mervyn Dymally, another ally, had just moved on to the private sector. It was a major loss for the Democrats and District residents during this pivotal time. We were simply outnumbered.

It was a low point for the District, and there was a lot of animosity against the Republicans in the city due to years of objecting to D.C. voting rights, ignoring the political will of District residents and overturning locally passed laws. After the Control Board was established and the members appointed by President Bill Clinton, Newt Gingrich asked Eleanor to help him organize a town hall meeting on education at Eastern High School. Newt Gingrich was an interesting man. During the day he managed the GOP daily assault on President Clinton; at night he wanted to talk history and diversity with Black lawmakers. One thing is for sure—Speaker Gingrich was a fierce partisan. He was a visionary of sorts for the emerging Republican majority and he represented everything I despised.

I'll never forget going into Gingrich's office at the U.S. Capitol and seeing this huge dinosaur. I looked at it and thought, "That's what the Republicans are all about, they are a bunch of old dinosaurs who want to eat the rest of us." Still, I was assigned to work with Jack Howard and Robert George from Gingrich's office to organize the meeting at Eastern High School in August. This was going to be tricky. Black folks were not interested in just talking about education. I knew they wanted to grill Newt on everything from South Africa to affirmative action. Newt's appearance would be seen as a proxy for Blacks' pent-up frustration with the double talk of the Republican Party. The perception existed that the Republican Party talked about outreach to minorities and opening doors for all citizens, while they simultaneously and deliberately shut people out of the housing markets, job markets and financial markets.

Nevertheless, I did for Newt what I had done for countless other Black leaders. I organized a huge town hall meeting in a predominantly Black neighborhood with a majority Black local audience. In the end, over a thousand people showed up. We had to turn people away and hold back hundreds of protesters outside who wanted to have their own audience with the powerful Republican leader. Newt Gingrich was not bothered one bit by the long-winded questions or the angry mob outside who wanted a piece of him before and after the town hall meeting. The process made me sick to my stomach, but I learned a lot about how Republicans thought—and how I could take them on in the next election.

In spite of the Republican majority in Congress, Eleanor negotiated a number of proposals to solve the District's financial crisis, like giving first-time home buyers in the District a $5,000 tax credit because the city was hemorrhaging residents and we needed a wider tax base. The Clinton administration, led by former budget director Franklin Raines, worked tirelessly to help the D.C. government. Today, D.C. residents continue to lack full voting rights and must rely on the federal government for assistance. D.C. returned to its former colonial status, and many local residents hated it. As in other times of despair in my life, I turned to organizing as a way to win back hope. Minister Louis Farrakhan was planning a major national mobilization on Capitol Hill. No one seemed to know what it was about. So I called Sister Claudette Marie Muhammad, one of his lieutenants and a District resident, to learn more. I immediately got sucked in.

I had met Louis Farrakhan in 1983 during the twentieth anniversary of the historic 1963 March on Washington, and again in 1984 during Reverend Jackson's presidential campaign. I encountered him again as he was planning the Million Man March to focus on the plight of Black men in America, scheduled for October 16, 1995, in Washington. The more I learned about the march, the clearer it was that despite attention to the publicity and controversy surrounding it, nobody was handling the day-to-day logistics. I volunteered to be their liaison with the Capitol Police and the Metropolitan Police. They all knew me and trusted my skills as a manager and organizer. Chief Gary Albrecht, a neighbor of mine, called me to say he was concerned that the march organizers had not applied for the permits they needed. I got on the phone with march organizer Ben Chavis Muhammad (he's now back to Ben Chavis) to push him to act fast to apply for all their permits. I had good contacts at the Park Service and used my status as Eleanor's chief of staff to place calls and arrange meetings. I was in support of the goal of the march—to bring Black men together—and I wanted to avoid all the drama surrounding Farrakhan and what he had or had not said about the Jews and should not have said. At the same time, I didn't want to piss off my Jewish friends or feel as if I had to explain why I supported the march.

Eleanor wanted little or nothing to do with the march because of her respect for all the groups in our society. In fact, many Black leaders on the Hill and in the civil rights movement were slow in embracing the Million Man March. The Black community perceived Farrakhan as a free agent, unbeholden to anyone or any interests. The leadership didn't trust him. But I knew this was going to be huge; I felt "these brothers are coming." I could tell it was going to be a helluva march, just based on the number of buses ordered by local participants. I received information from the bus companies as well up and down the East Coast, and by the bus count I knew we were going to have close to a million people in attendance.

I went to the District government and helped the march planners to obtain use of RFK Stadium for parking. They didn't have a clue on the logistical end of things. I was arranging parking and putting in requests without authorization from the march planners because I cared about my city and, as an African American, I cared about my brothers. I felt that if there were logistical or other problems during the march that I could've helped them avoid, I'd bear the blame.

Given the city's high crime rate and the image of Marion Barry smoking crack cocaine on an FBI video, the march was garnering ridicule from many corners. But I was about the brothers, so I got access to the electricity at the U.S. Capitol and suggested to the organizers to bring backup generators. I tell you, the Muslim brothers were all very courteous to me; I wanted to hand over control of the event to them, but I had to establish a strong logistical structure first.

I went to Black Caucus members and told them they needed to be a part of the march, but they were still resisting. Eleanor had come around a bit after realizing the importance of the march for the city. I told every Black man in our congressional office that they were going to show up. I made a last-ditch effort to tell them that Dr. Dorothy Height and Maya Angelou were going to speak on the program. I was doing ten things at once: trying to get the Black Caucus to say yes; calling Senator Carol Moseley-Braun's office to get a room on the Senate side of the Hill to hold the speakers until they were ushered onto the stage; calling the sergeant-at-arms to get visitor tour passes because we didn't have a congressional resolution to allow parking on the Capitol complex. I knew the Nation of Islam, like most groups unfamiliar with the congressional bureaucracy, would never understand our byzantine rules. Besides, I heard that Farrakhan was planning to park right up near the Capitol complex without a permit. By six the night before the march I finally felt I could hand things over.

The first wave of brothers came in from Chicago and they arrived at sundown the night before and prayed as a group as soon as they got off the bus. Up until the morning of the march we were still pleading for a sound system. I went to all the Black men who worked for Republicans (who controlled Capitol Hill) and I pleaded with them for help in securing a sound system, stage and electricity. I said, "Please don't make these brothers look bad. They are coming here to ask America for help, not a handout." They agreed to help—behind the scenes.

The march was the most peaceful I had ever seen. That morning as I was walking back to the Capitol I saw brothers streaming into the streets. Black men were coming from everywhere. It was the most blessed day I've ever seen in D.C., right up to this day. I was able to place reporters in the Speaker's office, which had the best view of the Mall and the Washington Monument. For two hours while the office was free I rotated reporters in and out as they snapped pictures of this sea of Black men. It was inspiring and awesome. I knew there would be a dispute about the numbers so I called Minyon and Ben Johnson at the White House to get someone over to the Mall, the Washington Monument and the Lincoln Memorial to get a picture of this awesome crowd. As I was coming downstairs from the Speaker's office, members of the Black Caucus approached and asked me to get them a spot on the program. And I said, "Isn't this something!" It was a little late in the game, but I caved in and appealed to the Nation of Islam to allow the members to speak.

For me the highlights of the day were seeing Dr. Dorothy Height being wheeled onto the stage in her chair, and hearing Maya Angelou speak. As much as the civil rights leadership tried to steer clear of the march, they couldn't—it would be like turning their backs on Black people. So Rosa Parks, Dick Gregory and Jesse Jackson were among the speakers. Farrakhan spoke for two hours, and the whole event was covered live on CNN. We knew that a million men had come to the march, but the Park Service put out an official count of 400,000, which they later had to revise upward. The march turned out to be the fourth largest ever held on the Mall. For me the march symbolized the untapped power of so many Black men and the potential that is unused and sometimes destroyed but necessary to change the nation and themselves. The Million Man March was my last—I haven't organized a march since then.

By 1996 most of the people who had been in the Clinton campaign and cabinet had moved on or were working elsewhere in government because they saw the right-wing tide rising. Mike Espy, secretary of agriculture and the first African American to represent the state of Mississippi since reconstruction; Hazel O'Leary, secretary of energy; and Ron Brown, now commerce secretary—all were caught up in investigations. Everyone I knew had a lawyer or knew someone raising money to pay for their mounting legal bills. I had no ties to Arkansas, but was worried about Minyon because she was still over at the DNC. I never took money, and never wanted to be on anybody's payroll. I worked for the DNC for free because I didn't want to need a lawyer.

As the party prepared for the 1996 presidential campaign, Craig Smith, who was responsible for field and political operations, asked me if I would serve as a state director again for Clinton-Gore. I agreed. After all, it was Washington, D.C., and I would not have to pick up and move. I took a leave of absence from Eleanor's office and I set up my office at 1111 Pennsylvania Avenue, the old school board building that the city was planning to demolish. I asked for and received a separate budget and resources. I wanted to work for Clinton but I wanted to do it separate from the party structure. A mean-spirited witch hunt was going on, and I didn't want to get caught up in it. I hired a lot of African-American and Hispanic staffers and we worked to get out the vote in D.C. and across the country to ensure that Clinton would beat Bob Dole. Unlike the 1994 midterm, this time we were ready for the Republicans. Harold Ickes, Craig Smith and the team put together an A list of Democratic organizers. We made a conscious decision not to bow to Republican smear campaigns, but rather to run on the president's record of leadership in turning around the economy and improving the lives of ordinary citizens. Clinton captured 49 percent of the popular vote and 379 electoral votes to soundly defeat Dole. We were back in business—or so we thought.

To his credit, Bill Clinton surrounded himself with African Americans, and we were always strategizing. After all, we had made both of his victories possible in terms of the large Black voter turnout. So when it came to putting our needs on the table, we had no second thoughts about it. We decided we wanted Alexis Herman to become a cabinet secretary. Alexis had staffed the DNC and had worked with Reverend Jackson and in the Clinton White House. She made it clear that she wanted to be a cabinet secretary. So C. Delores Tucker and Dorothy Height led the charge. Along with Yvonne Scruggs-Leftwich and the Black Leadership Council, we all backed Alexis Herman for this important position.

Secretary Ron Brown was probably one of the few Black people, other than Vernon Jordan and Marian Wright Edelman, who could actually look Bill Clinton in the eye and talk to him as an equal. But that April he died in a tragic plane crash. He did an amazing job, and his death left a huge vacuum. The emotional loss of such a good man empowered us to fight harder for Alexis.

Ted Kennedy and AFL-CIO president John Sweeney were backing former Pennsylvania senator Harris Wofford for the spot of secretary of labor, but that didn't scare us. Then, within a week of Alexis's name circulating as a possible candidate, all sorts of negative stories about her began to appear in the press. Byron York of the *American Spectator* and Brian Ross of ABC News began writing and airing stories about alleged financial irregularities, saying that Alexis had accepted $10,000 in cash in an illegitimate transaction.

It was absolutely ludicrous that Alexis would be on the take. The charge was made by Laurent Yene, a friend of Vanessa Weaver. Alexis had done business with Vanessa, who had previously worked at Procter & Gamble and later started a consulting company. Alexis sold her business to Vanessa. This guy claimed that Alexis had given him $10,000 to hold but he never said why. It was obvious that she had been set up and it was awful. Alexis's entire life, all her bank statements and tax records were investigated. All this for a rumor. All this to tear her down and take her out of the running for a cabinet position.

I don't need to be called when a friend is in trouble. They just need to make room for me, because I'll be there, especially when the person is being unfairly attacked and maligned in the media.

Alexis was by now a very close friend and I dropped everything to help develop a strategy to deal with the charges. One of the things we did was to remind Ted Kennedy that he had called on us to save his butt back in 1994 when he was in serious jeopardy of losing his seat. Back then he was up for reelection running against Mitt Romney, a well-financed Republican. Kennedy needed every vote he could get, even from the three Black people who lived in Boston. Minyon and I went up to Massachusetts and did his organizing. We did a radio script, we put together conference calls with national Black leaders, and we even got Jesse Jackson to campaign for him. And we did it for free because we were all about the party.

After negotiating with Kennedy, we put together a group encompassing nearly every key Black woman in the country to help Alexis win her seat in Bill Clinton's cabinet. It consisted of C. Delores Tucker, Yvonne Scruggs of the Black Leadership Forum, Elaine Jones of the NAACP Legal Defense and Education Fund, Barbara Arnwine with the Lawyers' Committee for Civil Rights Under the Law and members of women's organizations and the Congressional Black Caucus. We not only lobbied the senators, we went back into the states as well. We were afraid the Clintons would back off because whenever controversy arose, they had a hands-off approach. But we said, "We'll take care of that." We had seen what happened with Lani Guinier, and at that time Hazel O'Leary was under tremendous pressure at the Energy Department. We also remembered Mike Espy at Agriculture. We decided to draw the line with Alexis. She was not going down, we were going to fight to the bitter end until she was confirmed. We met once a week to develop a response and a plan. Over potato salad, red beans and rice and fried chicken or fish, we talked about who was with us, who was stabbing us in the back and what states and which senators we had to shore up. In the end, Alexis's name was cleared, she was confirmed, and we all celebrated at her house over filé gumbo and crawfish bisque.

In 1998, Newt Gingrich started bragging that the Republicans were going to take over forty more congressional seats. Democrats had barely survived the 1996 elections, and the Republicans were coming back for the kill. I used to stay up late at night and watch Gingrich on C-SPAN making these predictions. I used to go down to the basement in the Rayburn and Longworth House office buildings just to see what propaganda they were printing up to send to their constituents back home. I'd still be at work at 10:00 PM, and I would go over to the Republican side where they had their printing offices and I looked at their newsletters—it was attack, attack, attack. When I tried to tell the DNC and the DCCC that they were coming after us again, and that this time they were aiming right at Clinton, nobody wanted to hear it.

When Gingrich made the announcement about the forty seats, I told Eleanor I had to take another leave of absence to go and help the Democratic Party. She understood and let me go. Charlie Rangel was now vice chair of the congressional wing of the party. So after my discussion with Minyon, who was now at the White House serving as the president's political director, I decided to work over at the DCCC. We always covered our bases inside the party.

Matt Angle, the executive director of the DCCC, and I were old friends. We had worked together on campaigns in the South. Martin Frost was chair of the DCCC. They gave me a budget and told me to go for it. We targeted thirty-five congressional districts that had 10 percent or more African-American voters, and I traveled to twenty-one states from June until the election in November. We put together a plan to get out a larger than expected Black vote because of the 1994 cycle during which the Republicans nearly wiped us out. The black turnout that year had dipped to almost 34 percent nationally, representing less than 8 percent of the turnout. In some minority districts it was even lower than that, around 20 percent. But we knew how to move our people. My first job was to target Blacks who had voted for Clinton in 1992 but had failed to vote in 1994. I would find a way to track them down, send them a mailing, knock on their doors and drag them to the polls.

With Minyon at the White House, I had instant access to the president and vice president and was able to persuade them to help out with phone calls to key leaders and to make campaign swings to some of our targeted districts. We put together a message-driven strategy that made the election about saving Clinton and keeping him in office. In the face of the pending call for impeachment being led by the Republicans, our message to Black voters was, "We voted for him, now they want to take him out." And that message resonated. We put Newt's mean-looking face on every poster, and we printed and posted as many as we could afford in key congressional districts. We had bright, colorful postcards made up that showed Newt's picture in a doorway with a caption that read, "He's trying to block you from voting." If this scared some people, it should have. It was true. I did all this the old-fashioned way, the way Reverend Jackson taught me. Convene the ministers first, then get the politicians, then bring in the community to hold them both accountable.

Black people loved Bill Clinton. Under his leadership, poverty and joblessness were being reduced. Clinton met with members of the Congressional Black Caucus and he worked with Black mayors across the country. We came within five seats of taking back the House of Representatives, and my political capital was as high as it's ever been. No other political consultant, Black or White, had wanted to stake their reputation on that election. The Republicans were so confident about their victory that two days before the election they put an additional $10 million into negative advertising. I said "Thank you, Lord" when I saw what they were doing, because I knew that the saturation of negative ads would just piss off Black people even more and assure a high Black voter turnout.

As the 1998 midterm election indicated, even slight increases in African-American turnout can be a deciding factor in who wins elections. There is always a desire inside the Democratic Party to ignore appeals to Black voters in urban areas and the South, and instead go after coveted White suburban types. While Democrats clearly needed to attract White voters in order to win, ignoring the African-American community would have virtually guaranteed more Democratic losses. Black voters stood with Bill Clinton, most especially through the darkest days of the impeachment scandal, because Black voters believed with conviction that Bill Clinton stood with them on important national issues like jobs, health care and education.

The day before the election, Minyon, Ben Johnson and I arranged for Bill Clinton to be interviewed by the phenomenally successful Tom Joyner, who hosted a popular African-American radio show with over ten million listeners daily. Clinton, in a raspy voice, pleaded with his audience for help. He said, "I am here fighting for you and taking the heat. Please do this for me and I promise never to let you down." The interview was a hit. We followed up with some one-on-one interviews with Al Gore on Black radio stations in targeted markets, and called on Reverend Jackson to help us push folks out to vote on election day. Black turnout was up all over the country, particularly in our targeted congressional districts in the South. Turnout jumped 5 percent over the 1994 midterm congressional campaigns. The Democratic Party picked up five seats in the House and decreased the Republican majority to a slim 223–211. The Senate makeup was unchanged, but we were on a roll. The morning after election day, the president, under heavy pressure of impeachment proceedings, told Minyon he wanted to call Black radio stations all over the country to express his gratitude for their support. A few days later, Congressman Rangel called me at home to give me some good news: Newt Gingrich was stepping down as House Speaker and resigning from his congressional seat.

I took a risk by going back to the party to help with outreach to minorities and women and it paid off. Congressman Gephardt also called to congratulate me on our success. The president sent me a warm letter, and I was approached by several unions to start my own grassroots consulting firm. Deep down I was happy to be back in the game and back at the table. I was ready to get back into national politics. Perhaps work on the 2000 presidential campaign. But first, I had to help my president, who looked to be facing impeachment.

Gephardt gave me a staff pass to work the House floor. I spent time lobbying members I had just helped to reelect to persuade them to stand with President Clinton against the Republican charade. On December 19, 1998, the House of Representatives voted to impeach President Clinton on two counts of perjury and obstruction of justice. The first impeachment article alleging Clinton lied under oath was adopted by a 228–206 margin, mostly along party lines. Although Articles II and IV failed, the GOP majority prevailed, 221–212, on Article III, charging President Clinton with obstruction of justice by tampering with witnesses and taking other steps to conceal his affair with Monica Lewinsky, then a White House intern.

Afterward, the House leaders took several buses over to the White House to console the president and first lady. I briefly saw the vice president and he whispered in my ear to get in touch with him soon. It was a cold and rainy day in Washington. As President Clinton addressed the large crowd of supporters on the South Lawn, I kept my eyes focused on Al Gore. He wasn't looking at the president or the crowd. Gore was looking down at the White House lawn. Sure, he was standing up for the president. But I wondered if Gore wanted to walk away from all the impeachment controversy and step out on his own journey to the presidency.

CHAPTER TWELVE

CREOLE SHRIMP BISQUE

A favorite in the fall, this Louisiana specialty is one of the most time-consuming but delightful seafood dishes. This buttery soup should be made with fresh crawfish meat. As I began to prepare to become a major player again in national politics, I realized that I had to return to my roots, and the fresh smell emanating from a hot pot of crawfish bisque always reminds me of home.

IN THE FALL of 1998 I was appointed to the Democratic National Committee as an at-large member from the District of Columbia. I had been recommended by both Dick Gephardt and Al Gore. I had never really wanted to be a member of the DNC, but I was thirty-six, Ron Brown was now dead, Alexis was a member of the cabinet and Minyon was in the White House. At some point I had to jump back into the political game. The Dukakis campaign was behind me, but I still had some lingering concern about the party. I was also getting up in age and worried that I would never reach one of my personal goals of managing a presidential campaign. Besides, I had begun to feel that I needed to help fill the vacuum and take over more responsibilities inside the party. This is what Reverend Jackson and Ron Brown had groomed my generation for. And I was ready to serve.

Gore wanted me to get deeply involved in the party and to participate in some of the meetings leading up to the 1998 midterm elections. Gephardt wanted me to serve on the Rules and Bylaws Committee, which determines the process of selecting a nominee for the presidency of the United States. It also acts as the governing body of the Democratic Party. After years of toiling in the fields of political campaigns, I was ready to take my seat at the table and get back in the thick of things. Somehow I grew more confident after assisting the party in winning back some congressional seats, which also made me feel more comfortable that others would have my back.

Gore called me one afternoon at work and told me that he wanted me to be his person on that body. I told him fine, but he had to remember that my first priority would always be helping minorities and women in the political process. I told him that I would do his bidding as long as he remembered that I would remain loyal to fighting for the inclusion of minorities and women in the political process. He supported those goals. He reminded me of my promise some years earlier to back him. Sure enough, Al Gore got the last word. I wasn't happy to commit so soon without having Gore beg and grovel a little, but I liked the man and I knew that I would have to support him at some point. I called my friend Tina Flournoy of Savannah, Georgia, who was working with Al Gore as his finance director. Tina gave me the inside scoop. Gore wanted to broaden his base and was confident I was of value to the team.

I had a good relationship with Al Gore because I was always able to talk straight with him. Neither he nor Clinton was intimidated by race. Gore asked me that afternoon if I was willing to make calls on his behalf and help him secure the support of key members of the Congressional Black Caucus. I told him yes because Dick Gephardt had decided not to run. During the King holiday weekend, Dick had gathered some of his key advisers from the DCCC to discuss his chances. Many of us in the room were veterans of Gephardt's 1988 bid and we all liked him. But this was not going to be his year. Clinton was throwing his considerable political support and financial backing behind Gore, and Gore's fund-raising was off to a good start. Dick would have to start out running against Clinton and Gore. Besides, we were no match for the Gore operation. Still, I had to talk to Reverend Jackson. After that little episode in 1988 when I switched over to support Dick over the Reverend, and the decision to work for

Mondale without his blessing, I needed to have a private talk before Gore announced anything.

The private and sometimes public beatings I took from Jesse Jackson in 1988 for endorsing Gephardt were painful. For years I could not face some of my friends without explaining why I had abandoned the Rainbow Coalition to work for Gephardt. I couldn't deal with that twice in one lifetime. And I felt that I owed Jackson that much. It had taken us years to heal our relationship and I didn't want anybody to come between us again. I wanted to make sure he wasn't running, and even if he wasn't running, I wanted to seek his advice as I made this decision.

Jackson was in Africa when I called him, so I spent a few hours catching up with Mrs. Jackson. She was always around when I needed to confide and get some advice. Mrs. Jackson, who was living in and out of Washington after Reverend Jackson had assumed his role as "Shadow Senator" for D.C. statehood, was a great sounding board and was totally a girl's girl. Jackie could also straighten you out and remind you of the bigger picture. She liked the Gores and thought this was a good move for me but encouraged me to confide in Reverend. "Donna, he loves you like a child. He respects your ability and wants you to go forward," she said. So as soon as Reverend returned from Africa, I was on the phone with him to get input and advice. He had plenty of both.

As one of Reverend Jackson's confidantes, I had to be careful when listening to him. Some of his information was for public consumption and the rest was to be kept close. Publicly, Reverend had not made up his mind; he was still "mulling over" his options. But privately, he was not planning on running. Running for president took too much time away from the family he loved and adored. It also required him to raise money for the campaign, in addition to raising money for PUSH and his other pet projects. He asked me to keep his decision private, but that my working with Gore was fine with him; there would be no problems. I told him that he was my brother and he would always be number one. I had to say that, otherwise Reverend and I would still be talking about his options. I knew the way he thought things through and I was eager to keep my close friendship with the man who had given me my first big national break in politics.

Eleanor had also been very, very good to me. She had allowed me to take time off so I could work on campaigns or travel around the country to assist my Democratic friends. I usually took off in an even year. But 1999 was an odd year. Odd years were usually devoted to recuperating financially and resting up to go back out there and fight. So I asked Gore to call Eleanor and ask for her support. I had my own profile as a Democratic campaign operative and I was a super-delegate or party official inside the DNC. Eleanor was a member of Congress and I was her chief of staff and press secretary. So I gave Gore a script and he called Eleanor and asked both for her support and if I could join his campaign and help him out. Eleanor said yes to both and I knew that this was the moment I had put off for years, the moment when I would have to hire my replacement in Eleanor's office and help with the transition. Gore wanted me to be his deputy campaign manager and national political director. For the first time, I was jumping back into national politics with both feet firmly planted with Al Gore.

Physically, I was ready for the challenge of a presidential campaign. My body was in great shape. I had lost forty pounds since the 1996 campaign and my head was clear of demons that often made me doubt my abilities. Grandma had taught me to walk with my head up high, but I often looked down on myself. At certain times in my career I didn't feel good enough or even ready for the challenges that I faced. Sometimes I did not want to grow up and learn the minutiae of public policy or the political connections on issues of importance to the party or to me personally. Both Jackson and Eleanor were easy to work for and to stand behind because they were my own voice and represented my values. But with certain White candidates, you had to compromise your values and beliefs and look at the bigger picture. Before I started to work for Gore, I needed an emotional tune-up and I went to see one of my friends to get some help. I had to protect my soul and my heart from the disappointment of a long presidential campaign. I'm well aware that you win some and you lose some. But I could not afford to lose myself and my concerns for minorities and women. I built a wall inside my soul and prayed daily for guidance and protection. Spiritually, I was ready to fight for what I cared for in politics—inclusion, opportunity and prosperity for all.

Clinton had recommended Craig Smith, who was from Arkansas, as campaign manager. I had worked with him in the 1996 cycle and we worked together very well, but I wanted to get some clarification of my job description. I wanted to make sure that Craig understood that I was not going to take orders from anybody. I don't take orders; I take direction. Jesse taught us that. As campaign manager, Craig's job was to hire deputies to handle finance, communications, politics and compliance. Deputies were responsible for the bottom line. A campaign manager is someone who gives advice to the candidate and acts as the liaison between the candidate and the campaign staff and consultants. I did not want to answer to anybody but Al, Tipper and Craig. Lesson one: stand your ground. I was not about to get caught up in myriad political games.

Gore was positioned as a political moderate or centrist. The 1990s were good for Democrats. After years of losing presidential elections, Clinton steered the party from the fringes and into the political mainstream. This took the kind of skills that Bill Clinton possessed. He could maintain his Democratic base of liberals and progressives and appeal to swing or moderate voters. I had disagreements with Clinton and Gore about the death penalty, welfare reform and some of their crime proposals. I strongly disagreed with Gore's vote in the first Gulf War, which he supported and I didn't. Working for Eleanor, I never had to compromise my positions on national or local issues. She was pro-choice and against the death penalty and vouchers. Everything was clear as day with Eleanor, not nuanced or fudged. But working for the vice president of the United States, I would have to articulate his positions even when I didn't really agree with them. This would require some fancy footwork and adjustment on my part. I would have to act and behave as if Gore's views were my own. Good God, I thought. Did I have the stomach for this type of bullshit again? Some people can lie with a straight face, but as a practicing Catholic I often confess my sins when I am in the process of sinning. I'd already lost it once during the Dukakis campaign. Privately, I decided to share this concern with Al and Tipper, whom I trusted with my faith and values.

When we met at the vice presidential mansion at the Naval Observatory on Massachusetts Avenue, the vice president was sitting in his study before a nice warm fire. He was always a Southern gentleman, so he stood when I arrived and helped me sit down in a cushy chair. He called Dewayne, one of his personal assistants, to bring me some tea and cookies. (When I started the campaign, I was on one of my caffeine-free diets. It didn't last long under the constant pressure of working eighteen-plus-hour days.) Gore and I discussed everything that was on my mind. My title, my responsibilities and our own relationship, which we both valued and respected. I was about to give up my job as one of the most highly paid Black and female congressional staffers. I was actually going to take a $25,000-a-year pay cut to work on a national campaign because of the stakes involved. I wanted Gore to understand I was in it for the right reasons and that I had grown spiritually and politically since my last presidential campaign. Thus, I asked him to take me seriously even if we disagreed, that we would never air our dirty laundry in public. Second, I wanted to assure him that I understood his positions even when I didn't agree with them. I was coming on board because I had enormous respect and affection for the Gores. They, too, were my friends.

I spent the first couple of weeks doing transition on the Hill during the day and by night working at the campaign office trying to understand all his positions so I could relax when I had to state a position I disagreed with. But Gore was someone I definitely could support. Throughout my first couple of months in the campaign, I saw that the campaign was basically several different pockets or. factions. There was the vice president's White House staff, which included Monica Maples Dixon, Ron Klain, Charles Burson and Maurice Daniels. Then there was the group that had worked on his previous presidential run—Roy Neel, Johnny Hayes, Jeanie Nelson, Peter Knight and all the Tennesseans. The last faction, which was the one I was moving into, where Craig managed a highly competitive group of individuals, included Karen Hancock, chief of staff; Stacy

Specter, communications coordinator; Eric Kleinfeld, legal counsel; and Tina Flournoy, finance director. Our consultant list was even longer, with, among others, Bob Squire, Mark Penn, Mark Mellman and Paul Maslin.

Going into the Gore campaign was a little different from all the other jobs I'd had because I had to promote and defend the vice president. For the first time in a long political journey I wasn't the only Black person at the table. With Maurice at the White House and Tina inside, I avoided becoming the token Black person in the room. Minyon and I had also recommended that they hire a young organizer named Tamara Wilds who was just out of college and wanted to get her feet wet. Tamara was my eyes and ears and could be trusted to watch my back while I transitioned from Eleanor's office. Our little team was coming together internally, but before I could even get my foot in the door and set up my office space, I was dealing with the media attacks on Gore. They were making fun of his clothes, his weight, reporting that he said he had invented the Internet. I thought to myself: Forget the man's position on major public policy issues. The press was focusing on matters that most Americans did not care about, but it was a daily distraction and a waste of time. I could see through it.

Our offices were located at 2121 K Street, and on the first day, as I walked onto the executive floor, the fourth floor, I remembered the experience with Dukakis. I was the deputy campaign manager but I was still waiting to see where they were going to put me. It's very important and revealing where they put any person of color, let alone a woman. Following my meeting with Gore, I had worked out my role and my salary. They gave me authority to hire state directors in forty-eight states. I got forty-eight out of fifty. In the Gephardt campaign I got twenty-five out of fifty, so I had made some progress. And they told me that they wanted Craig to keep his hands on Iowa and New Hampshire. I said, "Hey, no problem, you can take those two small states. I'll take the rest of America." We had cut all the necessary deals. I had my salary, my authority, my budget down pat. I knew when I could hire; how much my deputies would make. I knew how much my assistants would make. Everything was worked out and then when I arrived for my first full day I asked, "Where am I going to sit?"

I looked around and saw two conference rooms, so I knew if I had to I could take over a conference room again—and I was prepared to do it. Karen Hancock came in to talk to me because she was doing the administrative part. When I asked her where my office was, she pointed to the end of the hall in the back near a window overlooking an alley with a trash bin. I couldn't believe it. I was number two in the campaign, higher in the pecking order than she was, but her office was right near the campaign manager's and soon-to-be-announced chairman's office.

I looked at her and then went to check out my office. I thought it was a damn shame when I considered the distance between my office and the rest of the management offices up front. But I made a strategic decision at that moment. I looked out that window and right on the corner was a local elementary school. I told Karen, "I'll take this office. You know why? Because it's not where you sit in life, it's where you stand in the end and I'm going to be standing. I'm going to be the last person standing in this campaign."

I knew that I had a reputation for not taking any back talk and I knew people were holding their breath, waiting to see what I was going to do. But I refused to rise to the bait. It was such an insult to be a football field's length away from the rest of the management team, to have been given a seat literally in the back of the bus. It really bothered me, but I was not about to have one of my outbursts. I brought in pictures of my family and some paintings from my brother Teddy Man, who had died of an aneurism a few years earlier. Teddy Man's paintings of various scenes of the French Quarter reminded me of home, so on hot days I could just drift back to the sound and smell of my native city. I was a happy camper, more mature and even more balanced than ever. My personal life was improving. I was trying to go out on dates and open up my life to socializing with my new neighbors. When I looked in the mirror, I no longer saw the anger or bitterness in my face. I looked and felt radiant. The sun was on me, not behind me. I was ready to shine.

I hired people I trusted and pulled interns into my department

where the campaign should be headed. James Carville, my
[fr]iend, gave me the best advice ever: "Girl, focus on a strong
[ ] and don't allow Republicans to paint Gore into a corner."
[ ] also suggested that I hire some tough state directors. As al-
[ ] thanked James for being helpful. He agreed to serve as a ma-
[ ]rogate for the campaign.

[Fra]nkly, I prayed. I said, "You know, God. I need help. This is
[ ] prayed for when I was sixteen. Now I'm here and I need
[ ] Craig Smith still had to relinquish control of the campaign, re-
[ ]sh control of the books. He wanted to cut deals and I tried my
[ ] honor his wishes, but my loyalty was to Gore, not Craig.
[M]y first act as campaign manager was to go to Tony Coelho
[ ] tell him that we had to freeze the books so that no new checks
[would] be written. I was totally paranoid in the face of all the back-
[stabbing], backstabbing and reactions of folks to Gore dismissing them
[and] moving the campaign headquarters. I needed allies. Michael
[W]houley said he would work with me. This was important because
[Mi]chael was inheriting Craig's two states, Iowa and New Hampshire,
[the] two states that mattered most in terms of getting the nomina-
[tio]n. Suddenly everything was in my lap, from the finances to the
[pr]ess strategy. Boy, was I scared, and this forced me to reach out more
[and] more to everyone I could ever remember working on a presi-
[d]ential campaign with, going as far back as the McGovern, Muskie
[a]nd Carter days.

Craig went around and asked each department head which person they wanted to keep. Well, Gore had fired everybody so why did
I have to keep anyone? I wasn't about to play that game so I said,
"Oh, thanks so much for the suggestions—the lists of names." I accepted everybody's letters and notes and flowers. But the only person
I was answering to was Al Gore. I wasn't answering to anybody else.
I didn't even tell the paid consultants what I was about to do. Boy, we
had too many paid consultants and countless advisers. My direction
was clearly based on Scripture. The night after he asked me to head
the campaign everybody wanted to go out, to take me to dinner. I
was like, forget dinner, I need to read the Scripture again, because
there was a hidden meaning in the book of Judges and I wanted to

from every region of the country. My goal was to build an incredible
grassroots operation the way Gore wanted it to be—loose but highly
disciplined. I reached out to every elected official across America.
We developed call sheets for the superdelegates and every member of
Congress. Senator Bill Bradley (D-N.J.), meanwhile, jumped into
the race and began to give us a serious run for our money. At the
time, I was not deeply involved in the day-to-day strategy. Craig
pored over the polling data every hour as if it were a romance novel—
with lust and hunger for a glimpse into the political unknown. Paul
Tully forced me to understand the science of polling and the objec-
tivity of the process, but I relied on good old-fashioned expertise
from people on the ground. While many of the top brass burned the
midnight oil seeking clues on message and strategy, I was racking
up unpledged delegates and doing the tedious work of getting Al
Gore on the ballot in all fifty states, the District of Columbia and
territories. My eyes were focused on winning and locking down the
nomination—Bill Bradley, in my judgment, was a distraction, one
that came back to haunt us in the late summer months.

We did not have to wait for the polls to tell us that things were
shifting. Normally, bad things happen in threes. All of a sudden, Bob
Squire, one of our top consultants and a dear friend of Al Gore's, was
dying of colon cancer. A sign, I suppose, but no one understood it
because he was no longer serving as the lead media consultant. Gore
was already looking to bring someone else in to do the media. Second, Bill Bradley became a serious distraction and was threatening to
take away our substantial lead in the polls. Last, our money was beginning to dry up, or as my mama would say, "We were spending it
faster than we could print it." Gore desperately tried to get the campaign back on track. He took the lack of message, emergence of
Bradley and fund-raising all in stride. Privately, he was complaining
and so was Tipper. They were upset with us but did not make immediate changes. We got through the campaign kickoff in June 1999
and brought in a seasoned veteran, Tony Coelho, a former member
of Congress, to chair the campaign and coordinate the consultants.
We also got the Clintons involved in our fund-raising activities.
Things were being fixed or at least seemed to be better until one day

---

in late September. Gore was angry. He was fuming. The rumors were being heard all across Washington. Gore was about to clean house. After hearing the news from some of my reporter friends, I went home and had a couple of glasses of wine. A few hours later, I was ready to face the music.

You know, when you have been fired on national TV, the fear of being run out of town is not so great. I was ready for Al Gore on the morning of September 29, 1999. When I got up, I made myself some garlic grits, scrambled eggs, apple walnut sausages and buttermilk biscuits. My dieting was now over. If I was going to be fired, I thought to myself, it would be on a full stomach. This was going to be a long day at the office and I had to be ready. It was raining outside—another sign, I thought. Somebody was going to cry today, but it damn sure wasn't going to be me. I took my time driving down Constitution Avenue past the Supreme Court, the Capitol, the Washington Monument and the White House to K Street. I did a loop and parked my car and headed for the elevators.

Gore rarely came to the campaign office. Whenever we briefed him, the staff normally went to him. This time he was coming to us. Tony saw me and said, "Hey, come here. Gore wants to see you." I looked up and saw the Secret Service. I always counted the folks with guns around. I had a little bit of Lionel in me. The Secret Service men and women didn't even look my way. Their eyes were fixed on Gore, who was stuck in some corner office.

When I reached the room, Gore grabbed my hand and took me inside one of the vacant offices on the fifth floor. He grabbed two chairs and took them and me to the back corner. Weird position, I thought to myself. But then, this was Al Gore and I knew he had something up his sleeve. After we were seated facing each other with my back literally up against the wall, I looked into his eyes. Gore has strong, reassuring eyes. He then grabbed my hands and I felt some coolness there. I squirmed a little but kept looking him in the eyes. It was so strange and I could not read his body language.

"Donna, you and I have come a long way," he said. "But we are now moving into a new phase of the campaign. One where I would like to make some major changes in both my style and my message. I

figure it out. I wanted to see not just the Baptist but the Catholic interpretation. I read all the different versions and forty interpretations and it was clear to me that he wanted me to clean house. He wanted a fresh start; he wanted his enemies gone.

And in private, I told Al and Tipper what I had not told anyone else: The campaign was hemorrhaging money. We were about to go into the third quarter and the FEC report was going to show that we were spending an astronomical amount of money, $5 to $6 million a quarter, and we were only bringing in $7 to $8 million. At that rate we were going to be in the red by the end of December. Meanwhile, Bill Bradley was not only building a lead, he was gaining on us in Iowa and New Hampshire. Bill Bradley was raising money but he was holding on to it so he would have a bigger cash flow at the end of the year than we would have at our current level of spending.

So my first task, as the daughter of the coupon clipper, was to get control of the budget. And Gore gave me, the person who once sat way in the back, a free hand: he said he trusted my judgment and I never once exposed my hand. Craig asked me to take several people that he had hired down to Nashville and I told him I couldn't commit to doing that because Gore had not asked me to take anybody. Besides, everybody had to take a major pay cut, starting with the campaign manager.

I made the decision that the only staff I would keep through the end of the year would be the finance staff, but I would close down the financial centers of the campaign—the Chicago, Austin, Los Angeles, San Francisco, Seattle, New York, Atlanta and Miami offices. And nobody just handed me the books, I had to request them. I wanted the FEC reports. I wanted to see all the different budgetary items. I went over the budgets thoroughly, with a fine-tooth comb. People were hiding stuff in those books and I wanted to see what was being hidden.

I didn't call my family and tell them about this change until the morning of October 6, the day of the official announcement. I knew it would be covered live on CNN and I wanted to tell my daddy. I called Lionel and told him I was going to be on CNN, and I wanted him to know I wasn't going to be fired. I told him that Al Gore had asked me to run his campaign and he said "Oh, really?" To Lionel it was just another job. And ironically, that morning when I left my house, I tried twice to hail a taxi and couldn't get one to stop for me. I had to walk all the way to Union Station. I almost missed my ride on Air Force Two because I couldn't get a damn cab, but I was the campaign manager for the vice president of the United States.

Flying down to Nashville on Air Force Two, Gore wanted me up front in the cabin with him and Tony. He sat me down and said, "The reason I named you campaign manager is because you clearly know how to organize, you know how to put together a campaign. I want to focus on getting the campaign under control, removing all the factions we had. You report to me. I didn't hire you because you're Black: I hired you because you're the best." Tipper was there listening as well. He was trying to pump me up, to give me confidence to do this, to feel that I was really in charge. And as he was talking, Tipper and I were holding hands. For the announcement in Nashville, everybody Black showed up and they were so happy. They told me that if I needed anything, they'd get it. They had places for me to stay around Fisk University and at Tennessee State University, whatever I needed. They knew I taught at the University of Maryland and asked me if I wanted to teach in Tennessee. They were so wonderful, the Tennesseans, I fell in love with them, and I said, "Lord, thank you, at least I'm in a nice environment."

But behind the scenes people in the campaign were trying to save their jobs. And after we cut the ribbon to officially open the headquarters, Al and Tipper took me aside to assure me that I had full authority. And that meant *full* authority. We had flown down to Nashville on Air Force Two; on another trip, we took Marine Two. I asked Gore how much it cost to fly from Nashville to Andrews Air Force Base, outside of Washington. When he asked why, I told him that we had to cut the budget. "But I'm vice president of the United States," he reminded me. I said, "Okay." I later learned the cost was $6,000 so I cut it out, which pissed him off. But I reminded him that he put me in charge. And, in fact, the first thing I did was to cut my own salary.

The Nashville campaign headquarters was on Charlotte Avenue, in a pretty raunchy, run-down part of the city, an area where at night you don't want to be caught on the streets. We had to put lights outside. But I had grown up behind the railroad tracks, so I felt at home—from K Street to being behind the railroad tracks. For a while I was living in a Howard Johnson's motel twenty minutes outside the city, and I began to wonder what I had done with my life. Every time I looked at the bloated budget I felt as if I'd been set up for failure.

Then Tipper came and said she had found a place for me. Tipper had this wonderful group of friends and she asked them to find me a comfortable house to live in. She wanted me to have a garage, because she knew I'd be getting home late, and a fireplace, so I could sit in front of it and relax. I ended up house-sitting for one of their friends, a venture capitalist who was living in California. It was a beautiful house with marble floors, expensive art on the walls, a huge kitchen, and a den. Her *bouvetroire* was a knockout with a big-screen TV, stereo system and piano. I thought I had died and gone to heaven. She had left her BMW, a car I had always wanted to drive. And upstairs was a huge master bedroom with a Jacuzzi. I called Tipper and told her that everything she and Al had put me through, with the budget and firing people, had been erased by that house. I started inviting people to visit and I had some place for my family to stay.

The neighborhood where the house was located was quiet and peaceful, and after a while I missed the urban ghetto sounds. So I'd turn on all the TVs in the house to get the right noise balance. Downstairs I kept the music on. I was afraid, even though it was a gated community, because the house was so big. Most of the staff lived in apartments downtown. Since I took another pay cut when I became campaign manager, I had to conserve my cash. The consultants lived in the Loew's for a while and Tony found a nice house somewhere in the city away from all of us.

My first week on the job was about really trying to figure out how to fulfill my new responsibilities as campaign manager. Tina Flournoy, who was bringing in the money, was as upset as I was that she was raising money and they were spending it like it was going out of style. I told her that I needed her help. I told her that I needed to know how the money was coming in and how it was going out in order for me to make the tough decisions that had to be made. The first thing Tina told me was that we were going to have to cut the consultants. "Go to every department—every department has a consultant." Now, here I am taking a pay cut to work for Gore, bringing in interns who are working for free. I've been told not to hire staff for several months because we don't have the money. And when I looked at my own department's budget, I saw people on the payroll as consultants for Iowa and New Hampshire who were being paid out of my budget even though they weren't on my staff. I figured that if this was happening in my department, it was probably happening across the board. So I went department by department and I separated the staff from the consultants and found consultants earning $10,000 a month who had been retained to do direct mail. And there was one direct-mail firm that had three people on the payroll. I was like, "Wait a minute, if I'm paying your firm $10,000, why am I also paying your people?" I was ready to cut the budget, ready to make the sacrifices. And then people wanted to negotiate how they were let go, asking for severance and continued health insurance and the like. I cut the campaign staff from four hundred down to about eighty people, and it was an unbelievably hard process. I was planning to build up in Iowa and New Hampshire, which were the first two contests.

Under the previous leadership, the Gore campaign was being run like a corporation—huge salaries, benefits and a load of consultants. Naomi Wolf, a personal friend of the Gores and a noted writer and feminist thinker, was being paid through the media firm. Ms. Wolf's financial arrangements came to light after weeks of trying to explain to the press her exact role. I did not want to hide her from the media, but some inside the campaign did not wish to discuss her relationship with the campaign. I felt differently after meeting Naomi on a campaign trip and made the decision to keep her in the loop, though at a reduced rate. We just could not afford her services or those of many Washington-based consultants.

The media detailed my every move in the early days of the campaign. "Brazile Slashed the Vice President's Bloated Budget" read the headline for one story in the *Washington Post*. The Associated Press reported that I was forcing campaign staffers to double up in hotel rooms.

Gore had given me carte blanche but everybody who was cut resisted my authority. I decided to help Craig, the former campaign manager, line up clients to continue helping me out with my new duties. In most cases, I dealt with the cuts as humanely as possible, giving people as much of an extension, like extending health coverage, as I could. I knew how it felt to be in their shoes. But we all had to pay for the months of squandering that had caught up with us. Everybody in the press knew about the campaign's budget problems, but I put a positive face on it all, saying we were a poor campaign with a rich message.

While I was struggling to cut the campaign budget I was also under scrutiny by the press. Initially, my appointment as campaign manager was met with praise. There were a lot of articles saying I was one of the most prominent Democrats in the country. Then overnight my appointment became controversial. I had promised not to repeat the kind of charges I had made about the elder Bush in the current campaign, telling the press that I was just going to spread joy and good news about Al Gore as a great fighter and proven leader. But that didn't stop then-governor George Bush from accusing me of practicing slash-and-burn politics. And there was a lot of mudslinging, some of it from the inside as well as outside of the campaign.

I was profiled by a *Washington Post* reporter doing a piece on me for the Style section, and during the interview she asked me how it felt to be the first Black woman to run a major presidential campaign. And I told her quite honestly that I felt that as a Black woman, I was the most invisible person on the planet. And I told her, "I'm in the White boys' world now and I've got to beat them just to get a seat at the table, but I'm ready for them. I can deal with them."

Well, the article was published and by the end of the week I was being called a racist. And the controversy over my firing from the Dukakis campaign was dredged up and the press beat it to death. Then they took my congressional financial disclosure forms, which I was required to file annually, and began to circulate rumors that I was wealthy because we had to average out our financial assets to the nearest dollar. I dealt with rumors for weeks about my private life and my public comments. In defense, I decided to become "notable but unquotable," to just clam up and stop talking to reporters. But I still returned their calls and fought back when they threw mud and kicked me around. I was fair game, but I disapproved of reporters trying to bring my family and my close friends into the public eye. I tried to draw a line in the sand, but the truth was I would never win the battle with the media.

I called my friends Minyon and Tina and told them, "This was a mistake!" I was wrong to take the job as campaign manager. The press is going after me the same way they were after both Clintons, Gore and just about everyone else. Soon I was going to need a fleet of defense lawyers. They listened and then began to talk. "You've got to hang tough, stay in there," Minyon urged me. But I felt as if I had lost control of my life. The battles over the budget were nothing compared to the press scrutiny.

The most amazing thing about the press coverage was how coordinated it was. It was pretty clear that the right wing was behind a lot of the attacks. There were charges that I had had several abortions, but I had never even been pregnant. I thought I was going to be excommunicated from the Catholic Church. It was horrible. The people attacking me woke up the anti-abortionists, the anti-Black people—every negative force in the country. I was on the board of the Millennium March on Washington for gay and lesbian rights and worked with homeless advocacy groups, and I felt so bad for my friends and the groups I was connected with.

The attacks would start as rumors late at night on the widely read Internet news site run by Matt Drudge. By the next day, conservative radio talk-show host Rush Limbaugh would pick it up and carry on for hours about my life. By the end of the day the daily papers, including the *Washington Times,* had follow-up stories. Most of it was untrue, but in the day-to-day environment of a presidential campaign, we had little time to respond to allegations, especially when Al Gore was under tremendous daily assault from the same sources.

And you'd have thought I was the leader of the Black version of the Ku Klux Klan. They went back and dug up into my childhood. I was portrayed as an angry Black militant. I was supposed to be ashamed of anger at racism and poverty. Then the death threats started. I felt so sorry for the receptionist at our Nashville office because the threats started almost as soon as I got settled in down there. She'd look at me sheepishly and say, "You got another one of them calls."

"What did they call me this time, Aunt Jemima? Sappho? Nigger bitch? What was it?"

"Now they're gonna shoot you," she'd say.

"Oh really? Now they're gonna kill me?" I just laughed it off.

One day the office was flooded with death-threat calls. I had brought my little-friends network to Nashville with me—my friend Tamara and Kristina Kiehl's daughter Alison Friedman, along with Debbie Jansen—and they all had my back. These kids I had hired as interns had to walk me to my car. They would get in their cars and follow me home. I had no security protection. Deep down, I wanted to move my dad up to Tennessee with all his old guns. But Lionel was not interested in the campaign drama.

Finally, I talked to Tony Coelho about the phone calls and he said that Bob, his staff person and assistant, or Eric would drive me home at night. Tony and I became very close friends during the campaign. I was increasingly concerned about my personal safety, but I was also concerned about Republican dirty tricks. They had put up a huge billboard right near our office with a photo of Al Gore hugging Bill Clinton and Gore saying "The greatest president ever." I felt that in the Black community that billboard was right on target with what many people actually felt, but I knew how the Republicans intended it to be read, in the wake of the Lewinsky scandal, in the Tennessee Bible Belt.

Then somebody tried to break into the office, so we hired a twenty-four-hour security firm, changed all the locks and appealed to the Black city council members who represented the area to put up more streetlights—it was really quite desolate. We had chosen this area to save money. Our rent had decreased from $60,000 a month in D.C. to $5,000 a month.

October was a great month. Tony and I went out to Los Angeles, locked up the AFL-CIO endorsement and got Gore on the ballot across the country. I skipped the first big debate in New Hampshire, choosing to stay in Nashville and be with the staff people. And in November and December I spent a lot of time working with Whouley, helping him build support in Iowa and New Hampshire as I had done in the other forty-eight states. I was working hard but I was still concerned about the death threats, and one day it dawned on me that Dr. King had been killed in Tennessee. I feared for my safety but I had to do my job. Young campaign staff spent hours after work hanging around to make sure I was okay. They had my back.

Soon the holidays began and I felt homesick. I needed to be with my family. I missed my sisters and brothers and their families. My soul was aching for a visit to the Mississippi River to sit on the levee to pray. The year 2000 was going to be the biggest, hardest, toughest year of my life, and I needed the strength of David, the faith of Job and the courage of Esther. The only way to get myself up for the tasks ahead was to go to New Orleans, visit with my family and stir up some crawfish bisque or whatever was in season. They all loved me. They could protect me. I could let my hair down with them and cry if needed. They could restore me and remind me why I was on this journey. Southwest Airlines had a daily nonstop flight. I took it on Christmas Day and immediately went to Church at St. Louis Cathedral. Afterward I went to see Lionel, who would give me an honest reading of my situation. He told me to hold on. God would not allow me to fail. But, he cautioned, "You better put on your whole armor of God. The devil is busy."

CHAPTER THIRTEEN

BELL PEPPERS

Bell peppers, stuffed with a variety of ingredients, are a common side dish on many a New Orleans dinner plate. Jean stuffed our peppers with ground meat, rice, tomatoes, onions, garlic and many herbs and spices. Throughout the primaries in 2000, we were charged with assembling a variety of ingredients and stuffing them into a single primary season—just like the tasty pepper itself.

AFTER SOME HOME-COOKED Creole cuisine and the sound of jazz bands at the House of Blues in the Quarter, I arrived back in Nashville before the 2000 millennium celebration. Most of the campaign kids had stayed around Tennessee or were preparing to move to Iowa and New Hampshire, the first two major contests of the political season. The preprimary was hell. Nonstop campaigning without time to recuperate or recover from mistakes. Gore had tried to help me charge my political batteries by surprising me on my fortieth birthday at the Wild Horse Saloon, a favorite country-and-western hangout in downtown Nashville. The campaign was organizing its final major fund-raising event and we invited all of our campaign supporters and donors from across the country to join us and contribute some much-needed cash. We had a stellar line-up featuring Donna Summer, Eddie George of the Tennessee Titans football team, Kathy Mateo and my homeboy, Aaron Neville. It was a delightful evening of fun and camaraderie. The easy part of winning a presidential nomination—the invisible primary—was over, and the new season was just weeks away.

Ms. Pauline, the vice president's mother, made a guest appearance and so did many of Al's friends. Gore told me to sit next to him and Tipper, which I took as a sign that he was still behind me. Before the end of the evening, Aaron Neville, in that silky-soft and sexy-smooth Nu'Awlins voice, was serenading me before a crowd of thousands. I was so embarrassed that I turned to Gore and told him "I owe you one." He just cracked up. The man knew how to make you laugh when you least expected it. I wished more people could have seen Gore in this mood—relaxed and comfortable with his closest friends and family.

I was now forty and the campaign manager for the vice president of the United States of America—nothing to write home about because when I celebrated the Christmas holidays, the people in my home didn't even bother to bring up the campaign. We discussed what normal folks in Louisiana chat about daily: the weather, what's for dinner and how much liquor we drank the night before. Don't get me wrong, politics to us is like the weather with its shifting winds and dramatic storms. But my folks are not the touchy-feely types. Braziles are supposed to be strong and utterly disciplined. Though they never brought up the Dukakis campaign to my face, I was determined not to embarrass myself or my family. Still, I could not shake the uproar my comments about the Republican Party were causing internally and externally in the campaign. Clearly I not only wanted to put these comments behind me, but I had made a vow when I was sitting on the levee back home in Kenner to just shut up.

It took a month for the news to break over my comments suggesting that George Bush would "rather take pictures with Black children than feed them." All the while I was talking to this reporter from Bloomberg News, I kept asking, why is he trying to get me to discuss race and the presidential campaign? No other campaign manager has to talk about the color of their skin. Yet every five minutes some reporter was on the phone or stopping me in elevators wanting to know what every Black person in America felt about this, that or the other. I kept telling them to back off and ask Gina Glantz, Bradley's manager, about race. This was the same line of questioning that got me in trouble in 1988 when reporters pestered me about

Michael Dukakis and the campaign's outreach to Blacks. I broke then and I broke again. Jesse Jackson had taught me never to respond to someone else's line of questioning. He told us to prepare for every interview as if you wanted to ask the questions. Now, in addition to having Gore upset at me, I had also managed to piss off two people I deeply respected in the Republican Party—General Colin Powell and Congressman J. C. Watts (R-Okla.). I knew I had to get to them and I decided to head back to Washington to repair the damage personally.

On the way, I called my friends Armstrong Williams, Robert George and Phyllis Berry Myers, three respected Black Republican operatives, for advice. Both Robert and Phyllis encouraged me to call Powell and Watts. Armstrong, whom I had befriended and defended for over twenty years, went on conservative TV and radio and continued to pile on me for being a racist. I was so mad at him that I wanted to follow him home and slap the very Black off his ass. He was so disingenuous, even though I had gone out of my way to defend him in the past. That takes courage, but I have always stood up and defended my friends. Armstrong's betrayal emboldened me to reach out and I placed a call to Elroy Sailor in J. C. Watts's office and left a message. We played telephone-tag for days, but the congressman got the message. I was not after him and I was sorry if he thought so. Now I had to go to President Clinton's White House to hide out for a day to reach General Powell. Once again, Minyon had my back.

When I arrived, Phyllis had given me the general's number in northern Virginia. I was scared because Colin Powell was one of my heroes. I had so much respect for him and his service to the country. He called me back within hours and we chatted about our families. Then he got down to the point. "Girl, what did you say and why did you say it?" I had no easy answer so General Powell gave me some insight and advice that I am still grateful for to this day. "When you have something to say that is controversial or different, just keep it to yourself. Don't allow yourself to be used by anyone and never get into a battle on race in American politics." I thanked him for the time, advice and encouragement. He wanted me to succeed. He told me how proud he was of my accomplishments. I promised I would never forget the advice. When I hung up, I sat back in the chair on the second floor in the West Wing of the White House. I grabbed some candy and decided to call Gore and let him know what I did. Gore was pleased. By nightfall, Gore and Powell issued statements. For the time being, my job was saved. This time I would not be fired, but it left an awful, disgusting taste in my mouth. I could not share or even discuss my feelings about race in America. Better to discuss the weather or walk down the neutral ground but not racism in American politics or culture.

I would go back to Iowa before the last debate. The Black-Brown debate, sponsored by MSNBC to focus on the plight of minorities, was totally fun. Tavis Smiley and Soledad O'Brien were co-hosting for MSNBC. I had some time to brief Gore before the debate and he did well. The next day I rolled up my sleeves to prepare for the Iowa caucuses. As usual, Whouley had the state on lockdown. We had enough precinct captains, vans rented and phone banks to clean house on caucus night. Humbled by my mistakes and determined not to lose to anyone, I focused on eight precincts in Des Moines for minority turnout. I did rush-hour radio and waited for the results. On a cold, wintry night in January, Gore beat Bradley. After a short victory speech, we headed for the airport. Bob Shrum had some champagne and we celebrated as the plane crossed the heartland headed for the Northeast. We landed in the middle of the night in Manchester. It was so cold I couldn't stand to inhale the air. I looked for a van marked "staff" and jumped in for the ride to our hotel in Nashua. One down, but the next one was big. New Hampshire voters were known for making their own mark. They would not be content with the Iowa results. They would put their own stamp on the race, and the underdog, Bradley, was still a hot commodity. Thank God for the Republicans. As our race began, theirs was in full throttle. Bush had won the Iowa caucuses, but the maverick senator from Arizona, John McCain, was aiming to beat the GOP establishment. Bradley failed to catch fire with Democratic primary voters. Gore beat him, but not before we had to change tactics and pull out voters from our targeted communities.

The media can ruin your day. No sooner did we begin to figure out our next round of campaign stops than we got a call on some exit polls. The race was too close to call. All morning the Gores were literally pacing the hallways asking staffers for information. We did not know. Once we learned the exit numbers, we had to make a quick decision to go back on the phones to supporters who had committed to vote for Gore and remind them to get out before the polls closed at 7:00 PM. Then we made a strategic decision to send Gore, the motorcade and the media back to work some key precincts in Nashua and Manchester. In addition to Gore, we had several prominent Democrats, including Senators Ted Kennedy and John Kerry, to pull out our vote before the polls closed. All Gore wanted to do was win. Our job was to win—by any means necessary.

On Tuesday, February 1, 2000, Gore triumphed over Bradley in New Hampshire. The race was now on. Bradley had no momentum and he was running out of money. Gore was on a roll. Still, we had weeks to go before Super Tuesday on March 2, when big states like California, New York, Ohio and Missouri would all have their say. Bradley, desperate for a win after we beat him in a little old beauty contest on February 5 in Delaware, went public to challenge Gore to weekly debates. We ignored him. Then our opponent went negative. He went after Gore's lackluster record on reproductive rights following an endorsement from NARAL, one of the largest pro-choice groups in the country. Next, Bradley went to California to attack Gore's environmental record saying the vice president did "little more than give speeches and write books." Meanwhile, the Republicans were getting antsy and decided to lob some heat-seeking negative attacks at Gore for his failure to "come clean" over the 1996 DNC fund-raising flap. The political situation was growing dire daily as Gore sought both to defend his record and to begin the general election appeal to independent voters.

Finally, we got a lucky break. Bill Bradley announced that he was going to make Washington State his line in the sand with Al Gore. He made the announcement midmonth in February and everybody in the campaign freaked. Like Delaware, Washington was just supposed to be a beauty contest with no delegates at stake for the nomination. We weren't even supposed to really compete there. Al Gore called and said I had to call the governor, Labor, women's groups, environmental types and do a whole lot of other things. I was as cool as a cucumber. While the senior campaign team and strategists had argued to keep our focus on winning Iowa and New Hampshire, I was preparing for a fifty-state campaign. After weeks of keeping it secret from everyone but Chairman Coelho, who took my side when it came to grassroots organizing versus paid media, I strolled into a major strategy meeting before the Harlem debate and assured everyone that we were ready for Bill Bradley.

At one of the strategy meetings I told the vice president, "Well, we already got forty percent of the vote, sir." Everybody in the room just looked at me in disbelief and asked how.

"I sent Paul Tewes up there."

"When," Gore asked.

"Right after the Iowa caucuses."

"We told you not to," Tad Devine reminded me.

"I know. Look, we'll be okay. We got forty percent of the vote already," I said.

"How?" Gore wanted to know.

"We did a mail campaign," I said.

"Who paid for it?" Tad asked.

"Don't worry about it. We have the money and could still pay for your TV ads."

That was it. The bottom line was winning and I knew how to get out Gore votes. The paid consultants were elated even though I went around them to execute the strategy.

And we beat Bill Bradley. Then came March and our final debate in Los Angeles. We had been on a roll. We had not lost a contest. I was back in my saddle turning people out in Maine. I went back to Nashville to finalize plans for Super Tuesday. Sixteen states in every region of the country would give us enough delegates to chase Bill Bradley back into retirement and out of the race. My field director Donnie Fowler Jr. understood my style of play. We had conference calls daily with our state directors and key supporters. I warned the staff that if we failed to get Gore on the ballot or win, I would fire them. Actually, I admired and respected my staff. They were the truly committed types who would fight to the bitter end. For many of us, it was not about a salary; it was the energy of winning, of moving people out of their homes on cold winter days to vote, and of giving poor people their voice in the political process. My field staff, led by Donnie and Laurie Moscowitz, were so hungry that I had to curtail their enthusiasm. We wanted an early win to focus on Bush and the Republicans.

Gore came into town, arrived at the campaign headquarters, pulled me aside and asked, "How're we doing?"

"Hey, we turned out in all sixteen states. New York looks good, California looks good."

"Is Bradley going to win any state?"

I looked at Gore, thinking, "Y'all ain't giving me any money, I had to operate on fumes and call in some of my chits." But I chilled. "Yes, sir" was all I could tell him. I was confident of my organizing skills and the staff we had in place across the country.

So on Super Tuesday we won all sixteen states and Bill Bradley was about to step out the next day. Al Gore became on that day the first person ever in a contested primary season to win every caucus and every primary. You can't let anybody beat you, and that night Al Gore was truly my friend. After we got the results we traveled to Leon High School in Tallahassee to celebrate and all the Black people greeted me with love.

Although Bradley picked up some delegates, he did not have a pot to piss in. We took that away from him, too. It's all a sport. Bradley knew the way the game was played. He was a pro. Gore, who had told me earlier to bring home the victories, was ecstatic. His grin stretched from coast to coast. When we arrived at the hotel, there was more food and drink. Even the press got into the celebration. It had been a long, long journey in just a few months, but it felt like years, even decades. Gore came over and said to me, as he handed me some of his ribs, "You did a good job. We told you that those states didn't matter and you still went and organized them."

"I know. Y'all told me in the beginning I couldn't do Iowa and New Hampshire and I still helped you out on that, too."

"You know what you're doing?" he asked.

"Thank you, sir, I do."

Tipper gave me a big hug. She was so good at making me feel a part of the Gore family. She asked if I had taken or needed a vacation. In the middle of a primary, who would have time, I thought. Tipper leaned on me and said, "Al needs a break and so do you and the staff. Let's give them the weekend off." Well, I had been working them seven days a week, eighteen plus hours a day. No time off for Thanksgiving and one day off for Christmas. Tipper was right, our staff was tired. I agreed to announce that we would shut down the office over the weekend, but they had to return to work promptly at eight o'clock on Monday morning. No back talk, I warned. Like the Braziles, we had to be disciplined and ready to push on. The best was yet to come.

At one point it was so bad that I went to Tony and told him that something was wrong with the kids. "What," he wanted to know, "was wrong with our kids." They were so uptight and nervous with the back and forth that no one was "screwing around." Campaigns are notorious for sexual escapades and relationships. Although I have never found anyone inside one of the campaigns to want to bed down at night, most of my friends have. Tony told me to plan a party outside the office where we could take the kids and let them let their hair down.

The kids got down all night and so did Tony and I. We partied until the next morning, but all it did was bind the Nashville staff with the campaign leaders. The consultants did not show. The Washington insiders did not arrive to buy a round of beer. It was left up to Tony and me to keep the kids together, to help keep the campaign afloat.

The next week we returned to the campaign trail, unified the party and began to prepare for the general election. But the campaign began to come apart. Campaigns are notorious for turf battles, warring between factions, backbiting and the withholding of critical information needed to make strategic decisions. I thought I had experienced every game imaginable in politics, but the Gore campaign set a new low for backbiting and political drama. Every day somebody else wanted to be in charge. We had more Al Haig imitators popping up daily, not to mention the second-guessing of our campaign strategy that was coming from inside the Beltway and the Clinton White House.

Meanwhile, on the daily conference calls that began at 7:00 AM central time with all the key campaign leaders both inside the beltway and in Nashville, Tony soldiered on. "Laura, what's in the news? Lisa, where is Gore today? Carter, what's Bush doing? Monica, Charles, what's going on at the White House? Donna, anything else?" Yep, I was the last to get a word in edgewise. The campaign was shifting. Gore, who used to call me almost daily to discuss the news and campaign updates and to share stories from the road, must have lost my number. We did not talk for two weeks. I started to get sick to my stomach. After months of working around the clock, locking up the nomination, I felt as if someone was about to kick me to the curb. I don't mind being fired, but I do mind being locked out. I had worked too hard, sacrificed too much to be disrespected. Yet everywhere I turned the folks just lied to my face. Something was going down. I could feel it. They were not talking. Then I read in the paper that I was about to be demoted.

At this point I was so disgruntled, I thought this was a good moment to step aside and go home. I could face mad dogs, bad airplane rides and a pay cut, but the silence left me feeling totally rejected. All of a sudden I became that little poor, ugly Black girl with nowhere to go. I could not take it. Little by little, I heard there was some discussion, now that we had locked up the nomination, as to whether or not I should go back to Washington and run the DNC. Tony Coelho tried to convince me to go back to D.C., reminding me that Ron Brown was the first Black head of the DNC and I would be the first Black woman to run it. He wanted me to chair the DNC, he claimed, not to get rid of me but because we agreed on a lot of things and he saw me as an extension of himself and his power. I called Reverend Jackson for advice and he told me to stay in Nashville, that I was making a difference. I was physically tired and I had endured so much. Was Tony trying to get rid of me or was he trying to protect me. And from what? Who wanted my job?

A lot of people were calling for me to return to Washington because I controlled the campaign budget with an iron fist and they didn't like it. I had balanced the books and put the campaign on a sound financial footing. Alexis Herman even called and said, in effect, "Oh, just give them control of the budget." But I said, "No, the budget is a strategic instrument in a campaign and if I give the paid consultants control of it, then I can't determine exactly how resources are spent." The last thing I wanted was to be out of the loop on how the money was being spent.

I was the campaign manager but now it was mostly in name only. There was no question that after I secured the nomination, people wanted to dump me. I didn't feel it coming from the Gores as much as I felt it coming from some of the other senior-level people. It was like, hey, we won the nomination—meaning we got the Black vote. Then Tony forced me to sign a contract to guarantee my salary until election day. He, too, was worried about my job. To make matters worse, the vice president had a reputation for letting heads roll when things went bad. There was a sense that the campaign had begun to drift and lose focus after the big wins in the primaries, and there was division in the campaign with some feeling that the vice president should keep up his aggressive attacks on Bush and others feeling that the attacks made him appear too harsh. And all the while Bush's poll numbers were increasing.

Gore had already shifted from winning the nomination to beating Bush and I wasn't ready to make that shift. In addition, there was more turmoil brewing. There was bickering and jostling over positions with some of the people who had been left behind during the primary process wanting a larger role in the campaign, namely people who worked on the vice president's staff down in Nashville. And we were losing support because the vice president publicly disagreed with the president over the Elián González case, saying that he felt the young Cuban boy should stay in the United States rather than be returned to his father in Cuba. I had hoped we wouldn't be dragged into that mess, but we were.

Then the vice president began shaking up the campaign and assembled everyone over at the Adelphi Arena, the football stadium in

Nashville. We had a fund-raiser that night and he asked all the senior people to gather there. He brought everybody in—the people who traveled with him on the plane as well as people from his vice presidential staff—and there was the same kind of buzz that had preceded the shake-up in Washington. I figured I had been spared the first time but now they were coming after my head.

This was a fund-raiser to raise the last primary dollars and to begin raising money for the DNC. The state party chairs and various leaders from around the country were there. So while the party was going on, the vice president asked Tony and me to meet with him and ushered us into a private room. He took two chairs and set them down about two feet apart and told us to sit in them. Then he placed a table in front of the two chairs and placed his own chair on the other side of the table and sat. He told us that he was very disappointed in both of us.

He said that he was reading in the newspapers that Tony and I were having major battles about the direction of the campaign. The *New York Times* and other papers were running articles that gave him that impression. Tony and I were having the typical campaign manager/campaign chairman tensions. It was normal for us to disagree and to have some tensions but it never got personal. We still spent practically every evening together over dinner and drinks. So it was just during the day that we fought and neither of us gave in easily. He was a former member of Congress and I was not impressed with his background or title. I stood my ground and Tony would stand his.

Tony had put Chip Smith, a close ally of the consultants, around me to help with the budget and had called in Tad Devine to do the general election strategy. So it was clear to me that there was this need for them to take control of the campaign. I'd done my job and it was like "Hey, send her a postcard." Everyone I talked to on the outside of the campaign kept urging me to just give up the budget, but I wouldn't until I understood the strategy.

The vice president said he didn't like what he was reading in the newspapers and then he looked at Tony and said, "Tony, you have a bad attitude and can't get along with people." He beat up on Tony so bad and I finally looked at him and said, "Sir, with all due respect, Tony has a great attitude. He gets along with people very well, but Tony and I are like a married couple, we disagree, we fuss, we fight, but we hang out every night. Who are you to beat up on Tony?" Tony was actually quite furious at Gore's outburst, and I wanted to stand up for him.

Gore, too, was angry, nearly red in the face in response to what I was saying, but I continued, telling him, "I'm not afraid of you. I'm not afraid of my own father." He was coming on so strong, really overbearing, like he wanted to kill the world, and Tony and I were his prime targets. It was like after months of press criticism, he decided to blame the two of us for the campaign stalling and drifting without a message.

He told me that he did not hire me to be his Black campaign manager, that I was campaign manager. I told him that I knew that and that I knew every facet of his life. He was visibly very angry. Finally he left us and went back to the party. Tony and I were shaken. Gore had never given us any clue as to how upset he was or that he didn't like the way we were managing the campaign. Up until that moment there had been times when I was ready to kill Tony Coelho, but Gore's outburst had made me love him. It's like we bonded because of how badly we'd been treated and our friendship got really deep after that.

The following month, the vice president was going to give a big economic policy speech in New York, and Tony and I flew back to Washington for a strategy meeting the Saturday before the speech. Tony looked really bad. After the meeting with Gore, he had started losing weight. He was epileptic and he began having seizures. Well, the morning after we arrived in D.C. I drove with him to his home in Alexandria, Virginia, to tell his wife, Phyllis, that he had been getting really, really sick.

The vice president was losing confidence in Tony's ability to serve as chairman of the campaign. In that position, he provided oversight. He talked to members of Congress and tried to keep the important people happy, including President Clinton and the White House staff. He talked daily with labor leaders like John Sweeney, president of the AFL-CIO, and environmental leaders like Carl Pope of the Sierra Club. Well, that weekend, while we were in D.C., Tony had another seizure and this one almost killed him, and Phyllis rushed him to the hospital in Arlington. And I told the vice president and Tipper that the chairman of the campaign was in the hospital and he was not doing well.

Not only did Tony have a seizure, but there were problems with his colon, he had a brain tumor and his liver was inflamed. The campaign had drained every bit of spirit out of him. Tipper and I went to see him and she brought Tony a big stuffed animal. Tony told us that he felt that at some point the vice president was going to ask him to step down, and that perhaps because he was so ill, this was the best time to do it. Tony had already reached out to Gerald McEntee, president of the American Federation of State, County and Municipal Employees, and other allies in the campaign and he told us that he wanted to step down to prepare for what would happen next. He expressed concern about me so I told him, "Well, Tony, if you go, I go, too." He told me I had to stay.

At this point there was a part of me that just wanted to get the hell out of Dodge. I felt as if I was going through one of the roughest spiritual experiences in my life. It was a test of my faith. I told my friends Tina and Minyon that I understood the book of Job. Like Job, I was losing everything. Like Job, I was upset with God. Like Job, I wanted my old life back.

This was a campaign dominated by highly paid consultants and strategists who were either media gurus or pollsters. We spent months locking up the nomination, arguing over the bulk of the $30 million that the DNC had set aside for the summer months to launch the fall offensive. I had no problems with spending a huge chunk on paid advertising, but all I wanted was 10 percent of that $30 million—$3 million—to begin coordinated campaign and voter contact programs, along with early outreach to solidify the Party's base vote. I was so sick and tired of the party waiting until the very last minute to communicate with minorities. I also argued that the party should place more states in play, including Tennessee, Arkansas and West Virginia. But I lost that battle, too. The paid consultants, who outnumbered the staff in the room, decided to move most of the money to pay for advertisements, not to commence grassroots organizing in the key states. All I wanted was to hire more field staff, to transfer campaign staff from the Gore 2000 to the DNC payroll. This was DNC money; this was soft money and some hard dollars. This was money that was raised in huge chunks, often $100,000 and $1 million at a time, and so I needed those resources to help restart the campaign. The primary season ended on June 5, but you have this lull between the end of the primary and the convention when the federal government gives you $67 million. Gore 2000 had just enough money to keep Air Force Two and the vice president traveling party mobile until the convention.

Sitting in those strategy meetings was tough. If Audrey Haynes, Tipper's chief of staff, or Elaine Kamarck were not invited, I was the only woman. But it didn't matter. I was not afraid of being in a room full of men. With the title of campaign manager, my ass was on the line regardless. During that summer I literally begged to put people on the ground early, to start communicating with voters early. We were being painted by the Bushies and the Republicans as a bunch of liars and serial exaggerators who would "say and do anything to get elected." Members of Congress like Barney Frank and Barbara Lee called and warned me what was happening around the country. The Republicans and their conservative allies were already on the ground organizing in battleground states, including Tennessee and Arkansas. We had little or nothing to fight back with so early in the game. I called Joe Andrew, chair at the DNC, and he said his hands were tied, that he wasn't in control of the funds.

Before Tony resigned, after the dressing down we got from Gore in Nashville and before he got really sick, Tony and I had a meeting with the vice president in Washington. During that meeting I told the vice president, "Do you understand what strategy you are approving today? Don't you know we are writing off the South, including Tennessee?" The vice president objected to my characterization. He had full confidence in the outside consultants. He was convinced, based on polling and our standing with swing voters, that the consultant way was the right way. I couldn't have disagreed more. I lost the fight, but I did win one battle. Pollster Harrison Hickman went through the strategy and the map. When he was finished, I took a deep breath and decided to do a Rosa Parks on the team. I was about to take a stand. "Look at that map," I said. "There's not one Southern state on that map except Florida. Tennessee and Arkansas have got to be included and I think we can win Louisiana." I didn't want to give up my home state. That's embarrassing if you can't win your own damn home state.

The voters in Tennessee were all getting mail from the Republicans, and I argued that we had to start doing mailings in Arkansas and Tennessee. But the consultants argued that "If we start competing in those states the Republicans will know we're desperate."

"Well, hell, we *are* desperate," I said.

We wanted to convince Gore that the strategy for the summer months had to be a strong message. Message drives politics. And you can't rely just on television. You've got to drive your message home through the mail and by phone. We were struggling to get the right message. Up to this point the message was "fighting for you." After the convention we were going to highlight peace and prosperity in the land and that the Gore administration would mean four more years of peace and prosperity.

"When this map gets out—and you know it will get out," I told him, "people are going to think you have written off the Black vote, because sixty-eight percent of all African Americans reside in the South." We were trying to create a road map of how to get to the 270 electoral votes needed to win. And we had $40 million to Bush's $100 million.

Gore finally gave in to keeping some Southern states on the list. They were essentially on a do-or-die list—not like Wisconsin, Pennsylvania and Michigan. During that meeting we decided to keep Georgia and Louisiana on the map, and Ohio. These were designated battleground states. But the Carolinas and Kentucky—I couldn't get them on the map. They, like Arkansas and Tennessee, were either just written off or taken for granted. I felt pretty battered after the meeting. But I knew that in politics you win some and you lose some. After that meeting, Tony was out. I was barely hanging on.

Tony was very sick. We all thought he was going to die and I called my aunt and told her that I needed everybody in the family to pray for Tony. Light candles, say novenas, just help this poor man, he was in so much pain and looked awful lying there in the hospital drained of spirit and fighting for survival. They say campaigns don't kill you. Well, I saw this campaign almost kill someone. So Tony stepped down the Monday before the New York speech and on Wednesday Gore called another strategy meeting. That day on *Inside Politics* on CNN, it was reported that Coelho and Brazile were out. A new team had arrived. And by that time I was honestly ready to go.

Gore had called a meeting right after Tony resigned. So when the *Inside Politics* story came out, I figured I was fired and that I was sitting there waiting for Gore to tell me this to my face the same way he had told me to my face that he wanted me to go down to Tennessee.

Just to show you how the Lord works in mysterious ways, I was over at the Gore house for a while that day. I was upstairs updating Tipper on the campaign. This was really strange, because Tipper had never brought me upstairs to the family quarters, yet I was up there with her, talking about music, what had happened to Tony—just gossiping like girls do. Later, as I was on my way out of the house, I saw John Sweeney, head of the AFL-CIO; Steve Rosenthal, the political director of the AFL-CIO; Gerry Shea, the public policy director, and Jerry McEntee, head of AFSCME; Charles Burson from the vice president's office and Monica Dixon, Gore's deputy chief of staff.

So I looked at the vice president and asked. "Am I in this meeting?" Tipper answered, "You're all in this meeting." I had known nothing about this meeting, and it wasn't on the schedule. Clearly this was not a meeting I was supposed to know about. But Tipper had acted as my angel, inviting me to the house and keeping me there long enough so that there was no way I could not be included in the meeting.

The first few minutes were awkward and Al Gore looked at me and said, "Donna, is there any problem? Is there something wrong?"

"No sir, but I just saw on CNN's *Inside Politics* that I'm history."

"Who said that? Where did it come from?"

"I don't know."

"Nothing's gonna happen to you. You're still on board."

Jerry McEntee told the vice president to give me a raise. John Sweeney told Gore not to take my picture off the wall. "Donna, we know her. We know her roots. She is a labor Democrat." Even labor had my back. I would never ever forget that moment.

I will always remember those words from Al Gore, because right after I had heard the CNN report I had called Tony and he told me that everything was going to be all right. He told Al Gore that I was the glue of the campaign, that he couldn't get rid of me. All the staff down in Nashville had heard the report, seen *Inside Politics* and were ready to rebel. So I called Tony and told him I took a hit but nothing more.

Gore decided to bring on Commerce Secretary Bill Daley. He was the son of Chicago's mayor Daley and was made commerce secretary after Ron Brown's death. Daley, whom I did not know very well, was aloof at first. He did not want to take sides or get into the consultant versus staff fights over the budget. He wanted to stay above the fray. I was so disappointed because this was a fight over direction, not personalities. Within one week on the job, I was under attack again from the media. This time I took a hit from Bob Novak, the conservative columnist. He wrote that Gore had wanted to fire me like he got rid of Tony but I was saved because I was Black. Nobody said I was saved because I was competent, the only person who truly kept organizing labor and women and everybody else, or that I was the glue in the campaign. Nobody said I was saved because members of the Democratic Party and members of Congress would have lost their point of contact inside the campaign. I had a powerful constituency supporting me, but the column was par for the course.

I wondered whether Novak had a source inside the campaign or if he was informed by his own prejudice. I prayed one night for dignity and humility. I said, "God, this is going to be a battle. This is going to be a battle to the end, Ephesians 6:12, 'wickedness in high places.'" And I put on my whole armor every day. I read Psalm 27 and vowed to avoid my enemies at all costs—but first I had to go and cuss them out.

So I went to talk to Daley. I showed him an article about me and he acted as if he had no idea where the notions about me had come from. I said, "Bill, drop the secretarial routine. This is an insult to this campaign. If I drop off the planet tomorrow, I will be fine. But will Gore survive if his Black female campaign manager was to disappear tomorrow? What would your response to that be? Do you have a credible answer?"

Of course he denied that he was the source of the rumor. I said, "Call off the dogs. I can fight back, but I promised Gore that I would stay out of the media. I am not going to take the bait." Bill did not look me in the eye. He denied that he floated the rumor. And I wanted to believe him on this. But someone did it. "Now you're denying it. Fine, everybody has denied it. But let me tell you all, the next time I get hit, I'm gonna hit back and I'm going below the belt. I'm gonna take the lid off. Now I'm telling you all to stop. This is it. Do we have an agreement on that? And I'm calling the vice president and telling him the same thing.

"As of tomorrow I'm gonna put my people in charge of the day-to-day campaign operations and I'm out of here. I'm going to win this damned election." And I gathered my staff around me and I told them that I would be on the road three or four times a week. I told them that I would come back for a change of clothes. "But this place has grown evil and I can't live with evil spirits."

The only power I had left was the power to organize, so that's what I did. And every time I got on an airplane there were the worst thunderstorms. And those thunderstorms seemed to mirror the storms all around me. I had hired all these wonderful, bright, eager young interns to work with me on the campaign and I hated leaving them to go on the road. You hire them, raise them, you want to teach and fight for them. But I told them I simply couldn't survive in Nashville. I was on the road a lot but I would go back to the office and give them what I called my "Donna speeches" about how we still had our joy no matter what was going on. But I spent most of my time, after Tony left the campaign, on the road with Gore and sometimes with Clinton or Tipper.

I would hitchhike a ride from one place to the next and then get myself a flight back, but I flew three, sometimes four times a day. Some nights I would get up and would have to look at a phone book to know what city I was in. I was so tired, but I would wake up the next morning and say, "Okay I guess I'm in Pittsburgh, how do I get back?" And I would figure out a way, based on where everybody was going. But I was doing my job. I was making sure that, on the ground, people were happy, and I was training and hiring people in the states. The cumulative efforts of traveling left me disoriented at times and dehydrated. My body was tired and I was exhausted. Yet I could not rest because we had so much work to do.

I had a great relationship, and still do to this day, with Michael Whouley. If I told him I had to bring staff on board, or I needed to get an office opened up in some weird place, he would always figure out a way to siphon the money off for me. But as we neared the convention I made Nashville my headquarters again. Through all this, I had different working groups—a women's working group, a Black working group and of course Minyon and Tina to help keep me going and sane. They boosted me a lot. I would check in with them regularly through conference calls. I put a senior Black, Hispanic or woman in every department, scheduling included. I said I wanted to see more than White males in the campaign. I really wanted women everywhere. Even if we didn't win, I'd do it anyway so they could get political experience. But the hardest room to get a Black person in was the war room, where all the major decisions were made. In my absence I got Jano Cabrera, who was Hispanic, to be my man in the war room.

Jano was on the press staff in the vice president's office and he was third or fourth down on the totem pole. I had Jamal Simmons in the Communications Department. He was a Black guy I had convinced to leave Representative Caroline Kilpatrick's office to work in the communications shop. And of course I had Blacks on the road as advance people, including Kevin Jefferson and Craig Kirby. But getting a Black person in the war room was the toughest thing to accomplish. It was clear that I was going to be the only Black person allowed in the war room, and since I didn't want to be there every day, I didn't get someone in there.

I was biding my time until the convention and the kick-off of the fall campaign. "God wasn't finished," Jesse Jackson told me one day; help was on the way. I would never be alone in my struggle or fight if I was doing the right thing in trying to help people. So somehow my faith was restored. I understood my role inside the campaign and the larger political picture. I lost so many battles, but I also won some. And I knew how to organize on the ground. No one—not the media, the highly paid consultants or the cautious political insiders—could take that away from me. I was fighting for more than a playground now. I was fighting for prosperity, health care, job security, freedom and equality for all. I was cooking with grease.

CHAPTER FOURTEEN

DIRTY RICE

Louisianans like their rice and their politics the same way—colorful and dirty. I didn't realize just how low down and dirty the electoral process could become with citizens unable to cast their ballots and confusion on top of it all. The last few months of the 2000 presidential campaign were painful, to say the least.

IT DIDN'T TAKE ME LONG to size up Bill Daley. The man was like comfort food. All he wanted was the trains to run on time. After our little confrontation, we never crossed paths. I stayed clear of his office suite and he didn't bother to come into my little chambers. From time to time, we chatted about Reverend Jackson and the calls we received from members of Congress who were growing nervous. The convention was coming up and Bill wanted to handle all the "big-picture stuff," like the vice presidential selection process, the role of President Clinton and the first lady and handling the TV networks. My eyes were focused on the fall election and putting in place the best possible and most diverse political team in American history. The consultants decided to play with me again. This startled me. But somehow Daley brought some stability to the campaign and I stopped feeling like the entire world was against me. I gave God all the glory for helping to smooth things out.

After our appearance at the NAACP convention in Baltimore, Gore and I really got back on the same page. He was back calling me in Nashville or bringing me back into his private cabin on Air Force Two to discuss strategy. Little by little, he was starting to worry about motivating the base and wanted me to keep him posted. Privately, I wanted to talk to him about the vice presidential selection process, but he requested Alexis's help on that. So I had to channel my thoughts to her and kept my recommendations to myself. I liked Dick Gephardt. I will always like Dick Gephardt. But I wanted to make sure women, Blacks, Hispanics and others would be on the long or short lists. Gore told me to send names and I sent Black members of Congress, including Charlie Rangel and John Lewis. I wanted Black mayors like Marc Morial of New Orleans and Ron Kirk of Dallas. I thought of Franklin Raines, Clinton's budget director, who had helped to balance the federal budget and was so smart. I was having trouble finding someone like a Barbara Jordan or even a Ron Brown, but I kept thinking, So did Alexis.

When Jackson heard about the list and that it did not include him, he called the office to talk with Daley. Daley was away and so he asked to speak to me. "Donna, it's your brother. What the hell is Gore doing with an all-White list?" Reverend demanded to know. Hell, I did not know. I told Jackson to call Alexis. He demanded a number for Gore. Gore was vacationing with his family in North Carolina and did not wish to be disturbed. But when Jesse Jackson was on a mission, only God could stop him from reaching his goal. In order to get him off the phone, I told him that I would email Gore to let him know that Jackson wanted a call.

When I got off the phone, without thinking, I emailed Gore about the call. Gore was on the phone within minutes and cussed me out. "Why did you tell him I have an all-White list? Damn, you should know better." Gore wasn't a great cusser. He sounded so upset, so I said, "Sir, I have no clue. I am not in the loop and it doesn't really matter because my first choice, Dick Gephardt, is no longer in the running." Gore hung up on me and I burst out laughing. I just didn't have any names to contribute to the process, so I sent another email: "Rodney Slater. Why don't you consider Rodney Slater?" Slater, who was secretary of transportation, was Black and from the South. Gore did not bother to call or email me again for days. I told Daley of both conversations and he shrugged it off. I didn't know Warren Christopher, the former secretary of state, who was heading up the process of selecting a VP. I left one message for Alexis and then I turned my attention back to thinking ahead for the fall campaign.

Daley had given me an interesting role at the upcoming DNC convention in Los Angeles. My job was to fill the three hours of non-prime-time slots on the air during the convention and to work with the paid consultants and Mike Berman, the party's most trusted convention planner. Because of my previous political experience working on various campaigns and my presidential campaign experience, I knew what the actual day-to-day procedures were for the convention and I used this knowledge to keep myself in the daily loop and conference calls. All anyone else cared about was prime-time coverage, President Clinton's speech and Al Gore's remarks. I could give input on those matters plus focus on convention business, like the introduction of the platform and the roll call of states. Secretly, I was working with Charles Burson, the vice president's chief of staff, as well as Carter Eskew, one of my favorite paid consultants, and the vice president to identify a keynote speaker. This was my chance to have another Barbara Jordan moment, one that would inspire some young kid the way she had inspired me early on in my career.

I really didn't place too much focus on selecting the vice president. I didn't worry about prime-time speaking roles either. All I cared about was my daily three hours. I was happy with what the planning committee assigned me to do. Who wouldn't? I felt that I would have the most important three hours of the convention every night. I could do Gore politics, which involved bringing more women, minorities, young people and unknown folks into the convention hall. In the back of my head, I was thinking: Who would ever have conceived of a day when people like Kwame Kilpatrick, Kendrick Meek and Janet Napolitano would have a few minutes on cable TV and the local news. I was thinking ahead to the fall and the people we had to rally to get out and vote. My calculation was simple: summer exposure equals fall excitement. My regional field staff and state directors were ecstatic. This meant they could also take care of local politics and become heroes for a day or two.

So everybody who was rejected by the mainstream in American

politics—Blacks, females, Asians, seniors, veterans, disabled people, gays, lesbians, Indians, Hispanics, environmentalists and Labor—all got slotted from 3:00 PM until 6:00 PM. I also took care of my D.C. people and placed Eleanor's and the new D.C. mayor Tony Williams's names in the hopper. I took care of Mary Landrieu by advocating that she handle the Credential Report. I always took care of Washingtonians and Louisianans because I knew that one day I would have to come home.

When it was all said and done, Mike Berman called me in. He needed some of my time back. I had gathered too many names and not enough time. Rather than fight for my time, I said fine. They'll just have three minutes each. The staff made the adjustments. I told them to tell their folks on the ground, "You can use this to get your name in the paper back home, you'll be on C-SPAN. Who knows who might pick it up? See, that's prime time at home. Just in time for the 5:00 PM news. I took care of my politics. I made people happy.

When the Planning Committee reviewed my slots and figured out what I was doing and the impact the interviews were having they freaked. But I reminded them that all they cared about was CBS, NBC and ABC; what I cared about was CNN, MSNBC, FOX cable, local cable and C-SPAN. I was using those interviews to solidify our base. I used them strategically. What happens in campaigns is that consultants want all the power but they don't want to do half the work. So naturally they began saying they should do the same thing in prime time. And in the process of all this I became good friends with cabinet secretaries and others. I gave time to civil rights leaders like Kweisi Mfume. And then I told them that there were certain Black people who had to be on in prime time. So I began to focus on a Black keynote speaker. And I chose Harold Ford, a congressman from Tennessee who was twenty-nine at the time. Ford, the son of Harold Ford Sr., was a friend of the Gore family. Ben Hooks was supportive of this choice and I passed it on to Gore through Charles who had given his blessing.

I chose Ford after a long search. We wanted to send a message about the South. I was concerned about Tennessee and getting folks in the state mobilized and activated. Charles Burson agreed that

Harold Ford would be great. I was back working out of headquarters during this period of the campaign. Then on the Thursday before the August 7 date when he would announce his VP selection, I got a call from Gore. "I'm getting a lot of phone calls, a lot of negative stuff on the vice presidential selection process," he told me. I reminded him that I had nothing to do with that process. No one had bothered to call me or even discuss it with me. At the time, I was more focused on putting together my fall mobilization and GOTV (Get Out the Vote) plans. But the press kept calling and I kept saying, "Call Daley, I know nothing about the process or the top tier of candidates."

That Friday Gore was having meetings all day. He had flown back to Nashville from North Carolina. For months, there was a lot of speculation about the vice presidential candidate. There was talk in the media of John Edwards, Bob Kerrey and John Kerry. I read about Joe Lieberman, the senator from Connecticut, and consulted my Jewish colleagues inside the campaign. Some of them were alarmed. They feared that if Gore chose Lieberman, there would be an anti-Semitic backlash. There were no minorities or women on the final list. Some names were still under consideration. Elaine told me it would be Lieberman. I didn't know. Whenever the press saw these paid consultants and Warren Christopher trooping over to meet with Gore at the Loew's Hotel, they would always ask, "Where's Donna?" And the press would continue to burn up my phone lines and share information with me. It was all part of the game, "You show me yours, I show you mine." And I'd tell them this wasn't my issue. I was still strictly enforcing discipline on my mouth and wasn't about to go on background with the media, because people would recognize my quotes. I did not want Gore jumping in my face again.

I got a call from Mike Feldman telling me not to go anywhere because Gore might want me to come over to talk about the vice presidential selection process. We were called to the Loew's Vanderbilt Hotel around 6:30 that evening, but Gore wasn't ready to see us. Besides myself, Tad Devine, Bob Shrum, Carter Eskew and Bill Daley were there. One hour went by and still no word from Gore; another hour and still no word. We ordered room service after dispensing with all the snacks in the minibar. Then we started playing spin the bottle: Carter was Lieberman, Bob was Edwards or Kerry and Tad was Kerrey. At the end of each spin, it kept going to Carter or Lieberman. He didn't show his hands. Then we started drinking every beverage in the minibar. So we were spinning the bottle, drinking, spinning the bottle. And the bottle kept coming up Lieberman. I had all the consultants take turns being Lieberman and the bottle kept landing on whoever had been designated Lieberman, but everybody had a different hand they were going to play in the meeting with Gore.

I had overheard a conversation between one of the consultants and one of the advance staffers to take a black-and-white VHS tape to NBC News for Claire Shipman. And then Ron Fournier, a veteran AP reporter, had been told that he would get the first phone call when the decision was made. I placed my cell phone on mute. I wasn't about to discuss Gore business. Not me. So I sat there listening to all the gossip, eating peanuts and M&Ms and anything I could find in the minibar, drinking diet Coke and later Scotch. It's like we were sequestered for two or three hours. We couldn't leave because we were right down the hall from Gore. Finally we got the call to come in and Gore had us sit around the dining-room table in his suite.

I was on his immediate left along with Warren Christopher and Bob Shrum. Tad Devine was right in front followed by Bill Daley, Carter Eskew and Frank Hunger, Gore's brother-in-law. There was his daughter Sarah standing near the table and Tipper on his immediate right side. Gore had placed Tipper and me right next to him. He began the meeting by saying, "You all know what we've been discussing all day. I've not yet made up my mind, but I know which way I'm going. I just want to get your input. Donna, why don't we go to you first?"

I looked around the room and wanted to make a joke. I knew where everybody else stood. So I said "Joe Lieberman."

"Lieberman?"

"Yeah, Lieberman."

"Why?"

"Because of what it would say about you, sir."

"What would it say about me?"

"It would say that you are your own person. That you chose some-body who had clearly defined himself during these last couple of months."

I could tell from his body language and his facial expression that my recommendation had stunned Al Gore. I was emphatic, too. I wanted someone Black or Brown or even a female. But all of my choices had been ruled out earlier in the process according to Alexis. Now I was going for the Jewish guys because it would be different. Gore could make history like Mondale did with Ferraro.

He went around the room and everyone else gave up their opin-ion. And then the vice president came back to me and he said, "Donna, if your first choice is not the person that will be chosen, do you have a second choice?"

"Well, my first choice stands as Lieberman, and you know I was for Gephardt. But because I am a Southerner and you're a South-erner, I always fight for the South and John Edwards would be my second choice as a Southerner. But choosing Lieberman would be similar to what Clinton did when he selected you."

He went around the room a second time and everyone settled in to listen to each other.

It was after midnight by the time we were dismissed. We went back to the minibar room and realized half an hour later that he wasn't going to make his decision right then, so we could go home. While we had been in the hotel the press had gathered in the lobby and we were questioned about who the vice presidential candidate would be. When I got home I called Donnie Fowler, who was my ace in the hole, and I said, "Donnie, I just argued for Lieberman." Donnie was my first hire as campaign manager. Since Teddy Man's death, he had become my little brother. I was his big sister and we were very close. I could trust Donnie with my life.

I told Donnie to call Sherry Brown, a senior aide and campaign adviser, who worked for Lieberman. I knew Christopher and his team had background information, but I wanted to get my practiced team in motion. Just in case, I told him to find out everything he could about Lieberman. Because Gore and the VP selection team had been so discreet, we worked feverishly to complete our task. Donnie made his calls and by the time I went to bed at 2:00 AM I knew that Lieberman had gone to high school in Stamford, Connecticut. I knew about his wife, Hadassah. I knew about his mother. I knew everything I needed to know about him. I had even called Eleanor to get more information about Lieberman because they attended Yale together. She didn't think Lieberman was a good choice because he had grown to be very conservative. Then at 4:00 in the morning Alexis called and I told her that I went with Lieberman. When she asked me why I told her what I had told Eleanor, that I wanted to propose someone who could help Gore in key states, including Florida. At 5:15 I got a call from Michael Feldman saying that the vice president wanted me to know right away that it was Lieberman.

When I hung up I closed my eyes for five minutes and just said "Whoa," because I was still half asleep and hung over from the conversation we had just hours ago. Lieberman, who had criticized Clinton during the Lewinsky mess, was Gore's choice. Lieberman, the chair of the Democratic Leadership Council and an orthodox Jew, was the nominee. I had to call Tom Nides, who was selected to manage the VP campaign, right away to tell him about the decision. But first I ran downstairs to make some coffee and get some ginger ale, and then it really hit me and I said, "Ooh, Lieberman, oh my God!" I called Donnie right away and told him that it was Lieberman. I didn't think it was out yet but it was breaking on AP and Claire Shipman was preparing to report it at the top of the *Today* show at 7:00 AM. And I was getting all these calls from people telling me that Lieberman was my guy, which I was getting accustomed to. I got to the office by 7:15 and everybody was looking at me for an explanation.

Before I could call Reverend Jackson and the civil rights leadership, the groups I was expected to call, I asked one of the Jewish staff why the Jewish community was alarmed about Lieberman. He said, "Well, we don't oppose him, but as Jews we don't like to draw attention to ourselves." I knew nothing about that. I called other Jewish friends at AIPAC, one of the most influential pro-Israel lobbying organizations, to find out more about this perceived fear of drawing attention to Judaism and how I could be helpful. Many of AIPAC's officials were shocked when I told them it was Lieberman. I was so puzzled, but it would have to wait. I had to get to the Black leadership and explain Gore's decision before the media got to them.

Every member of Gore's senior team was on the phone. The vice president had to call the people who were not selected. I had members of Congress on my list as well as civil rights leaders, women's leaders, all of the constituency leaders. I started making my phone calls. I had to call the Arab community. I had to call Jim Zogby, and so I got pulled into all the Middle East stuff. I had to call Kweisi Mfume. I had to call Reverend Jackson again because he had already gotten his call from Gore. I had to call the Nation of Islam, Louis Farrakhan and Reverend Al Sharpton. I was wondering what I had gotten myself into.

I had to put together a conference call by 9:00 AM with members of the Black Caucus because they wanted to be told as a group what the rationale for choosing Lieberman was. I called Senator Chris Dodd of Connecticut and asked him to help me with that one. I was in damage control from the moment I hit the office until that afternoon. We had all of the Black-Jewish stuff. And I told the Black men, "Let's button up, this ain't our fight." But then I got a call saying that I had to do Larry King Live at 6:30 PM. I said no, I was still in my notable but unquotable phase, which had lasted since March. I absolutely refused. I went to all the strong men in the campaign and told them to do the interview, but they told me it was time to get back out there beyond the camera.

So I went on Larry King, which was my first appearance on the show, to defend the selection of Joe Lieberman. I had to do all of the local Tennessee networks, even though it had been months since I had been prepped or briefed for a media hit. No one briefed me. No one prepped me. They just sent me out to defend Lieberman. And the questions were why was he selected, what will he bring to the ticket? I had answers to the questions thanks to Eleanor and some of my friends on the Hill. Elaine Kamarck was also helpful in drafting talking points and I reached out to Al From of the DLC to give me some of their talking points. That evening I met Joe Lieberman for the first time. He was very appreciative. Sherry, whom Donnie had called the night before, had broken the news to him. I was just happy for the day to come to an end. I gave him the quarter we flipped the night before. What I hadn't noticed until that moment was the flip side of the coin. It was a Connecticut quarter. I gave it to his son Matt. The next day my worst fear was realized. Some Black leader was criticizing the choice of Lieberman and had uttered something anti-Semitic. I had to rush to put the fire out.

The Democratic Party was filled with people who were uncomfortable with Lieberman. Clearly, I was not one of them. Although he was not my first or second choice, I got to size him up pretty quickly. He had spirit and I like a man with joy. Lieberman also had a way of bringing you in, the same way Jesse could when he wasn't just preaching to you. I took time to write out a number of things for Joe to do and he was eager to make the phone calls to civil rights leaders. The president of the Dallas chapter of the NAACP, Lee Alcorn, called the selection of a "Jew person . . . suspicious . . . because their interest primarily has to do with money." Kweisi Mfume immediately condemned his comments and placed him under suspension. The *Amsterdam News* was about to come up with an editorial and I immediately called Charlie Rangel and David Dinkins, the first Black mayor of New York City, to help me control this furor. Just days before the convention, the Black Caucus of the DNC became agitated and went public.

Hamil Harris, a reporter with the *Washington Post,* called to say he had spoken with several delegates and they were upset. I asked him why the *Washington Post* was stirring up trouble. In the end, Lieberman had to meet privately with Black leaders to shore up Black support heading into the convention. Rumors were spreading that Joe had fought against affirmative action at a time when Bill Clinton was trying to "mend it and not end it." There were hourly negative votes or comments and I had to bat them down one by one. It got so bad that I appealed to Alexis and Eleanor to help Lieberman out. Joe had to sit down and face the music. When Black folks circle a White politician, it's best to advise the person to sit down and get their lesson. In the end, Blacks will always come around, they just have to make their point first. And the point was simple: Lieberman was a lot more conservative than anyone had imagined. He had to find common ground with Black leaders. He had to walk the walk and speak from the heart. Blacks wanted to see him up close, smell his clothes and look at his shoes. He had to make an appeal for our help and if he succeeded, he would be regarded like Clinton and Gore, as a brother. I had less than one hour to prepare him for this baptism.

The convention was held at the Staples Center in Los Angeles. This was home to the NBA world champion Los Angeles Lakers. We were in Shaquille O'Neal's arena but on Maxine Waters's turf. Congresswoman Waters represents Watts and South Central Los Angeles. This is a woman who can walk in any ghetto in America and force both sides to stop the violence. Her reputation as a tough, take-no-prisoners, abrasive, strong and demanding diva has always made me blush. Maxine is a walking bottle of Tabasco sauce—spicy hot but smooth. Before Lieberman could get in a call to Maxine, she went public demanding to know what he would do for "poor Black people." When it came to communicating with Maxine, she regarded my calls as complementary; she had to hear from Joe. He had to beg for her support. No one—not Jackson, Mfume, Lewis, Norton, Clinton or Gore—could deliver this blackish red pepper. Lieberman would have to taste her fiery sauce and listen to her before becoming a part of the family.

Maxine walked into the small conference room at the Convention Center and did not bother to look at Eleanor or me. She went straight to the table where the senator was sitting and began laying down the rules. This was not a conversation for staff to hear, so I told Lieberman's traveling party to leave. The senator was about to go to church and only the truly converted could witness this remarkable but transforming ceremony. Someone must have given Maxine a list of Joe's voting record, because she started calling the roll from affirmative action to welfare reform. Senator Lieberman did not flinch. He took his time, gave her an answer and kept glancing over to Alexis and Eleanor to see how he was doing. When Maxine finished talking, Joe smiled and said, "Congresswoman, I really want your support. As vice president, I will follow the president's lead on these issues." With those words, the church ended. We walked out the side door where the press had gathered and told them that the senator and congresswoman would make a statement shortly.

Eleanor left the room to go to the stage and gather the other members of the Black Caucus. Maxine went to the restroom to freshen up before going into the arena. Joe was reunited with his staff. He was upbeat. The man had just been through three hundred years of Black history and it never wore out his face or spirit. He was ready for prime time. The moment Eleanor got up to introduce her old classmate to Black America, Senator Lieberman was officially baptized into the struggle for civil rights—a struggle he learned as a young man who marched in the sixties and registered Black voters in Mississippi. He was now cooking with grease. Maxine's comments sent a shock wave through the audience. This man, she said, would respect us and help Democrats win in November. The truth was Joe was very spiritual. He understood Scripture, and the Old Testament was the part of the Bible Blacks relied on in understanding their own pain and suffering. Soon Lieberman was the most requested White politician in America to speak before Black audiences, a man who started each day by praising the Lord and shouting the good news. He also hired Tina Flournoy to serve as his political director and to be part of his traveling staff. I had survived my first big controversy of the convention. The rest seemed easy. I had to learn how to entertain, something I was not so good at. I needed help. It came from strange corners.

The political part of my job came natural to me. I took care of all the people who were normally locked out of the political process. I made sure that the system was as equitable as possible. And I had a nice suite at the Biltmore Hotel. I was one of the people to know, but I didn't care about that stuff. My mission was to get my people into the arena in as safely and orderly a way as possible. I was also assigned to do Black media, but that did not stop CNN and the networks from calling me hourly for an interview.

Cindy Adams, the famous columnist at the *New York Post,* decided to follow me around. At times I treated her like one of my staffers. I told her we could talk later. Right now, I needed a big sister. Cindy, who was so cheerful and excited to be in the middle of the convention, brought me food and we spent the day and night running around that big arena. I will never forget her friendship. We bonded. We dined and we had so much fun pretending to be in charge of the convention. The campaign also gave me a suite to entertain people and have people come in, have wine, dine and watch the proceeding. But my budget was not enough to handle the constant flow of people looking for food and drink.

My cousins Ethel Mae and Josie, one from each side of my family, came in from New Orleans to help me stay afloat. Ethel Mae was my daddy's older sister's child, who lives in the house I grew up in. She decided to come because by this time she and my daddy had kissed and made up about the house. My daddy wanted her to come and be with me, and from my momma's side of the family they sent Josie. So both sides of the family were there to support me. Every day they came to open up the suite and they made sure I had food for anyone who dropped in. Don't ask me how they got the food there, but they got food and liquor and they had that suite looking like I was the person they had advertised me to be. It was a great feeling to have my family beside me. In all my political battles, I never recruited them to fight because I never wanted to see them get hurt the way I got hurt.

My suite was tiny compared to the other campaign leaders. I had made a decision to get tickets to the other larger suites because my little place was jammed. Kerry Lobel and Margie Adam, two friends from California, came up with a novel idea on how to feed the masses. Give 'em popcorn. By the third day of the convention, I was out of food and liquor. Ethel Mae and Josie went to the local liquor stores and filled the refrigerator with beer and wine. They put the hard stuff in their bags. Kerry and Margie would go to the Labor suites and take trays of cold cuts and bread. Somehow we made it. Just like growing up, poor but never hungry.

I was so grateful to have a suite that I said "I'm gonna invite every Black person in America to come to my suite." And sure enough, if Jesse Jackson wanted to come use the bathroom and watch TV and have something to eat, he was welcomed. It became a kind of running joke that inside the convention, my suite was where all the Black people were. When the others noticed that their suites didn't have any Black people in them, they would call me, the lonesome Black, for color. I had more than enough to offer people.

After months of fearing the media and the comments that came out of my mouth, I did press interviews for two hours before the convention started, giving a sense of the day's events and programs. I did the *Today* show with Bryant Gumbel and ABC with Charlie Gibson and *Inside Politics* with Judy Woodruff. I got around because I had decided that after having to go out and defend the choice of Lieberman, I would not be silent anymore. I had to talk again. And I did. I talked about the fall campaign and what I thought we had to do in order to win, which was to focus on building the largest grassroots army in the nation's history. Our goal was to turn out more votes than Bush, which we did, and to use the convention to help showcase the talent of the party.

Gore was staying at the Century Plaza Hotel and everyone was asking me if I wanted to stay with the vice president in his suite of rooms, or with the campaign staff. I said I wanted to stay with the campaign staff. But he constantly called looking for me. I had washed my hands of a lot of the emotional stuff around the campaign and I was just doing my job. I mean I did not have to worry. I had been with this man for over a year. I was the only person in the inner circle who had been on that campaign for that long and I was just so tired. But on the night he gave his acceptance speech and gave Tipper that long kiss, I said to him, "You're gonna make it. You're gonna win." And he said, "You feel it." I told him, "I feel it." Indeed I felt good about our chances against George Bush and the Republican Party.

I told Gore that I prayed for him that night. I said, "I want you to get out there and let it come from here." I pointed to my heart. Sometimes, before a speech, the guys would just beat him up and not let him be himself. They would always try to put words in his mouth. I always liked Gore. I liked him personally, despite all the drama of the campaign, because I could talk to him honestly. Gore was great if you allowed him to absorb what he had to do. He was very grateful for my words and he asked me where I would be after the speech. I told him I would be backstage, that was where I was going to watch him give his speech, which I did.

He gave his speech and then all the balloons came down from the ceiling. Everything was so emotional at that moment. He was reaching out to grab people. He knew he'd won the nomination. I was in the back telling people like Harold Ford and Kweisi to be ready to go on stage after the speech. And after the acceptance speech your family comes out, then your VP and his family. And then all of a sudden I felt somebody tap me on my shoulder and it was Al and Tipper pulling on me. They wanted me to be visible and on stage. And I'm thinking, "Oh please, don't kiss me like you just kissed Tipper or it'll ruin my reputation." So I made a quick appearance on stage, said my thank-yous and quickly returned backstage.

And it was backstage that Gore asked me to go with him and Lieberman on a two-day ride down the Mississippi. I looked at him and said, "Honey, I'm not riding on the Mississippi River with nobody." I love that river. It flows through me to this day, but to actually ride on it—no way. And he asked me where I was going and I told him I was headed back to Nashville. "I'm tired. I got to get some rest."

Sure enough, the next day I was sick. My body just shut down. I had to spend an extra day in Los Angeles, and I didn't leave until Saturday. I had some kind of intestinal flu, a virus of some sort, and it just knocked me out. I knew that I had to get physically ready for the fall campaign, and the best way for me to do that was to get back to New Orleans for some filé gumbo or frogmore stew. Otherwise, my body would not take the pressure.

Gore called me to ask about my health because word had gotten back that I didn't get back to Nashville because I was sick, and he wanted to know when I would be back on the road with him. I told him that I was going back home to get my body back into shape and then I would get back on the road with him, which I did. I got well and I got back on the road with him and I never got back off. I'd go back for a change of clothes and to check on staff, but I stayed on the road just to avoid the drama in Nashville. It was so competitive and hostile. I had made it to the final stretch. Starting with Labor Day, when I ate three Philadelphia cheesesteak sandwiches with Gore, I understood what Gore wanted from me. All I had to do was read the good book and remember the story of Gideon. We could win this battle.

Prior to the Democratic National Convention in Los Angeles, Bush was leading Gore in all the national polls among likely voters—voters who were registered and indicated a willingness to vote in November. The Republican convention, which was held in Philadelphia before the Democratic convention, gave the Bush team a head start on defining the race between old versus new. The Democrats were the old guard. The Clinton-Gore administration, according to Republican spin, was corrupt, scandal ridden and immoral. Bush, in his acceptance speech at the convention, called himself a compassionate conservative. He said, "They [Democrats] have not led. We will."

Along with his vice presidential running mate, Dick Cheney, the GOP left their convention energized and focused. On the last night of their convention, the GOP celebrated their successes. With the theme President with a Purpose: A Strong Leader Who Can Unite Our Country and Get Things Done, they took their minstrel show on the road. The Republicans wasted no time in running against us and painting Al Gore as a continuation of Bill Clinton, whom they hated more than Satan himself. Gore was not seen as a leader, and therefore the GOP wasted no time in going negative and energizing their right-wing base. But the early assaults on Gore and his campaign did not stick. We got our chance during the convention to fight back. And we did.

The selection of Joe Lieberman forced voters to give Al Gore a second look and a fresh new start. Clinton's speech on opening night and that long, soulful walk into the hall mesmerized the convention delegates and the viewing public. Night after night leading up to Gore's speech, we used the prime-time slots to tell our story. And our story was simple: Gore would stand up for the middle class. Gore would use his clout and power to protect them from special interests.

Gore would continue the peace and prosperity of the Clinton years, but also solve and tackle more problems, like the rising costs of health care and prescription drugs. There would be a renewed fight to save and protect the environment and a woman's right to choose. It was one of Al Gore's best speeches. He was on. The campaign was on. Al Gore was ready to make a fresh new start with the voters.

Leaving the convention, Gore was very manic and he decided to start the fall campaign going nonstop. Soon after I recovered I met with Michael Whouley to plot the fall season. Michael Matthews would have my back at the Nashville office, along with Donnie Fowler. I wanted to take care of Labor myself, because they always stood up to help me out in campaigns. Donnie was going to keep in touch with state directors and activists. That left me on the road to see the ground operations, look after many of the constituency leaders and train some of the young folks working in the field. The senior leadership was focused on paid advertisement and the upcoming debates between Gore and Bush. I stayed away from those decisions and worked with Chip, our COO, to develop a sound budget for our ground game and surrogate travel. Ralph Nader, who had announced his campaign earlier on the Green Party ticket, was threatening us in several states, but no one paid attention.

We got a new pollster, Stan Greenberg, who had helped Clinton win in 1992. Stan was smart and extremely sensitive. The first thing he did was to bring on Celinda Lake to do some polling in the women's community and Diane Feldman to help put together an African-American poll. I needed some research in order to improve my voter contact programs and outreach. Harrison's research gave me a glimpse into some turnout patterns, but I had to know what Black voters in the battleground states thought of Gore. After my Black business was completed, I began to focus on Hispanics, who would be very influential in the outcome in several key states, including New Mexico, Nevada and Florida.

I had to make a stop in Washington, D.C., to attend the Congressional Black Caucus legislative weekend. Gore wanted to attend. Clinton was also planning on attending, and I had to go and light the way for Gore. Some bad blood had developed between Clinton and Gore, but I did not want any part of it. I liked both men. They were my friends. I worked for Gore, but privately, I was still talking to Clinton. Some days I would send over polling data and information to the White House and swore all of them to secrecy. The last thing Gore needed was some major leaks from the White House. When it came to strategizing, Clinton was the best in America. He has the mind of six men and could take the long and short of any problem. We needed Clinton, who had strong ties, to motivate the base of the Democratic Party to turn out. They both attended the Caucus dinner, but barely talked. I gave the president a nice firm handshake and he gave me one of those Clinton bear hugs that went all around your back. After the Black Caucus weekend, we stayed in Washington to shore up our game plan and to work with the vice president, who wanted to unveil his own economic plan.

Gore held the meeting on Sunday afternoon at the mansion. I was in the room with all these smart people like Leon Fuerth, his foreign policy adviser, and Elaine Kamarck, my friend from Harvard. Tipper and Audrey Haynes were in the room, along with the paid consultants. Gore began to outline the projected budget surplus. He wrote down "$5 trillion over 10 years." I said, "Wow, that's a lot of money. What are we going to solve?" Gore then went down a long list of categories from education to the environment. When he finally got around to health care, I spoke up. "Mr. Vice President" (I was always formal in meetings like this), "can we make sure every child, no matter where they are born, has health care?"

The vice president looked at me and said, "Of course, I will support that and include it in my plans." At that moment, I walked out of the room. I had to cry. All my life I wanted to hear someone say every kid would have health care. I was born in Charity Hospital for the poor. My mama was born and died in Charity Hospital. As children, we could not go out and play because Jean told us we could "not afford to get sick." With Al Gore as president, every child could play until they were tired of what they were doing. I had finally come full circle. That little girl inside me was happy. I washed my face, put on fresh lipstick, walked back inside the room and took my seat at the table. Gore was now discussing how to make college tuition tax-free. I was so happy to be a Democrat that afternoon and to have a seat at the table where the blueprints of a ten-year budget were being discussed.

CHAPTER FIFTEEN

COCHON DE LAIT
(ROAST SUCKLING PIG)

Suckling pig, a real Cajun specialty, is seasoned and stuffed with garlic, shal-
lots and seasonings, and then slow-roasted over an open flame for up to sixteen
hours. By November 7, I realized that the campaign was similar to roasting a
pig—we faced constant heat with seemingly no end in sight.

FOR THE FIRST TIME the polls showed Gore leading Bush 45
to 41 percent. Nader was at 5 percent and I knew Gore could not afford to allow Nader to take away our votes. The election was too
close. Stan was polling Nader, and the entire campaign had finally
caught on to the threat he could pose in some states. I was dispatched
to rally the environmental and pro-choice communities in Wisconsin, Minnesota, Maine, Oregon and Washington State. Lieberman
was sent to many of these states, but mainly we sent Joe to Florida.
The *St. Petersburg Times* reported that Florida was a battleground state
and "they [voters] might determine our next President" because they
are "swing voters in the largest swing state." We had a lot of resources, including paid advertising in all the battleground states. A
decision was made to drop Ohio, Georgia and Louisiana from our
line-up. The polls in those states had us too far behind and there was
a certain limitation to our funds.

In October we began to prepare for the debates. The first was going to take place in Boston; the second in Winston-Salem, North
Carolina; the third in St. Louis, Missouri. In between the first two

It was actually the best possible job, the best place for me to do my job. I got to meet with the people on the ground. In addition, I held daily conference calls with all of the state directors. I knew every-thing. I knew what the left hand and the right hand were doing. At this point I just wanted to get out the damn vote, win the election and go back home and have a life outside politics.

Our last debate was in St. Louis and we decided that rather than prep Gore back in Florida, we would do a final debate prep outside St. Louis at a resort in Wright City. The place was so remote and des-olate I thought we were sitting ducks for hunters. We were out in the middle of nowhere doing the debate prep. Then I got a call from the governor of Alabama asking if I could come down to Birming-ham to do a big rally. Alabama was not a target state, but Karenna, the vice president's oldest child, wanted to go. And so we found a crop duster for her to fly to Alabama in. That night, October 16, the night before the debate, we got a call from the Secret Service that a small plane had gone down en route back to the airport in St. Louis. I'm thinking "Oh, my God, I've got to go tell the vice president that I put his daughter on a crop duster"—I was always trying to save money any way I could. Soon we found out it was Mel Carnahan, the governor of Missouri, whose plane had crashed. My heart went out to the people of Missouri. He was a great leader and friend.

That, of course, cast a terribly negative spell over the campaign. The next day, for the whole day, it rained. And we had to go back to St. Louis; it was just awful. So all during the last two weeks of the campaign I was haunted by Mel Carnahan's death. We went to the funeral and I marched in the procession with all the Black ministers. Mel Carnahan was a good man who was really loved by the people his state. He had been running for the U.S. Senate against Ashcroft. Carnahan beat Ashcroft posthumously, and Gov. Wilson kept his promise to name Carnahan's wife, Jean, to husband's place. Only in America can the dead be revived the political process. It didn't just happen in Chicago o leans, it happened in Missouri.

The final debate was set up like a town hall meetir inated by discussion of domestic issues, including th

---

debates there would be a vice presidential debate in Louisville, Ken-tucky. So I made the decision that I would get involved in debate prep if for no other reason than to be there. Debate prep was not my strength but I wanted to make sure that somebody Black was in the room so that we could try to inject some issues and analysis that would be helpful in terms of motivating African Americans.

Alexis Herman was also coming in for debate prep and for the debate sessions. As a member of the Clinton administration, Alexis was very close to the vice president. She and I were the only two African Americans involved in debate prep. Elaine Kamarck was there, along with Audrey Haynes, so Gore had lots of women around him for these daily sessions in a battleground state. The sessions were held right outside Sarasota, Florida, at the Longboat Key Club. Bill Daley also liked Alexis a lot and felt comfortable around her, as Bill had been a cabinet secretary. Alexis and I talked about what we wanted to emphasize in the debate prep and to make sure that we were on the same page. The debate prep went fine. Gore could ab-sorb every detail and understood how his delivery should be. Paul Begala, an old friend from the Gephardt days, was the Bush stand-in. He did very well. Bob Shrum played Jim Lehrer, the moderator. Everyone else, including Tom Donilon and Carter Eskew, were there to help Gore digest all the materials.

After the first debate, according to pollsters and analysts, the vice president came across as too cold. And they criticized the amount of makeup he had on. We were promised there would be no split screen but there was and every time Bush was talking, Gore was shown rolling his eyes. He had had a lot of diet Cokes and PowerBars and I think the sugar made him hyper. But still I thought he had done great. That was how we felt in the spin room after the debates. I thought he was on his game and that he was in command of the is-sues and facts. Bush clearly gave soft answers. But the next day the press was writing that we lost the debate. We were all baffled, won-dering how we lost it. The press said he was overprepared, that we had coached him too much and that he was cold.

So we decided that at the next debate—in Winston-Salem, North Carolina—we would try to bring in "real people" he had met along the campaign to sit in the audience. The candidates agreed on so many issues that the press thought Gore was too soft or warm. We couldn't win for losing. Bush, who had mangled sentences and mispronounced every word under the sun, kept racking up points just by showing up. The press did not give us a bounce. It was clear to us that the press corps did not like us. They captured every mistake and blew it up so big that it dominated the daily news cycle. Gore didn't help the situation much because he was prone to making mistakes. And then, of course, there was the furor over comparing the cost of prescription drugs for his mother-in-law and his dog. So reporters started asking how much he was paying for his dog's medicine and how much his mother-in-law was paying for hers. The media jumped all over him and trivialized everything. It was like we couldn't get a foothold.

After the North Carolina debate there was a terrorist bombing in Yemen. We got a wake-up call in the middle of the night and I suddenly remembered that Al Gore was the vice president of the United States. The wake-up call informed him that he had to hurry up and leave the state for a briefing. I did not feel safe. Something was happening all around us, but I could not put a finger on it. Gore knew, but he didn't share it with anyone. The country was on alert. The staff was kept in the dark for hours until we were finally told that one of our ships had been hit in Yemen. As dramatic as all this was, it didn't alter our schedule. We thought we would have to fly him back to Washington. Often we would have to fly back for congressional votes, but that didn't happen.

We spent some time back on the campaign trail in battleground states shoring up support after the bad press reviews. The polls shifted again. This time Bush was in the lead among likely voters, 48 to 44 percent. Nader was at 4 percent, a number that was still unacceptable to many of us inside the campaign. Campaign staff both in Nashville and in the battleground states were as good as they come. We had assembled some old hands from the successful Clinton-Gore campaigns and some new talent from recent congressional campaigns. The staff was diverse and everyone was finally singing from

the same hymnbook. The attacks on Gore's character made us bolder and stronger.

We refused to be cowed by the ruthless and persistent attacks from the Bush-Cheney committee. We pulled together and became the fighting team Gore wanted all along. I gave up fighting the consultants. After a long and tough year, I saw them as my brothers. On the night before we headed to St. Louis for the final debate, Shrum gave me a cigar. I had finally arrived. We brought our chairs outside and sat near the Gulf of Mexico drinking wine and beer. Carter, Stan, Bill, Frank, Jim, Tom and I were all talking about the days ahead. The final weeks of the campaign were in sight. With two and a half weeks to go before election day, we all bonded. The only thing missing on that clear, cool evening was someone with a guitar to start us singing "Kumbayah" or "Amazing Grace"—depending on your taste in music. I used this moment of relaxation to think ahead.

At this point in the campaign, our message was that Gore was a champion for the average citizen. In our polling we saw that people didn't feel prosperous. They felt something was missing in their lives and there was nobody to fight for them. Nobody to take on the big oil companies, the big pharmaceuticals. And our message was that Gore would do that for them, that he would fight for the average American. The race was still pretty close, too close to call for weeks. It was a four- or five-point game with Bush leading sometimes and then Gore creeping up on him. But I really did feel that we could make up five or six points in the final weeks. And I was sure that we could rally the troops better than the Republicans.

So I was worried. Every day we hit the ground while Gore was out there giving speeches. I was having staff meetings on location, and asking how many mailings we were doing, how many phone calls we had done. I was still writing my campaign ads. I was doing the African-American media part of it. I was making sure we had Hispanic media. I was still doing my job. I was not just sitting on the airplane to sit on the airplane. Every time I got back on the plane, I would call back or email back to Nashville, "Just met with the folks running Michigan [or wherever] and here's what's up."

health care and Social Security. Gore was in his element this time. Not too hot or cold, according to most of the postdebate reviews. The Get-Out-the-Vote efforts were under way. With the debates behind us, I had to focus on the weather, which could have a dramatic impact on our GOTV operations. Again, I took time to focus on Ralph Nader, to look at his schedule and to see what, if anything, we could do to slow his growth and momentum.

Nader needed 5 percent in order to qualify for federal funding in 2004. The Greens did not target independents or swing voters. They were aiming dead straight at the Democratic base. I did not like what the Green folks were up to in some of the battleground states. They could easily have found their 5 percent in the red states where George Bush and the Republicans dominated. I called up one of my Nader friends to suggest they campaign in Mississippi, Alabama, South Carolina and Virginia, where the Black vote would be useful. Gore was not running ads in those states. He could pull the Black vote. They ignored me. I went after them with every legal maneuver at my disposal. It worked. We brought him down in some of the battleground states, but he still kept coming after Gore, not Bush.

So we decided, with Paul Wellstone's help, God bless his soul, and with Gloria Steinem, Barney Frank, Barbara Lee, Jesse Jackson, Tom Hayden and many other progressives, that we were going to fight back, we were going to go after the environment vote. We reached out to Carl Pope, the president of the Sierra Club. We called Kate Michelman of NARAL because Nader was siphoning off White women and liberals from us, and the last thing we could afford was to lose votes from our left. We were already fighting for the middle. The middle 10 percent of the American people were undecided to the bitter end, and we spent close to $80 million from the DNC and the Gore campaign to get them to come our way.

So we had to fly back into those states—Oregon, Wisconsin, Maine and Minnesota. We had to get Lieberman to fly back in the closing days of the campaign to solidify those states. And we couldn't break any new territory. We took Nader on by using surrogates. And the last couple of days we spent time just focusing on turnout, so we looked for big crowds. We wanted to make sure that we had our base turnout, our core Democrats.

In the final stretch of campaign 2000 two things happened. One, the polling showed we were behind in Tennessee. That was October 4, right after the Boston debate. I wasn't surprised, because Bush had been campaigning there since June. So we were scrambling. I went back to try to shore up Tennessee and the only money I had left was $250,000 that was not earmarked for Get-Out-the-Vote programs. So I was stealing from my overall budget to buy posters and other materials and to get organizers on the ground. It was too late, but I did what I had to do. It wasn't enough. Politically, Tennessee, like many other Southern states, had grown conservative. The Black vote was not as large as it was in states like Louisiana and Mississippi. Without a strong White vote, we would be in trouble. The same was true for Arkansas. Clinton, who was back in Washington, anxious to hit the campaign trail, was fuming that we were not calling on him. I was. But I was told by Daley to keep quiet. This was the campaign's decision and I had to respect that. Stan Greenberg had some polling to help us make an informed decision on where to send Bill Clinton. Ten days before the election, we agreed to come up with a light schedule for the president to travel to Arkansas, California and per- haps Maryland to do a Black church. Under no circumstances would he campaign in a battleground state. This made many of the civil rights leaders upset. They argued that Clinton could help Gore get out the largest Black vote. I agreed with them, but I had lost that battle and moved on. With Minyon's help, I would find time on the president's schedule for him to talk with Black and Hispanic leaders in every state. Like in the primaries, I knew Gore wanted me to win it all. The details were left for me to work out.

The last two weeks of the campaign I felt really good. I was telling everyone that the only thing that would stop us from winning or getting out the vote was the weather. I didn't focus on any other de- tail but turnout, turnout all the time. I was a woman on a mission. I was only really worried about the weather. Ohio was no longer in play, Georgia and Louisiana were off the map. We were down to nineteen battleground states and I was begging the consultants for money, telling them I needed money for Jacksonville for paid radio in order to get out the vote. They still had funds for media. I was now negotiating to get both Gore and Clinton on every gospel station in America. My goal was to expand the Black vote in key areas, target Black seniors, rally Black women and get them to pull Black men out on election day.

Our field program targeting suburban women and Hispanics was also one of the best I had ever seen in the Democratic Party. We pushed our field staff to identify precinct captains and to turn over local operations to volunteers rather than rely solely on paid staff from the outside. This gave the campaign a source of energy and more people on the ground than ever before in the history of modern politics. We did not do all of this by ourselves. Big Labor, with their phone banks and seven-point program to contact their members, was also out there working the ground operations. They recruited members to talk to Labor households. Labor helped us to canvass tens of thousands of Democratic voters before election day. The RNC was reported to be spending $40 to $50 million. The DNC was planning on spending a lot less, $10 to $15 million. So we needed the extra resources provided by labor organizations and other Democratic allies. And I had no problems begging. Whouley and I developed a new policy. It was called no excuse. When I called Rob Tully, the chairman of the Iowa Democratic Party, to discuss his plan, I would say, "What do you need? I do not want to wake up on November 8 and read your excuses in the media." Rob needed more than $50,000. I do not know how Whouley did it, but the money was there in twenty-four hours. We were both Catholic and begging must come natural to us, because we did it without even feeling the least bit embarrassed.

The last forty-eight hours of the campaign we started off in St. Louis and traveled to Waterloo, Iowa. I got Babyface—Kenneth Edmonds—to campaign with us for a couple of days. Weeks earlier, Jon Bon Jovi was with Gore all through Wisconsin and Michigan. Bill Cosby made a trip to West Virginia and Pennsylvania. Cher was stomping up and down the West Coast. Melissa Etheridge was going from campus to campus. At this point it was all hands on deck—

Stevie Wonder, Robert De Niro, Jessica Lange, Elton John, Whoopi Goldberg, Robin Williams all stood with us. We flooded every major media market where we knew we had to make a tremendous effort and the crowds were awesome. Twenty thousand people came out in Madison, Wisconsin, for Melissa on our behalf. And Gore just loved it. You could see the relief on his face. We had help in turning out the vote.

Every morning I got up with less than two hours of sleep and we did early-morning drive-time radio in key battleground markets. Gore did not seem to mind. He wanted to win. Tipper did her part and crisscrossed America. The Liebermans were troupers, too. The Clintons settled into the groove and they did as instructed, plus what they knew they had to do. They kept the money flowing to us. They kept doing those conference calls to rally the base. We were cooking with grease. I could feel a little surging. Bush was back home in Texas relaxing on the final weekend of play—typical Republican action. Leave the game before it's all over and declare a victory, I assumed. We were fighting as if the campaign was neck and neck and we headed into election day feeling joyful.

On Monday night we had one last rally in Flint, Michigan, then headed down to Miami for a rally in South Beach at midnight. Everybody on that plane buckled up and took a nap. I looked over and saw Babyface and winked. He had become my lucky charm and I enjoyed his presence on the campaign those last few hours. He was uplifting, not to mention talented and a gifted singer. When he arrived at the site, our motorcade had difficulty getting through the streets. It felt like Mardi Gras under the palm trees. The crowds were awesome. We had a huge rally on the beach with all these celebrities and thirty thousand people all around us. Florida congresswoman Carrie Meek pulled me aside and told me to get some rest. Everything would work out fine. I looked at her and looked at the crowd and felt Florida would go for Gore. I could feel it. I could smell it. We got back into our vans and boarded Air Force Two for a short ride to Tampa. I stayed on the plane to take a nap. I needed some sleep. That's how we began election day.

We met up with Lieberman at 4:00 in the morning. They had an event at a local hospital and we started off our day at 6:00. I woke Gore early to get him on the radio and I got him talking to Tom Joyner and Steve Harvey, Donnie Simpson and Doug Banks. We did drive-time radio until 7:00. He was exhausted, but prepared to make his calls. I told him this was our last day together. I would no longer bother or pester him. Gore laughed it off and gave me a big hug and a high five. I had him on the radio for two straight hours talking to people. I had Bill Clinton on the radio, too, and Gore was telling me not to let Clinton go on the air before him. Clinton enjoyed talking to the disc jockeys, and Gore just wanted to hit as many markets as possible. I reminded him that his voice was up and running in all those markets. On this, the last day of the campaign, the entire party was on board pushing people out the door, dragging or driving voters to the polling stations. But something strange was happening.

The first inkling we got of trouble at the polls was when we talked to WTMP in Tampa in Pinellas County in the Hillsborough area. I had called ahead to see if they were ready to talk with the vice president. Stacy, the host and producer, bent my ear saying that people were having problems voting. It was too early for people to have problems voting so I asked her what kind of problems. She said that people were being told that the absentee ballots would be disqualified because they were not certified. I told her that you don't need to certify them. You don't have to get a notary to certify your ballot. You just need your signature. I told her I would look into it.

I called Arthenia Joyner, who is a Florida state representative, and I asked her what was going on. She said "Oh yeah, my momma had this problem and so did my aunt."

"Well, are you gonna fight it?" I asked.

"Yeah, we'll fight it."

"Okay."

Then we got back on the phone and I placed a call to Bishop Curry down in Miami. Whenever you're in a state you always call the local stations first and then you fan yourself out. Bishop Victor Curry, who was active in the Haitian community, called me back and told me that there were problems because there were no ballots in Creole. So I knew that Florida was a mess—and this was 8:00 in the morning. We flew up to Nashville and I finally got to take another short nap. At this point, we were so tired that coffee could not keep our eyes open. I just napped the entire time and I did not care who sat next to me on the plane. When we got to Nashville, we had a big welcome-home rally planned, welcoming the vice president and Tipper back home. That's where we were going to spend election day. Lieberman went back to New Haven, Connecticut, to vote. On the plane the vice president hugged me again and said, "Donna, thank you so much for everything." I thanked him. For two solid years I had given my all to the party and Vice President Gore. He was appreciative. I was so happy this was over. But I knew I had a long day ahead, so I reminded him that we needed to do drive-time radio in the afternoon and evening. I was going to have him do radio all during the day. We were going to hit at least thirty or forty stations across the country before the polls closed in Washington State. I even had numbers for stations in Hawaii.

Black radio personalities easily open up their radio stations and will cut through a rap song to give the vice president a minute. And Gore said, "No problem." He told me to check in with him about turnout and I assured him that I would check turnout throughout the day. We had been together almost forty-eight hours and I couldn't wait to take a shower and change my clothes. So we got off Air Force Two and everybody applauded us at the airport, where we were met by a huge rally. I just dropped my bags down. I'd been on the plane for two whole weeks and I was ready to talk to the friends I saw in the crowd that had come out to welcome us back to Tennessee. When I came back I couldn't find my bags. I didn't carry a purse. I carried a small duffle bag. It had my CD player, my wallet and my Bible. I carried my Bible because at any time Gore might want to read or refer to Scripture, and he and I would argue on what book it came from. So I carried a Bible just to engage him in a conversation on Scripture and its meaning. I had my little diary, all my personal stuff. I had my clothes in another bag and my cell phone. I couldn't find it and I wondered, "Who removed my bag?"

But then I thought that the bags had been taken to the hotel.

When I got to the hotel, Audrey Haynes, who was giving me a ride, didn't know where my bags were, either. I went back to the airport and they couldn't find them. I was worried, so I called my father from campaign headquarters. Lionel has many gifts and talents and one of them is the gift of sight. When he answered the phone I told him, "I just got down to Tennessee and I can't find my bags."

"Don't worry about your bags; they're trying to steal the election."

"What did you say?" I wanted him to repeat what he just told me. I was startled. He did not back off. The election was in trouble. He sensed desperation and a lot of people being turned away from the polls. He was not playing. Lionel was worried. I hung up and was about to leave my office to talk with Joe Sandler, the DNC's legal counsel for advice. Then I got a call from Demetria, my sister in Orlando, Florida. I had planned to call my family later in the day to check on everybody's vote and she said, "Girl, how many forms of ID you need to vote?"

"One."

"Well, Miss Jones and I just went to vote and they asked us for more than one form of ID." Miss Jones was her neighbor and good friend. Leroy, my brother-in-law, and Demetria looked out for them.

"No, Demetria, you only need one form of ID. You only need a driver's license or a voter registration card."

"Well, I had both and they wouldn't let me vote until I also showed them a utility bill."

Leroy didn't have a problem voting because he had a couple of IDs on him, but Miss Jones, who is elderly, couldn't vote and Demetria felt so bad about what happened to her when they had driven her to the polls. Demetria is the cussing type and she told them at the polling station "I know one damned thing, y'all gonna let me vote." But they didn't. I told her to go back and ask for a provisional ballot.

The conversation with Demetria started me wondering what was happening around the country, so I started making phone calls to other states. This was 11:00 in the morning. I went into the offices and told Bill Daley that people were having trouble voting. I told him about my conversation with Demetria and that I had just gotten similar reports from Virginia and Michigan. Daley was worried. He had also gotten news from Chicago that people were having difficulty at the polls.

Then when I went to the war room I got a call from Reverend Willie Barrow in Chicago and she told me that the police were giving tickets to cabdrivers who were taking low-income people to the polls. I told Daley, "You better get your brother on the phone and tell the police to back down." Then I called the Fraternal Order of Police and lit into them about what was happening. They had flip-flopped on us, saying they were going to endorse Gore and then endorsed Bush three days before the election. Now I became pissed off about intimidation at the polls. Like previous elections in New Jersey and New York, where the Republican Party was caught red-handed trying to harass or intimidate Black voters, they were back at their old game. I was not impressed. I am frustrated and wondering whom do we call?

Then I knew whom to call. I put in a call to Eric Holder. Working for Eleanor we had made him U.S. Attorney for the District of Columbia, and then he became number two at the Justice Department. But I decided to talk to the campaign lawyers first to see if they wanted to make the call. I was more than a bit hyper. I hadn't slept and I had lost my bags. I hadn't eaten and I was disoriented. But what was happening had given me an adrenaline rush and I was back to functioning. I told Joe Sandler and Lyn Utrecht, Gore's counsel, what I had learned, how I had told Daley what was happening and that we needed to call the Justice Department and put them on notice that people were violating the Voting Rights Act all over the country. And I had gotten a call from Gayle Andrews from Leon County in Tallahassee about police blocking the polling site. I had no idea how all these people were getting my number, but I was getting lots of calls.

"The war room is not set up to talk about how many people turn out. People can't even get to the polls. The damn police are stopping them," I said. And then I told them that I was making an executive decision to call Eric Holder and asked if anyone had other ideas. We were in trouble.

I got through to Eric, who was a personal friend, and told him what I knew and that he had to get someone on this situation right away.

I then went to the storage place where I had left my junk to get a change of clothes, went back to the hotel and explained to the woman at the front desk that I needed my room.

"Ma'am, I have a room here. Trust me. I am Donna Brazile. I do not have an ID or any credit cards. I can't explain where my bags are. I have no money, but please, I have to take a shower. You can call Tipper, she knows me." I got checked into my room, and went right to the ninth floor, the vice president's floor. I knew I had to tell him because I had more than enough information about voter intimidation. He was still the vice president of the United States. I can't even tell you how angry I was.

When I met with the vice president I said, "I know you're working on your victory speech but we got a problem."

"Well, I'm not supposed to make my calls until four o'clock."

"No, it ain't about your calls right now."

"What is it?"

"They're stealing this election. We're getting our vote out but people are having a hard time voting. You need to call Janet Reno. I've called Eric, but it's still happening all across the country. Every time I think I've got it isolated to a particular state I hear from other people."

He didn't fully understand what was happening. He heard that we were getting out the vote, but that's all. He didn't get it. So I went over to the staff room to tell Tipper and she understood a bit more. So I started working the phones, making calls to all these Black radio stations, asking about turnout, what are you hearing? This is afternoon drive-time and I start just telling people, "Even if you're in line when the polls close you can still vote. Please stay in line." I was getting calls in my hotel room from the office telling me to call stations all over the country and urge people to stay in line, even if the polls closed on them. I called the White House and informed Minyon and Ben to work the phones, too. Turnout around the country was just awesome. And in many Black communities people were showing up late. The polls close at 7:00 PM in certain locations on the East Coast, but we still had to turn people out in the Midwest and South. Some voters were arriving at 6:45 PM and being told they had run out of ballots. No one was really prepared for this kind of turnout. Around 7:30 PM that night I was talking to Julie Gibson and Joyce Aboussie, my two lieutenants and friends from the Gephardt campaign in Missouri. There was an incident where people were in line and being told to go home. Joe was on top of it. We decided to file an injunction to keep the polls open and the polls were kept open and then they were closed down again.

Meanwhile, Peter Jennings had reported that Gore won Florida and everybody was jubilant. We all jumped for joy because Florida was key to an electoral victory. The way the map was being called that night, early returns gave us New York and Pennsylvania; they called Florida, and Michigan was about to be called. There was no way Bush was going to win. Even if we lost West Virginia, we still had it in the bag. Of course we didn't know for another twenty minutes that we lost Tennessee; we still thought that by winning Florida with twenty-five electoral votes, we had won the ball game. That was around 7:45 PM.

I took some time to check in with my family at home. This was the first presidential election for my little niece Janika. I talked to my siblings and other relatives and everyone was reporting long lines and the difficulties they had experienced voting that day. Demetria did finally vote after pushing her way in the polling place later that day. She was so angry that my little apathetic sister took people to the polling place until quitting time.

I went back upstairs to the vice president's suite and reported again that people were still having problems, and I told him what was going on in Missouri with the polls being shut down while people were still in line and that we had filed an injunction. And at that point I got a beer and thought it was over with.

The exit polls had shown Gore as the winner in Florida and they had been a reliable tool in politics for almost a decade. So when the reporters in TV came back on and said there was a dispute, that Florida was now in Bush's column, we were wondering how that

could happen. For a few hours we didn't know what wa
down in Florida. The results from the rest of the country
coming in. Oregon and New Mexico were too close to ca
that point we knew we were in for a long, long, night.

They called Tennessee at around 8:00 PM for Bush. W
stunned. And then in the same breath, they called Minneso
Gore. We kept switching back and forth between the cable cha
and the networks. We had three television sets going simultaneo
on mute. Iowa was too close to call. Missouri, where we had had
sorts of problems, went with Bush. I was furious. It takes months
convince people to vote, and on election day, many of these peopl
who were excited about a candidate got sent home without ever casting their vote. Tony Coelho had come to Nashville to watch the returns. I pulled him aside to let out my frustration at what was
happening with voter suppression and intimidation. Here I was sitting in Nashville unable to help anyone cast their vote or to fight
back. If only I could provide those anonymous citizens with a thank-
you note for trying, I kept thinking. I felt so bad for them. What an
embarrassment to get up to vote and be turned around for lack of an
ID or because someone had mistakenly purged your name from the
voter rolls.

It looked pretty grim but we decided to regroup at 9:00 PM
on the eighth floor to go over all our options. Stan Greenberg, Bill
Daley, Carter Eskew, Tad Devine, Frank Hunger, Bob Shrum and I
were in the room. Gore came up, Lieberman, who had returned to
Nashville, came up, and we kept looking at results. Gore wanted
to get our best advice on what he should do and he got on the floor to
watch the returns while Lieberman and I were discussing Florida and
what happened. Lieberman was telling me what had happened with
Jewish voters. Apparently they had problems in West Palm Beach
and other places. I told him that Black voters had encountered a lot
of problems in Florida, too. I told him what had happened in Pinellas
County with the absentee ballots being decertified and that we had
to fight this. I told him what I had heard from my sister.

At this point Bush's lead had grown to over five thousand votes in
Florida—the key state at the time for our march to victory. It was

clear that Bush was picking up votes as the total came in, which was strange because nighttime votes tend to be Democratic, not Republican. So we all got prepared to leave for the War Memorial in downtown Nashville where Gore would give his concession speech. He wanted to go up and talk to his family and also to call Governor Bush. He asked Bill Daley for the number because Daley was in touch with Don Evans, Bush's campaign chairman and now the secretary of commerce. Although I had met Karl Rove earlier in the year and sent him a postcard from time to time to remind him of our campaign bet, I was not ready to call anyone on the Republican side. Suddenly, I got my second wind. I wanted to fight. I looked around the room for some support. No one was willing to fight at that moment. So I went to get my BlackBerry, which I had on me and not in my bags. Thank God, I thought, I can communicate with Gore as he goes up the stairs.

My email to him was that we are not to surrender and those were the exact words that I used. I said, "Never surrender." Bill Pickle, the lead Secret Service agent, was walking slowly to the elevator. I was behind him with my borrowed umbrella in my hand because it was raining, and I was emailing Gore again to never surrender. Everybody left the floor crying or with their head down. There was Audrey Haynes who was with Tipper. I hugged Frank Hunger, Gore's brother-in-law, and his girlfriend, Valerie. I got in my staff car; I was so disgusted. I put my head down on the front seat and prayed for a miracle. "Please God, just let us hang in there for another day or two because something is wrong, something is happening." I just felt it.

When I got out of the car I was willing to do anything. I was ready for another bargaining session with God. I have learned my lesson since then, but I used to still bargain back then. I prayed, "If you will let this man just hold on for two days I promise I will turn my life and intentions back to whatever you will for me to do."

Then Michael Feldman started screaming, "I need to reach the vice president, I need to reach the vice president."

"Well, he's up there."

"I just got a call from Whouley."

"Why?"

"We're within a thousand votes."

"Yes!!!!" I shouted. "We're gonna win. We're gonna win!" I was the happiest person in the world.

I ran to find Lieberman, who was in the car behind Gore, and I told him, "We're within a thousand votes and that means an automatic recount. Your people's votes will be counted. My people's votes will be counted. Oh man, we're gonna win this thing!!!" He was as ecstatic as I was. By this time Joe Lieberman and I were as thick as thieves. The man had replaced Tony Coelho as my brother on the campaign trail. We both had faith, we enjoyed the book of Psalms and were proud to talk about our relationship with God.

God was not finished with Al Gore, either. The rain kept coming down heavy. The tears stopped, and for a brief moment I heard the sound of angels. I looked up at the cloudy sky and whispered, "Thank you, God."

For Fannie Lou Hamer; for Martin Luther King Jr.; for Emmett Till; Rosa Parks; Ella Baker; Medgar Evers; Septima Clark; Malcolm X and every living soul who cared about the right to vote. I thanked God for this miracle. I walked upstairs to join the Gores and Liebermans. The night was still young. It wasn't over yet.

CHAPTER SIXTEEN

OYSTERS BIENVILLE

Oysters Bienville is named for Jean Baptiste Le Moyne, Sieur de Bienville, the founder of New Orleans. The oysters are served on the half shell and topped with shrimp, mushrooms and grated Parmesan cheese and heavily seasoned. Throughout the Gore campaign, I attempted to expand the Democratic base beyond its core—the oyster—by adding spices and novel ingredients—new voters and a broader message.

ONCE UPSTAIRS AT THE WAR MEMORIAL, the mood shifted from doom and gloom to heightened expectation. We all looked around to see what was going on, but the little black-and-white TV was hardly functioning. So we got Whouley on the phone and he explained it all to Gore and he understood what this meant. Whouley was back in the war room. A veteran of numerous presidential campaigns, he understood the ground rules on recount and statewide election procedures.

Gore finally understood that he couldn't concede. He said, "I'm gonna have to call the governor." So he got on the phone with Bush and it was the testiest conversation I had ever witnessed the vice president have with anyone. Gore's body language was so revealing. We heard him say, "I don't care what your brother says, and the law's the law, with all due respect to your brother." And I was so happy that we were standing up for ourselves. I was near the window cheering him on. "Go Al, go Al, go for it!" If they wanted a fight, then we were going to fight for the last count.

That was the beginning of the next phase of the campaign. The decision was made to send chairman Bill Daley out to issue a statement explaining to the American people what had happened. The rest of us headed back to the headquarters for a strategy meeting to figure our next move. It was 3:30 in the morning. This was the end of Gore-Lieberman 2000 and the beginning of the Gore-Lieberman Recount Committee.

Peter Knight had convened a meeting with fund-raisers at the hotel. Gore asked Warren Christopher to come to Nashville and do the legal part of the strategy. Ron Klain would head up the team that would hit the ground immediately and I sent Donnie Fowler from the political team. We told the staff to get a week's worth of clothes so we could head to Florida. Meanwhile I had to close down the campaign office. At 4:00 in the morning we're sitting in this meeting and I see all these lawyers in the room. I raised my hand and asked if there would be any voting rights specialists on the team. "Can I call Kweisi, Elaine Jones from the NAACP Legal Defense Fund? Can I call Barbara Arwine of the Lawyers Committee? Can I call Wade Henderson of the Leadership Conference on Civil Rights? Can I call Eleanor Holmes Norton? We need a civil rights lawyer. I understand Mr. Christopher is a very important lawyer, but he's a corporate lawyer. We need somebody who knows how to deal with election laws."

Their response was "We've got all these election law experts on staff."

"Yeah, but who's gonna deal with voting rights violations?" I asked.

No one in the room really addressed my concerns. I was totally ignored. At this point I became, once again, the odd person out. We had been up all night. I went back to the hotel to sleep on it. Actually, I couldn't sleep. I was wide-awake thinking about the next move. I was so tired, but I could not stop or give up right when Gore needed his staff more than ever.

I did not set an alarm clock because I knew my daily preacher would call me sooner or later. Reverend Jackson came over to the hotel and called up to my room. He told me to come down; we had to talk. "We're gonna have to fight," he said.

"Reverend, I know we need a voting rights lawyer but I just lost that battle two hours ago at the strategy meeting."

"Well, we ain't gonna lose this battle," he told me. "You've done your job. I'll take it from here."

"Thank you, Reverend."

Reverend Jackson wanted to meet with Gore, so I called him. But Gore said, "I don't want to meet with him, tell him I'm busy."

There are a lot of things I can do, but one thing I can't is lie to Reverend. So Gore talked to him by phone and not in person and then Gore wanted him to meet with Daley. Daley didn't want to meet with Reverend. Some people thought I had set Jackson up to do this but I told them "You know Reverend Jackson. He did this on his own." So I told Reverend to meet me over at the campaign head-quarters, where we had to go, and talk to the staff and tell them what was going on.

At the campaign office, Reverend Jackson and I did a combined rally and prayer vigil with the staff. It was our last full staff meeting of the campaign. It was just the two of us talking to the staff, and we let them know that "weeping may endure for a night but joy cometh in the morning" and that we were going to fight. No one told us to say this, but we had to tell the staff something. They were sitting there in the headquarters watching CNN for clues as to our next steps.

We were willing to fight but the campaign had not made that strategic decision. Mike Glover, a reporter from the Associated Press, asked me what I thought the next move was. I said I didn't know. And I told Reverend Jackson, "They're not gonna let us be involved in this." Gore called everyone back later in the day. He wanted to take control of the situation. Warren Christopher was expected to arrive in town any minute and he wanted to do a press conference. It was the day after the election and I still had not had a chance to change clothes. I looked a mess, but my looks never bothered me. I did shower, however, and that mattered.

Gore told me that he wanted me to publicly thank the staff and all the people who helped get out the vote all over the country. I was surprised to have a role at the press conference. Gore decided to introduce Warren Christopher as the man who would take over the next phase. So Christopher, Bill Daley and I would talk to the national press about the next step. Gore looked at me as if to say, "You're not going out there dressed like that, are you?" I reminded him I had not slept and had not had a chance to change clothes. Hadassah came to my defense, saying "She looks fine, there's nothing wrong with her." It reminded me of my childhood when my mom used to tell me I couldn't go outside because I didn't look the part. But I figured this was an opportunity to say thank you to the entire world and to thank Al Gore and leave the stage. This was, for me, the end of the campaign. My job as campaign manager ended the day Warren Christopher took charge of the recount.

Just as he had done when he named me campaign manager, Gore had to find the people he wanted to take on this phase of the operation. My role was clearly to close down the Nashville office, help the staff with transition and assist anyone who needed help with the recount in Florida. I was committed, as always, to take care of the kids, take care of the workers. I did not want them to leave the campaign disillusioned or sad. I tried to encourage them to hang around or drive to Florida or Washington, D.C.

I thought, "Let me do what I do best, let me close this campaign." If the election turned out right, as I hoped it would, I would help with the inaugural. Throughout the campaign, I never spent any time thinking about what was ahead after it was over. Would I return to Capitol Hill? Would I finally go to law school? Would I start my own business? Would I just take it easy and go to Europe? I did not know if Bush, who had a slight lead that kept disappearing, or Gore, who needed every vote to be counted, would come out ahead.

I was so tired. My legs were weak. I felt a cold coming on, but I couldn't afford to get sick. All of my credit cards were being canceled. My bank did not allow me to take any money without the proper ID. In the last forty-eight hours, I had hit every emotional note in my soul. My spirit beckoned me to relax. I sat in my office listening to gospel music, pondering the entire campaign and all the what-ifs. What if we had just won Tennessee? What if Clinton had campaigned in more states? What if we had more resources to get more people out? I did not have any answers, but I knew I had given Al

Gore everything I had. Now I was lost. I could not predict the outcome. Lionel, who had a wonderful sense and gift for predicting things unseen, went totally underground. He was an emotional wreck, too.

The press conference was my only opportunity to tell the world what was going on. I wanted to tell America that all the votes must be counted in Florida. I wanted to tell America that people had trouble getting to the polls and that someone should investigate how so many people could have stood in line only to be turned away later. I wanted to discuss the students who were denied the right to vote. When my turn came, I looked into those cameras and had an instant flashback to the Dukakis campaign. Deep down, I wanted to let it rip, but I held back. "Thank you, America, for your votes and support. Al Gore thanks you, too. To the best field staff in America, you won yesterday." These were the only words I could muster. I was too tired to shout and too drained to take a bold stand. I wanted to go home and sleep. I was told to come to another strategy meeting. This would be my last of the campaign and recount.

I didn't get back home to Washington until late Saturday afternoon. Southwest Airlines was going to allow me to fly home without an ID. I had convinced the people at the airport who I was. They saw me on TV and were going to allow me to fly to Baltimore. I had arranged a car from one of Eleanor's staffers. My Jeep was packed and I gave the keys and all my junk to a couple of strangers who promised to get it to me by midnight. Like on my trip to Tennessee, I relied on strangers sent by angels to watch over me. Then I got a call from Donnie and he asked me if I was missing a bag. I told him I was. "Two bags?" he asked. "Yes."

He asked me to describe the contents and I told him what was in them. "I found your bags." They had been found in West Palm Beach, and he overnighted them on Southwest Airlines and I went to the airport, picked up my bags, got my ID and flew home. My bags had been put on Lieberman's plane by mistake and sent to Florida with the recount staff.

I got home late Saturday night and got a call from Gore the next morning. He wanted to know what I was going to be doing during the recount. I told him that I would help with getting surrogates to help us explain our role in the recount; I would help with sending staff and raising money for the recount and work out of the DNC. And that's what I did. I didn't go back to Florida until April 2002. I was so worried about our recount strategy of targeting only four counties that I went into a silent rage. I placed calls to so many people, among them Johnnie Cochran. I did not care that he was not a voting rights specialist. Warren Christopher wasn't an election lawyer. I tried to push for their inclusion in the process and when I emailed my thoughts about this to the vice president, he forwarded them to Ron Klain who understood my concern. As one of our top lawyers, he began to hire several Black lawyers to augment the legal team.

I then called Alexis and gave her my list of seven voting rights experts who could work around the Gore campaign. The legal strategy that Warren Christopher and the new team had adopted was a narrow one. It challenged the votes in four counties and the undervotes. I was worried because of what I heard about the ballot confusion in other, less populous counties. I was worried about excluding counties like Pinellas, like Hillsborough, like Duval, like Gaston and Lee. Based on conversations I'd had and on the information that was still coming out in press accounts, I knew there were problems in those counties. Congressman Alcee Hastings was calling me hourly, as was Congresswoman Corrine Brown, who wanted to get in somebody's face. All along, I took from these leaders all the jabs they were sending Gore. Some of the remarks wounded me spiritually because I knew we were doing the best we could do, but it did not stop people from wanting to beat us up day in and day out.

For three days, I raised these issues in conference calls with the vice president, Warren Christopher and Lieberman, and whenever I raised the voting rights violation strategy they knocked me off the calls. It was very painful. Gore wouldn't take my emails or my calls anymore. I felt shut out. Their message was so contradictory. They told me to go and find voting rights specialists and then they wouldn't call them.

One thing was clear: Our opponent was not about to lose. The

Bush team, under the leadership of former secretary of state James Baker, had both a political and legal strategy. Their goal was to stop the recount by any means necessary, arguing that it was damaging to the constitutional process. They were also contacting Florida legislators. I started contacting Florida Democratic legislators just to get them on board. Nobody on our side was making those calls. The Bush team had a very comprehensive strategy, a very broad strategy that included both stopping the count and bringing in people to create a moblike atmosphere. They were paying round-trip plus per diem, hotel, everything for people to leave Capitol Hill to go down to Florida and protest. I learned later that my neighbors two doors down, who worked for House Republican leader Tom DeLay, were planning to take a whole busload of people down there.

I was so upset and it was hard to maintain silence in the face of all that the Bushies were doing and all that we weren't doing. So I just supported the team and did what I was told. If they wanted some troops to come to the mansion to rally for the Gores, I called around to organize it. If they needed more warm bodies in Florida, I sent them. I did this in order to keep my sanity and not give up. We were looking for a break. The lawyers were good but the strategy was awful.

Finally, on Friday, December 8, the weeping stopped. Good news was on the horizon. We got the message that the Supreme Court in Florida had ruled that they would count all the votes statewide, undervotes and overvotes. You're talking about joy! I emailed Tipper Psalm 30 and Joe Lieberman and I talked. Joe was a fighter, too. He was on the same page with me about the voting rights strategy. Gore had given an interview to the *Investor's Business Daily* and said he disagreed with his campaign manager and that Jesse Jackson had injected race into the process. "It is time to end all talk of the disenfranchisement of Black voters in Florida. It is time to stop accusing the Republicans of racism. Yes, bigotry still exists. And we must never relax in our fight to end it. But name-calling on either side does nothing to achieve that end." I was furious and felt as if I'd been thrown overboard.

I wanted to say "That's okay," but it really wasn't, because by this time we had a pretty clear picture of the scope of the massive voting irregularities that had occurred. Black men were being singled out for criminal background checks before being allowed to vote. Black voters were being required to show as many as three different proofs of identification. Black voters were being required to show photo identification while White voters were not.

So when the Florida Supreme Court made this ruling I felt vindicated, I felt that they were the saviors. When the Florida Supreme Court made its ruling, I had dinner at the vice president's mansion. It was Shabbat. The Liebermans were coming over for dinner. Gore asked me to stay. Carter Eskew, Bob Shrum, Alexis Herman and Bill Daley were all going out to eat. I had to stay because I wanted to see Joe and Hadassah.

Gore sat there, looking at the news. He was ecstatic; he was hugging everybody, and he told me to take my seat right next to him. But I was rolling my eyes. I didn't want to be there. It was very uncomfortable.

Everyone had warned me, from day one, that at some point I would get on Gore's bad side. But it didn't happen to me until the recount. And I got kicked over a principle—the right to vote—and that didn't sit well with me. I was very upset. I had spent my entire career fighting to expand the electorate, helping people to learn how to register people to vote, and I thought about Gore's daddy, who lost his Tennessee Senate seat in 1966 because he took a principled position in support of the Voting Rights Act. I was sitting there looking at this man and I wanted him to understand how important it was to have every single vote counted—across the state. I kept thinking in support of his candidacy I had moved heaven and earth to get people out to vote for him and now they needed his voice.

But everybody was happy. I pretended to be happy, too, but I wasn't, not really. I was glad to see that every vote would be counted. I kept thinking my life would dramatically change after the recount. I had to get on with being a forty-year-old woman. I could not go back to being a kid anymore. I had to take charge of my life—not some politician or even my family. It was time for me to begin to settle down and become someone worth loving. I had no idea what I was thinking about, but I wrote it in my diary. So, I knew it was in my heart.

Philip Dufour, Tipper's deputy chief of staff, went to the Safeway and got some rotisserie chicken. So we had rotisserie chicken and salad and bread that Hadassah made. Because it was Shabbat, Lieberman asked me to give the prayer. We were sitting around the big dining room table, a table we often sat around to discuss message and to develop strategy. The fire was burning and everyone was relaxed— the first time in weeks. Joe asked me to say the prayer that he and I had been saying since the election night. "Weeping may endure for a night but joy cometh in the morning." I got that prayer from Reverend Jackson and so I said the prayer and we had Shabbat and afterward I hugged the vice president and said, "I'll see you later, I have to go back and do some work." But actually I was headed over to the Palm. I hung out at the Palm with the boys until two in the morning.

The next day was a beautiful Saturday and I got up early because I had to give a speech at NARAL, the National Abortion Rights Action League. I was giving my speech to one of our main constituencies and updating them on what was happening in the campaign when somebody ran up to the podium and told me that I had to call my office right away. My BlackBerry wasn't working so they had not been able to reach me. I asked what was up and the person told me that the U.S. Supreme Court had just stopped the count.

So I am standing before five hundred people and I had to tell them what had just taken place and then I quoted from the book of Amos: "May justice roll down like water but righteousness like a mighty stream" (5:24). Justice Antonin Scalia had argued that the recount would do irreparable harm to Bush. I went back to headquarters feeling as if the lights had gone out. It was still a bright day, the sun was out, but I felt plunged into darkness. At headquarters we sat and waited. The next forty-eight hours were the longest ever. David Boies, our lead attorney, had to prepare arguments for *Bush v. Gore*. The Florida Supreme Court decision was now under the jurisdiction of the U.S. Supreme Court.

During the recount we learned more about evidence of voter intimidation and harassment. Twenty-seven thousand spoiled ballots in Duval County, Florida, about 19 percent of all votes cast in four heavily Black precincts in Jacksonville, where Gore was favored, were tossed out, compared to 7.5 percent tossed out in a predominately White precinct in Jacksonville, where 64 percent of the voters favored Bush. And from the discarding of hundreds of absentee ballots in Hillsborough County, we learned many Black Floridians had been purged from the voter rolls. The stories were so painful that I stopped answering my phones and going on Black radio stations. There was nothing I could do but document all the stories and pass them on to the NAACP and others who would never stop fighting for civil rights.

On the day the case was scheduled for argument before the Supreme Court, Eleanor called and told me she was going over because she was a member of Congress. I called somebody I knew in Justice Clarence Thomas's office to see what the procedure was for getting tickets. I had met Clarence Thomas years before and we got along peacefully and respectfully. I didn't bother to talk to him or anyone from the Republican side. This was a battle. The White House was at stake. Why would any of them help the Democrats or me? I was told that the Court had only a limited number of seats and, of course, they were not sharing.

The vice president's daughter Karenna, as well as some other people, wanted to go. And so I was told I had one seat. I decided to give my seat to Reverend Jackson because during this crisis he had called me every day, he stuck with me, and he was at my side every day of the 2000 campaign. I called Reverend and told him how to pick up his ticket and I said, "Go and sit down. Let them know that we will always fight for our rights." I really didn't have to preach to the Reverend, he had taught me how to remain faithful. Jackson went and he saw Eleanor there and after the arguments were made, he told her that he thought our case was weak. I did not understand our arguments, but I had heard the Republicans were using the Equal Protection Clause of the Fourteenth Amendment. When Eleanor and I talked about it she told me, "You know David is brilliant but they focused on equal protection."

"You mean the civil rights statutes?"

"Yes. Your guy acted as if he knew nothing about voting rights and civil rights. Why did they have him lead the case?"

"Eleanor, I'm not a lawyer. But I thought Boies was brilliant."

When the Supreme Court decision was finally handed down it was late in the evening; at the campaign headquarters and the DNC everybody was speculating what Gore would do next. The 5–4 decision to stop the count and essentially declare Bush the winner came down and we were faxed the decision, and I'm telling you, there was nothing that could have made me angrier! And I was especially angry with the Supreme Court because I had to drive past the damn building to get home. Before I went to sleep, I underlined all the offending parts of the decision regarding equal protection and I faxed it to Reverend Jackson.

I had my normal morning phone call with Daley, Greenberg, Eskew and Shrum—we talked every morning. When I got off the phone I thought about my sister, and I thought about all the phone calls I got on election day and about all the radio calls. And I called Shrum, because Bob usually helped out on important speeches. I said, "Bob I'm not gonna BlackBerry Al Gore, I'm not gonna call him because I don't believe he wants to hear from me anymore." And then I just let all my feelings out. I burst into tears and told him, "But please let him know that on election day people tried to vote and they were stopped because they were Black. He cannot give a speech to the country, he cannot concede without at least acknowledging that fact. I don't care what he says. I don't care what he thinks. I don't care about any of that. Just let the world know people tried to vote."

I cried because I had to face the prospect that we had lost. Gore had lost. I had lost. My people would now lose. The people who lived on a minimum wage would lose. The children without health care would lose. The people living in poverty would lose. They were my people. This was my journey and my mission to help the poor. I had held my tongue for weeks. Now, I thought about my sister—a resident of Seminole County, Florida—and what had happened to her. I thought about all the other people I didn't know but whose stories I had heard; I thought about the police blockades, the cabdrivers who got tickets for driving people to the polls under the guise of being ticketed for driving without a permit, and all these crazy things. I felt so bad.

I was the first Black person to run a major presidential campaign and that campaign ended up not going the distance to get every vote counted. I had quit my previous job for the Gore campaign. I had taken a pay cut. I had sacrificed. I had taken more shit than most people. I had endured death threats and I kept going every day. But the campaign was now officially over. I sat in my living room and just cried until I got a headache.

Shrum shared tears with me. We had gone through so much together. The campaign team was going to gather later in the day to mourn. We wanted to gather once more. It was a stormy day and that reflected my mood. I got a call that afternoon saying that the vice president wanted me and others from the campaign staff at his house at 6:00 PM. I immediately thought, "I can't do that." Normally I'm always thinking about what I have to do for the sake of my kids, and for the sake of the people in the campaign, and so I talked myself into going. By the end of that day it was starting to sleet, so I tried to talk myself out of going with the argument that I don't drive in sleet. I said, "I'm not even gonna get myself in the car." Then I got a Black-Berry from Tipper, a very lovely message saying she was so grateful for all my hard work.

Then I got a BlackBerry and a call from Lieberman and I decided to go. I got there right before Gore was about to get in the car to go give his concession speech at the White House. I just looked at him and said nothing. I knew if I opened my mouth I would say something I would later regret. He was giving his speech at the Old Executive Office Building. Tipper and Lieberman told me to get in the car. But I told them I would watch it at the vice president's house, and that I would be there when they got back. I did not want to be window dressing for that photo-op. I had thought about all the things I had ever fought for in politics—issues, people and, most of all, inclusion. That's when I really thought about my entire life, and knowing what I had stood for all of my life.

I poured myself the biggest glass of wine I could find. We went out back to a heated tent on the lawn. I saw many of my friends and hugged everyone. We had just gone through hell. I was dressed in all black down to my shoes. This was hard. I could barely swallow my wine, I was so upset. Gore was so graceful. That night, he wanted to begin the healing process. He wanted to help America move on and accept the verdict of the U.S. Supreme Court. I wanted to lead a massive march on Washington. I wanted to lead a protest up the steps of the Supreme Court. But as I watched the speech on television, I thought it was the best speech he gave since the convention. He mentioned what happened in Florida in passing. Clearly, he had decided to take the high road and spoke like a statesman. He was no longer Al Gore the candidate. He was back to being vice president.

They came back to the mansion and Gore went around and talked with his key supporters and the staff who had assembled. I made the rounds and walked out before the dancing started. The sleet was coming down hard and the roads were very icy. I took Rock Creek Parkway home to avoid driving past the White House, the U.S. Capitol and the U.S. Supreme Court.

Something happened to me during that campaign. For the first time in my life I realized something that Tony Coelho had drilled into me for months. I had resented him for it, I hated him for saying it, but he kept telling me, "You're a principal now. You have your own voice. You don't have to wait for someone else." I was not ready during the campaign, but driving home I decided to become my own person.

All my professional life I waited for someone else to make the important decisions that I would then implement. I was an implementer. I now saw myself as an instigator, someone who could, like Jesse Jackson, decide what I wanted to do and what I wanted to say. With the Gore campaign and the recount behind me, I no longer had a boss. And that led me into thinking my own thoughts. I wanted to write an op-ed for the *Washington Post* to discuss what happened in Florida. Driving home in the sleet forced me to focus not only on the road I was driving but on the life road I would have to learn now that I was no longer a staff person. I knew my career in politics was over for the time being. No one would hire Gore people to manage the next race unless Gore ran himself. He was tired and did not talk about the future. He still had six weeks as vice president of the United States. I was now unemployed and without health insurance or future job prospects. As campaign manager, I never entertained job offers or discussed my future. I had given Gore my word to keep my focus on his campaign and future. Now I had to face the sad music playing in the background.

I felt as if I had just left a funeral. People were crying and falling out. Many more were just as emotional but did not shed tears. They wanted to fight like me. I understood losing. Losing is part of the political game. It is after all like sports, where the preseason often lasts longer than the season. I had been in the longest political season of my life and I had the battle scars and wounds to prove it.

Physical wounds are often healed with medication and time. But this wound went deeper than the surface of my skin—I was hurting inside. My pride was wounded. My joy was nowhere to be found. My optimism about American politics was shattered. I could no longer preach the gospel of political participation after what I had just experienced. No matter what the media was saying, Gore was right to try to get a recount to settle the 2000 presidential campaign. But I learned a valuable lesson about running against Republicans: be prepared to fight a bloody battle for control of government. They were ruthless. They were bullies and they took no prisoners. By the time I parked my Jeep and climbed the stairs to my home I was so weak I could have fainted. I made it inside and just fell out on the sofa and went to sleep. The campaign was over. My body ached and my muscles were no longer willing to carry my weight. That night I slept so hard that I didn't hear the phone ring. My family tried all night to reach me. They wanted to know if they needed to come to Washington.

We Braziles were still sticking together. I now needed my real family, because my political family was moving on.

CHAPTER SEVENTEEN

CAFÉ DU MONDE:
COFFEE AND BEIGNETS

The Café Du Monde was established in 1862 and is still open 24 hours a day, closing only for Christmas and hurricanes. Its famous coffee is flavored with chicory, made from the root of the endive plant. The coffee perfectly complements their beignets, square French-style doughnuts, smothered in powdered sugar. For me, the combination of the two evokes one thing: being home with my family.

THE NEXT MORNING, I wanted to take the first plane to New Orleans and stop by Café Du Monde for some hot coffee with chicory and French Market doughnuts. My house was quiet. I kept the blinds shut and the curtains closed. There was a real sense of loss all around me. Lionel had warned me that the election would be stolen and I blew him off. Yet I did everything to alert the proper officials at the Justice Department and in the civil rights community. Still, we were not prepared for the long battle of trying to recount the vote.

Throughout those long, anguishing thirty-six days that gripped the nation and the world, I spent each day retracing our steps and trying to keep the kids in the loop. I tried to keep cool under tremendous pressure. At times, I felt humiliated by Gore or Daley for not bringing me back in the loop to discuss strategy, but I tried to retain my dignity. For weeks I kept silent at the recount office. As during the campaign, I was often the last to leave at night. The consultants did all the talking. I kept getting reports from the staff down in Florida and watched CNN for any breaking news. No one, it seemed, cared about anything I was saying about voting rights. I tried not to play the race card even when the situation called for it because the intimidation down in Florida was clearly aimed at minorities and first-time voters. I just held back. I avoided any confrontations.

For months, Reverend Jesse Jackson was my best friend. In the end, he was there for me. He called me on the morning of December 14 and told me that I had "performed my job with grace and dignity." I was back with my political family now. Back with the boats stuck at the bottom, but I preferred to be with them than with people who did not care about the downtrodden in society. He told me to take some time off and get rested. I agreed. I was still operating on fumes and my fuel was running low. Once again I had to pack my bags, so I went over to the DNC and gathered up all my files. I sent Gore copies of all the campaign records just in case he wanted to send thank-you notes or run again in 2004. Gore was still the leader of the party and I was not about to leave without helping him prepare for the future.

As I sat at my desk reading the newspaper and listening to commentators talk about the recount on the news, I wanted to curl up like a baby and cry. This was one of the worst moments in my life. It was as if someone had cut me wide open and poured salt in the wound, and the wound kept growing deeper as stories poured in about the fate many citizens faced when they tried to vote. At 1:30 PM I decided to go home and call Lionel. He could help me sort this out.

I called but he wasn't home, which was weird because he rarely left the house anymore. Lisa didn't know his whereabouts and Sheila was not around. I called Sister Charlotte Ellzey, his good friend and my spiritual aunt, and asked for some advice. Like Reverend, she wanted me to get out of Washington and get some rest. She suggested Hawaii. My friend Kristina lived out there with her husband. I knew they would welcome me and I left a message with them. The plane ticket was $2,100 and I put it on my credit card. Lionel called back. He was at the doctor's office. My dad asked if I was sitting down because he had some news. My God, I couldn't take any more drama—throughout the course of the campaign, Lionel and I had grown to be very close. Al Gore helped me understand Lionel—his rage, his temperament, his humility and his humanity. The man was no saint, but he was my dad and I had come to respect and like him.

"Guess what, Donna?"

"What, Lionel?"

"I am cancer free."

"What?"

He began talking about his new diet and faith. For a moment I got lost listening to him talk about God, miracles and the power of faith. He should have been a priest. But then he indulged in things that men of the cloth were not supposed to enjoy. I wanted to know about Al Gore and why we lost. Lionel cleared his throat and said, "It's God's will and nobody should be upset." Lionel told me that I had done my job, but it was now over. I needed more than God's will. "What did we do wrong, Lionel?" I asked. "What could we have done differently?" He did not take the bait. He was my dad, not a political analyst. I got off the phone with him and called Eleanor. Unlike Lionel and Sister Charlotte, she would give me the nonbiblical answer I was looking for.

Eleanor was a woman of faith. But that was not the only way she drew her strength or passion. She was about the letter of the law. The Court, she told me, had given the election to Bush. After her review of the decision, it was clear Gore had to concede the election. Eleanor wanted to come over and check on me, but my house looked as if Hurricane Betsy had been through it. I told her that I needed to rest. By the end of the day I got a phone call from Dick Gephardt.

"Donna, you did great. You won that election and they took it from you. Now, get some rest. Do you need anything?"

"No, Congressman, I am going to be fine."

"What about health insurance? Do you want to come back to Capitol Hill to work for a few months just to keep your benefits?" he asked.

"No, I have to figure this all out, but I love you, Dick Gephardt."

"Jane and I love you, too," he said.

I went upstairs and took a long, hot bath. I had to clear my head again. My forty-first birthday was just hours away. I wanted to find a way to celebrate my life and accomplishments. When I emerged from the tub, I called Steven Damato and reserved a table at Nora's. Steve told me to come on by tomorrow. They would give me a private room upstairs. I immediately called Minyon, Julia, Tina, Eleanor, Ceci Connolly of the *Washington Post,* Kit Seelye of the *New York Times,* Karen Tumulty of *Time* magazine, Sandra Sobieraj of the Associated Press, Audrey Haynes and Tipper and told them all to come over to celebrate. I was treating. Although we did not win, I wanted to relax and hang out with some of my best friends and the reporters who had covered the Gore campaign. It was an odd mixture of old and new friends, Black and White women who had stood by me during one of the toughest periods of my life, plus the reporters who witnessed it all. Once gathered, we got down to real business and began talking about what women always talk about when we're not busy with our careers: good food and clothes.

A week after Al Gore officially ended his campaign, I received my last paycheck from the Recount Committee. It was just under $2,000 and I immediately cashed it and paid some of my bills. I went over to the DNC to say good-bye to the chairman and his staff, who had practically turned the party's headquarters over to the recount staff during those long thirty-six days and nights. Joe Andrew, who is usually cheerful and upbeat, was in a dour mood. His staff greeted me with suspicion and I was anxious to know why they were acting so silly. Joe looked up at me and said, "Have you spoken with the vice president?" I looked surprised because I had not spoken with Gore since his concession speech.

Apparently, Joe had learned that Gore had approved of the decision to allow Terry McAuliffe to run the Democratic National Committee. During all of our grieving and mourning, a small group of

White House aides were meeting privately to plot the next steps. When I heard the story, I blew up at Joe and demanded to know more. The first thing Joe told me was "Gore wanted Daley to handle the transition." Well, this was news to me. Throughout the campaign, Bill Daley showed no interest in the Democratic National Committee, its politics or its members. Why, I thought, would Gore move Daley in when the only two people on his team with DNC experience were Michael Whouley and me. As Joe shared more information about the plans under way to take the DNC away from Gore and place it back firmly in the hands of the Clintons, I grew alarmed.

For the first time in my association with the Clintons, whom I strongly supported, I was worried that they, too, were about to take the Black vote for granted. All I could do was pick up the phone and my BlackBerry and start emailing everyone inside the White House and over at the vice president's office. Gore had taken his BlackBerry off and did not answer his private lines at the residence. I received another call that afternoon from Joe Andrew who said he was going over to meet with Al Gore. I asked him to share with Gore my concerns. There had been another meeting earlier that day at the White House and the decision had been made to put forth Terry McAuliffe to serve as chair of the DNC. I said to myself, "Damn, we have not even buried this campaign and they are already making a move. This is back to the Gore versus Clinton war."

Without much thinking, the first thing I decided to do was to take on Terry McAuliffe. If Al Gore didn't want to fight, I did. I felt they were not taking over the party for the right reasons. They wanted to continue the status quo. I was not about the status quo. I felt that history would ultimately judge me not by the vote I got out but by what happened in Florida. So my entire focus was still on voting rights. I had decided to make that my crusade. What did Terry McAuliffe know about Florida or the Gore campaign? Terry, who had helped us raise money for the convention and two major DNC events, was not a strategist or an organizer. Why would anybody place him in charge of the oldest political party in the country? I decided to call Maxine Waters and Al Edwards, the chair of the DNC

Black Caucus, to see if they had heard about the decision to place Terry in charge of the party.

Maxine, as expected, was unaware of any new changes at the DNC, and because no one at the White House bothered to call her, she was pissed. I knew she would follow up and cuss out whoever was in charge. Al, a state legislator from Houston, was the chair of the largest constituency group inside the party. Without the support of that constituency, no one could win any position in the Democratic Party. Clinton knew that. Gore understood that. I was about to find out if anyone had the nerve to install a chairman without consulting the Black leadership.

Al was at work when I finally reached him. "Al, this is Donna. Have you approved Terry McAuliffe as chairman of the Democratic National Committee?" I demanded to know. Al was stunned. One of the things I liked most about Al was his candor. A good ol' Southern gentleman. He was out of the loop as well. I promised to get back to him. Maxine reached me on my cell. She was ready to rumble.

I did not have anything against Terry McAuliffe, whom I had gotten to know and work with in Gephardt's 1988 presidential campaign. A Syracuse, New York, native, Terry was one of the happiest men I had ever met. He could raise a dollar from a poor man or woman. But in the aftermath of a 49–49 election, I wanted to see someone like James Carville or Paul Begala take over the party. I wanted to see the Gore staffers stay on the payroll and perhaps go to work at the state and local levels. Of course, I wanted to stick around to help with the transition to place our field and political staff in congressional offices or with progressive organizations. But I did not need to be there physically to do my work. Donnie Fowler or another Gore senior staff person could take the lead. Instead, we were all being shoved right out the door without the courtesy of a thank-you note or call. The message, intended or not, to the Gore folks was: "Good-bye, warriors. The old team is coming back." I'm sorry, I did not expect to get shoved out the door so soon after not only "winning" an election but also getting out more votes for Gore than any Democrat in the history of American politics.

I called Minyon over at the White House and told her, "I'm very tired and I really don't want to call the vice president, but is it true that you are about to replace Joe Andrews with Terry McAuliffe?" She confirmed it, and told me that Bill Daley knew about it, and that the vice president was meeting with Terry in another hour. Now I was livid. Gore was in on it and did not have the guts to call me and discuss it. I did not understand the harm in discussing the future of the Democratic Party with people from inside the Gore campaign. Grandma taught me what truly must have come straight out of the Bible: The Lord said, "Let vengeance be mine."

My concern was that the party was going back to business as usual. I thought the party should be focusing on what had just happened, the fact that we had just lost an election because the Supreme Court of the United States had stopped the vote and because there were serious voting violations. It was time for me to go back to being Black. I called Maxine Waters again. I called Eleanor and Charlie Rangel. I told them that we had to come up with a response to this latest move. It was clear Gore didn't want us involved because he hadn't called any of us. "He's gonna put his boy Terry up to run, and we have to have a seat at the table. They cannot just tell us who they want." They asked me if I had an alternative candidate. I didn't, but I promised to have one in twenty-four hours. The next day, I had my candidate—Maynard Jackson.

A former mayor of Atlanta, Maynard was a giant inside the Democratic Party. He was a role model for urban mayors, transforming Atlanta into a thriving metropolis. After leaving office he established a lucrative business as an investment banker. We settled on Maynard because Maxine wanted someone who could go on TV and articulate our agenda. I agreed. He could sway some of the votes from Whites in the South who were upset that the Gore campaign had completely written off the Deep South. I called Maynard to offer my hand of support. I told him of my trip to Hawaii and that I could make phone calls from there to help shore up his support. No sooner was I off the phone with Maynard than Terry called to ask for support.

"Donna, Terry McAuliffe, how are you doing?" he asked. I felt like telling him, "None of your damn business." Instead I put on my finest hour of bullshit and political spin and began talking about the Florida recount. I could tell from Terry's silence that he could feel my pain and frustration. After a few minutes of letting some air out of my exhausted body, I cut to the chase.

"So, Terry, you are calling for my support?"

"Yes, I would like your help."

"Have you heard about Maynard Jackson?"

"No, what's he doing?"

"Sir, he is planning on running against you on a platform to change the way the party courts voters in the future."

Terry, who is an eternal optimist, quickly ceded the call and told me I would come around soon to support him. "Right," I said.

I was the former campaign manager and I decided to do a quick check to see if I could pull off an upset and beat Terry. Within days of the Christmas holidays, I learned that Terry had captured the chairs of New York, Pennsylvania, Illinois, Michigan and California. Maynard had the chair of Louisiana, the District of Columbia and Georgia. Terry had also locked up Dick Gephardt and Tom Daschle, the Democratic leaders in the U.S. Senate. One thing I learned to do as a child was count. We did not have the numbers. Even if Maynard could win all ninety-two members of the DNC Black Caucus, we did not have the votes. Maxine was convinced that regardless of the tally, Maynard could still win. I agreed. The same formula that worked for Jesse Jackson could work for Maynard. I decided to play broker, to get something in return for all my years of sacrifice. I wanted to find out how the Republicans stole the election and intimidated so many of our voters across the country. I had to learn the lessons not only in losing the electoral votes but of how to help future citizens secure their voting rights. Maynard and Maxine agreed. Now it was time to convince others inside the party to help me investigate what happened in Florida.

The DNC was the logical place to start an investigation. The Republicans had taken control of both houses of Congress and I knew they would never lead such an investigation. The party needed a complete inquiry into the numerous violations of the Voting Rights

Act and a staff inside to compile data to be passed on to the U.S. Civil Rights Commission and other groups, including the media, who had begun their own investigation. For me personally, this was the only reason to worry about the chairman of the party. I wanted to figure out how so many Americans had their ballots spoiled. I knew we would never allow this to happen again. This wasn't about making strategic blunders, even though we did those, too. This was about something bigger.

The choice of Terry McAuliffe was part of a bigger turf war. McAuliffe was Clinton's choice to head the party. When a presidential election is over, the party goes back to the people in charge. Gore was tired. He was not interested. Although I tried to get him to understand that the DNC was the ball game until the next election, he made it very clear to me when I talked to him that he didn't care. Gore would let the Clintons take over.

Lieberman called me. He was still upset. His call prompted me to call Gore again. Two years on the road with someone brings you quite close. I knew he was ready to move on, but I still had questions to figure out. When I asked how he was doing he was noncommunicative.

"What's up?"

"Nothing," he said.

"I hear you."

"What you gonna do now?"

"Nothing."

"Got you. Anymore on what's happening?"

"No."

"Thank you."

Gore was in no mood to share his feelings or to give me any direction about the future. He was hurting pretty badly. I wanted to help him, but he was not the kind of person who would ask for help. Tipper was there. He had a family.

I called Reverend Barrow and Reverend Jackson. I decided to spend as much time as I could afford in Hawaii to replenish myself. I was brokering for the Voting Rights Institute within the party so that the party would never again be the victim of what had happened in Florida. It didn't matter to me if it was just me against the whole party. I was determined that Black people would never be betrayed again. How could I ask my people to vote for a party that didn't value their votes? I was still angry and felt a responsibility to both the millions who voted and the tens of thousands who could not vote.

The *Washington Post* quoted a senior Republican strategist as saying, "Yes, the Democrats got out the vote, but their people were too stupid to know how to exercise that right." I was so pissed that I called the *Washington Post* editorial board and asked if I could write an op-ed to focus on the need for election reform across the country. Everybody was concentrating so much on swinging chads, pregnant chads, dimpled chads from the notorious antiquated punch-card ballot machines that they had forgotten all about the fundamental right to vote.

The piece was published on Christmas Day. I read it while flying twelve straight hours to Kona, Hawaii, to celebrate Christmas with Bob Friedman and Kristina Kiehl—two wonderful old friends who had nurtured me since my early twenties. After a few days in the sun, I got back on my computer, even though I needed to rest and relax. The members of the 107th Congress were about to take their seats and Gore emailed me and asked if he should attend the Black Caucus ceremony. I told him he should go and explain his position. I told him in my email, "Sir, with all due respect, they are a little angry. You're going into choppy waters but I'm sure they will be glad to see you."

Not only was the Black Caucus ready to see him, they were ready to tell him what they thought about Florida. They told him everything. And they told him that they still planned to protest, that when the time came for them to cast their ballots, they would be casting their ballots for him and not Bush. "No, no, no," he told them. He was trying to get me, from Hawaii, to tell these Black leaders to stop protesting. I emailed him back. "I can't help you, I'm protesting, too."

As Gore presided over the Senate for the actual votes, members of the Black Caucus wanted the Senate to protest. They looked for a senator to support the protest, but not one, including Lieberman, would launch the protest. The Black Caucus was very upset; it was pretty bad. So we thought the best way to channel our dissatisfaction was to create within the party an independent institute that would protect our rights.

When I finally got back to the mainland—after Bush was sworn in—I received an invite to come up to Harvard's Institute of Politics for the spring semester. I agreed and emailed Gore, who was also elated.

Even at Harvard, I was still working the phones to get the best possible deal for Maynard. Minyon was assisting Terry and was willing to help us negotiate. Maynard knew the votes were not there, but he was going to hold out. Terry wanted to meet with the Black Caucus before the official start of the DNC's winter meeting. It was being held in Washington, D.C., and I finally came back home.

When Terry arrived at the Caucus meeting, Maxine was about to come on stage to "rev up" the crowd. She held back for a moment. Terry was so nervous. He had built up an incredible base of support inside the party with donors and key leaders from across the country. Since Gore did not publicly object, I kept most of my fire off the record or on background with certain reporters I could trust. I was fine. My deal was done, but I had to be reassured that the party would never turn its back on African Americans or other minorities. Not only did Terry give me his word, I knew Minyon would make sure he would never turn his nose up at us. Besides, Terry agreed to raise money to launch an investigation into Florida and to hold town hall meetings across the country to find out what happened.

We didn't have the votes to put Maynard in as DNC chair, but he still wanted to play a major role in the party. So Minyon, Regena Thomas, another Jackson campaign alumna and the two vice chairs, Lottie Shackelford and Bill Lynch, decided to get together before the meeting to hammer out the details of our agreement. Terry could become chair if Maynard became the national development chair, meaning a separate chair with equal strength and a budget. We wanted his major responsibility to be the head of the National Voting Rights Institute. We established it based on my resolution. I was now brokering Black politics the way Jackson taught us: stand firm and never lose sight of the mission.

Terry won. Maynard hit the ground running the Voting Rights Institute (VRI) and raising money for the party, which he did until his death in 2003. During his tenure as chairman, he held town hall meetings in every region of the country and he demonstrated that with the proper reforms in place, Florida should never happen again. The Republican-controlled Congress, as expected, took its sweet time in passing a bipartisan Election Reform bill to improve the way we vote. The bill made its way through Congress and was signed by President Bush on October 29, 2002. The Help America Vote Act (HAVA) is designed to help correct many of the irregularities that took place on that awful day back in 2000. Many states went ahead to replace their punch ballot machines with sophisticated electronic voting machines that have proved to be just as controversial as the old machines.

I HAD SPOKEN TO GORE on January 20, the day of George W. Bush's inauguration. That was it for several months. He was so tired and beaten. Gore was weary and felt responsible for the loss and he took it hard. I felt sorry for him. Gore had his flaws, as we all do, yet his were always magnified much more than Bush's. I could only imagine Gore's anger and disgust. I wanted to make him some gumbo to help warm him up, but he did not want to talk. I felt the pain of separation. Gore was not rejecting me so much as pushing me away to avoid seeing the hurt and pain on my face. He could not take it, let alone console anyone else. Most of us who worked on the campaign found ourselves talking to each other because it was hard to transition back to our ordinary lives. We all felt bad for the country, too. We had let down the people we had fought for in the campaign. They took the hit for our mistakes, and all we could do was say, "We're sorry. We tried."

I spent 2001 and much of 2002 on the road to political recovery and preaching the virtues of voting. It's been a long way back, but I am now focused on training and educating a new generation of political activists to take their seats at the table. When I left Harvard, I went back to the DNC and asked to be an intern. Yep, an intern. I made a decision to help young people get excited about politics. Minyon was also in charge of the day-to-day operations of the party and I wanted to help her out the way she helped me in 2000. So, after having my photo taken, I received my intern badge. I made a decision to help the party win elections in 2001, and we were in for some big surprises. I went back to serving as an adjunct professor at the University of Maryland teaching African-American Participation in American Politics. I moved on, but without taking a long look back on my career and journey in American politics.

Of all of the war stories and major events of my life as the first Black to run a major presidential campaign, I'll never forget the meeting in April 2000 with Gore about the $5.6 trillion budget surplus. He sat us all in a room and asked what were the priorities we should have for using that money. Of course, his priorities were education and the environment. I raised my hand and said health care. I would never trade the ability to be there when those decisions are made. By getting involved, I was allowed to sit at the table.

I've worked on Capitol Hill and I know how laws are made. I know how decisions at the highest levels of government are made, and I would never give that up no matter what kind of hell you go through. This much I know: Democracy is worth fighting for.

I used to sit in the rooms with my colleagues and think, I'm the only person in this room who knows what it's like to live on minimum wage, and knowing that it won't get you anywhere. I knew the price of bread, the cost of a dozen eggs. I knew the price of a gallon of milk. I felt as if my purpose there was to be as real as anybody could be with people who had lost touch with reality. I used to tell Gore, "You know why I'm in this? I'm in it because when I was growing up, as one of nine children, we were poor." I told him about the food stamps. I told him about everything and said, "Throughout this campaign, I'm gonna remind you what people back home would tell you. I'm gonna be that voice."

There was also the fulfillment of a dream. Some people want to be doctors, lawyers, firefighters or teachers; I wanted to be a campaign manager. I wanted to run a presidential campaign. So I was living my dream. And all the intrigue and conflict—that's part of it. Politics is a blood sport. So I like being in the game. I'm a fighter. I am a survivor.

Soon after President Bush's inaugural in 2001, I called Karl Rove—Bush's right hand and some would say his brain—to congratulate him on their success. We agreed to maintain a civil and constructive dialogue. I can report that Karl is always gracious and has always returned my calls and responded to my letters. I have only lobbied him for one thing: improved elections.

We have continued to maintain a dialogue about current events. In 2002, I went home to help my friend Senator Mary Landrieu defend her seat. The Republicans spent over $22 million to defeat her. We spent less than $5 million and won the election by pulling Blacks out in record numbers.

Yet I know it will be difficult to pull Blacks or any other voters out in record numbers unless Congress fully funds the electoral reforms that the states must make in order to have an error-free and transparent election. These states not only need money to upgrade their voting systems and set uniform national standards for election procedures, they need resources to help update their voter registration lists.

I would gladly go back door-to-door urging citizens to register and vote. I wouldn't mind standing at bus and subway stops to run people down to the polls before they close. But I cannot face another Florida-style election.

No one, especially the citizens who were the last to receive the franchise, should be denied their constitutional right to vote. This is now my mission and my purpose for staying actively engaged and personally involved in the political arena.

It's about the right to vote. It's about exercising that right, too. It's about respecting that right and never denying it to anyone based on the color of his or her skin.

As long as there is breath in my body, I will stir the pots in American politics. For too many Americans, politics is boring. Some people believe that their votes will not make a difference. Well, we could have used some of those votes in 2000. While over 100 million Americans cast their ballots on November 7, 2000, over 75 million stayed home and did not even put up a fight. Many of these Americans are the people Al Gore was fighting for. He wanted to help ease the financial burden and the uncertainties of their lives with strong, capable leadership. Gore did not get a chance to lead America in the twenty-first century. Gore did not get a chance to meet my mother or my grandmothers.

Had they been alive, Al Gore would have enjoyed their company and vice versa. Jean would have stirred up some creamy red beans and rice and andouille sausages or a bowl of jambalaya. Grandma would have made him an okra dish with shrimp and corn and some crabmeat Lafitte. Mama would have made her favorite étouffée or bisque from the fresh seafood of the bayous, rivers or canals. My sisters and brothers did get a chance to meet Al Gore and I am proud to report that Gore won 100 percent of the Brazile vote.

I have since spoken and broken bread with Al Gore. He remains one of my friends and I seek his advice from time to time. Gore decided not to run in 2004. He thought the party needed a fresh start and a fresh face. He was right on both counts. He is now in the private sector and teaches a class at Fisk University. Tipper is busy writing and working with her favorite charities. She has long championed issues like women's rights, mental health and education. We remain close and in contact all the time. I am grateful for their love and friendship.

At times it was hard to understand my role and responsibility. But I always found time, whether flying on Air Force Two or back home in Louisiana, to pray to God for wisdom and strength. God never abandoned me on my long journey. I remain faithful to continue on my mission to stir more pots in American politics.

ELECTORAL GUMBO:
A NEW RECIPE
FOR VICTORY

ON MY FORTY-THIRD BIRTHDAY, in 2002, Al Gore announced that he would not be running again for the presidency. In his remarks, made after appearing on CBS's *60 Minutes,* Gore stated that he, as always, had made the right political calculation. Democrats were not anxious to replay the last presidential campaign. Many of us seasoned veterans wanted a new beginning, a fresh start. The fiasco in Florida seemed like ages ago.

For me, the last four years have allowed me some reflection on my role in American politics and the national landscape in general. Although I no longer work directly for political candidates, I have been astonished at the amount I am able to accomplish even from the sidelines. I am committed now more than ever to making sure all Americans have a voice in the political process, and that means encouraging the next generation of leaders to become actively engaged now.

There is no more important responsibility that we have as citizens than going to the ballot box and choosing our representatives. For years as a campaign organizer I registered tens of thousands of voters—bringing new voices to our political process. As a campaign manager I worked to get out the vote by convincing voters to go to the polls. I have long believed that there is no more important right we could have as citizens. Yet in 2000, that sacred right suffered immensely. Because of the closeness of the Florida vote, Americans got to take an up-close and personal look at our electoral system, warts and all. What we saw wasn't pretty.

Because many of the problems of the last presidential election are still with us, it is still my mission to make sure that every vote counts in America. After the 2000 election, and the hope of reform, I thought voting problems might be behind us. But then Katherine Harris, the Florida secretary of state who certified the election results there, won a congressional seat and moved in down the street from me on Capitol Hill. So I know this problem is going to follow me for a while.

I am also concerned about the future of the Democratic Party and the progressive movement for reform and change in American public policy. Throughout the 1990s, the American left was dead, the victim of centrist politics and a prosperous economy. In the 2000 presidential campaign, many rank-and-file Democrats had forgotten what they were all about. They forgot about the struggles of the 1980s. They forgot about injustice and millions of Americans still being left behind in poverty or with stagnant wages. With a Democrat in the White House in the 1990s, it was easy to believe that good times left no one behind. It was easy to turn a blind eye to the injustices that surrounded them. Those were good times. Democrats were in control of the executive branch. But for many leaders inside the beltway, there was no fight left in them. Today, though, things are changing. George Bush, Tom DeLay, John Ashcroft, Donald Rumsfeld and Antonin Scalia have breathed new life into the progressive movement and the Democratic Party.

Many of us have spent the last three years watching George W. Bush and the GOP-controlled Congress put into action the most extreme right-wing agenda this nation has ever seen. Liberals and progressives, awakened from their slumber, are now adamant that Bush must be beaten in 2004.

The Bush administration and the radical right-wing Congress gave rank-and-file Democrats something to be angry about. They brought moderates and liberals together again with policies that favored the rich, trashed the environment, trampled on a woman's right to choose, overlooked enforcement of civil rights laws and promoted policies for corporate special interests over average folks. The nation was thrown from a great budget surplus under the Democrats back into massive budget deficits under the Republican leadership. A national recession, followed by a jobless "recovery," cost millions of ordinary Americans their jobs. Corporate scandals and greed stole the pension savings and the hopes of workers across the nation. The seeds of change have finally taken root in American politics. It's time for Democrats and progressives to stir the pots in 2004 and beyond. The political landscape has shifted.

No one will ever forget September 11, 2001—the most horrific attack on our nation's soil since the attack on Pearl Harbor. For a moment, the president and his Democratic critics came together. We stood shoulder to shoulder with our commander in chief to go after those who ruthlessly murdered more than three thousand people. Democrats sought to work with the Bush administration, but Republicans never wanted our hand in battle, just acquiescence and silent agreement. That desire was affirmed by the decision to invade Iraq under the false pretense that they had weapons of mass destruction. President Bush's decision to rush the nation to war threw fuel on an already burning fire.

The Iraq war brought out the progressive movement in full force. Not since the heyday of the 1960s had war protests been so large. The progressive movement hit the streets in multitudes to protest the decision to go to war. Although they did not garner the type of attention and headlines of the past, they have helped to revive the Democratic Party. Many of those individuals were organized with the help of the Internet. These groups and leaders are still actively engaged in the electoral arena and will make a difference in 2004 and beyond.

As I write this, Republicans not only control the White House but the Senate, the House and the majority of state houses across the country. Democrats cannot afford to spend future electoral seasons wringing their hands. In order to defeat this president and future ones like him, Democrats must bring forth a new recipe for victory. In this new recipe, Democrats must go back to the twenty states and the District of Columbia that voted for Al Gore in 2000 and reengage voters there to take back their country. The party must also compete in the Deep South and capture Democrats who often vote during the primary season but who are not courted to vote in the general election. States like Louisiana, Arkansas, Tennessee and Florida are fertile ground for a new generation of Democratic activists and leaders. Democrats should also enlarge the electorate, bringing in more young voters and reawakening voters who have tuned out of politics. Democrats must energize their core base of voters and reach out to as many nonvoters as possible. We must expand geographically and redouble our efforts to win Nevada and Arizona—two more western states to add to our electoral gumbo.

Unless Democrats put up a fight in 2004 and beyond at all levels, we face possible political extinction. Karl Rove, Bush's political guru and someone I have come to respect for his personal tenacity and strategic understanding of the political landscape, is putting all his chips on giving the GOP a supermajority in Congress in this electoral cycle. The Democratic Party must not allow this to happen.

Fortunately, the sentiments of citizens across the country show that Democrats have every opportunity to stop Karl Rove and the countless Republican strategists who will follow in his footsteps. When average citizens are asked to describe the mood of our nation, their answers are stark; for them, this age is marked by uncertainty, chaos and fear. This pervasive anxiety does not come just from the fear of terrorism, as the Bush administration would like the nation to believe. The real problem is the sense that our nation has lost its way and that politicians have lost our trust. Americans are calling for leadership and stability—in education, in jobs, in the economy, in the cost of health insurance and in foreign policy. The president promised to unite Americans; instead, he has consistently divided them. Yet the American people will not be divided in calling for a renewed vision of justice and fairness for every citizen.

Democrats in Washington and progressive leaders across the country are beginning to get smarter. They have done what strong minority parties need to do in order to survive and reemerge as the dominant political party once again, using the Republican Party and its allies of the 1970s and early 1980s as an example. They have founded left-leaning think tanks, like the Center for American Progress, to compete against such groups as the CATO Institute, the Heritage Foundation and the American Enterprise Institute. They have organized groups, such as Americans Coming Together (ACT) and Unity '04, dedicated to registering new voters and getting out the vote. Plans are in place to communicate a broad, uplifting message at the local level and to organize. Democrats are even trying to purchase local radio stations to communicate directly with voters. In both Washington and across the country, Democrats are poised to bring new, fresh, inspiring, passionate leadership to America again.

Above all, my party must not run away from its core beliefs. Americans are tired of the same rhetoric, the same safe messages, the same meaningless banter. As a party, we must remind Americans what the Democratic Party stands for. My fellow Americans say they are apprehensive about the direction of the country. They feel like their voice is silenced by the much louder yelp of corporate America and its interests. They believe their government can be bought and sold. Being a Democrat means standing up for these people and for their voices.

Over the last several years I have had the opportunity to educate young people about American politics. We all must do a better job of bringing younger Americans into the political process. So many issues that we face today—the looming Social Security crisis, the national debt, the future of foreign policy—will have a direct impact on the next generation. We must encourage them to follow politics, to take positions and, most important, to vote.

Even from the sidelines of professional politics I'm working to make a difference. From traveling to college towns all over America to teaching at the University of Maryland, Harvard's Institute of Politics and Georgetown University, I have renewed my vows to help the next generation of Americans take their seats at the table. I have found joy in writing political columns for *Roll Call,* one of the newspapers of Capitol Hill, and in serving as a weekly commentator on CNN's *Inside Politics.*

I have come a long way, from riding my bicycle door-to-door

in Kenner, Louisiana, to registering my neighbors to managing the day-to-day political activities for my party's presidential nominee. Throughout my journey my faith in God and my passion for people have helped make the difference. I truly believe that one person can make a difference—and many Americans working together can make a big difference. The direction of our nation is too important to ignore, too important to leave to others. It's time for every citizen to reassess their commitment to our country and participate in the political process.

There is an ebb and flow to politics. Sometimes you're up, and then you're down. Things go your way, and then they don't. It can be frustrating. It can get bitter. The road toward victory is paved with stumbling blocks. I have spent my entire life removing barriers to participation, and I know the real obstacles that keep change from being made. Yet I also know that real progress can be made in this country. I have seen African Americans and women serve in the highest levels of our government. One day, I know America will finally elect a minority or a woman to the White House. I know America will live up to its ideals.

My own journey in American politics is a testament to that hope. The struggle for inclusion is hard, but the prizes are great. They are the ideals of this nation itself: freedom, liberty, equality and justice for all Americans. So long as I have breath in my body, I will continue to work toward them. I was raised to stir the pots, and I'm not stopping now.

PICKLED OKRA

A LITTLE AFTER MIDNIGHT on election night 2004, I caught a bad case of the blues when the results began to pour in from across America. After months of campaigning across the country for the Democratic Party and some of my progressive causes, I went into instant shock as a fresh batch of exit polls caught up with reality.

Senator John Kerry, who defeated a large number of Democrats in the primaries, along with his running mate, former senator John Edwards (D-North Carolina), was beginning to lose some key battleground states. No sooner had the polls closed in Florida than the networks began to make their early projections. President George W. Bush, who was behind all day in the exit polls posted throughout the blogosphere, was now slightly leading Kerry. This news made me downright sick and tired. Unless we Democrats captured Ohio—a state where citizens were still standing in long lines to vote—the night would soon be over.

On Election Day, I was on the phone literally all day talking up Kerry and the need to get out to vote. Although I had talking points provided by the campaign, I felt more comfortable using my own words.

> *This is Donna Brazile calling from the Democratic National Committee to remind you today is Freedom Day. This is a day to free yourself from the war in Iraq. A day to free your families and communities from a jobless recovery. A day to free yourself of four more years of George W. Bush. Vote today. Urge your friends and family to stand with you.*

I enjoyed working the phones and walking the streets urging complete strangers to vote. There's nothing quite like seeing people vote for the first time. The weekend before, I was down in Orlando with Congresswoman Corrine Brown (D-Florida), urging citizens to vote early. Our message was "Vote early for Kerry and you will not have to stay up all night waiting for the results." Clearly, the results still coming in on election night were sobering. Slowly, my mood began to shift from the merely blue to a total funk. I was hungry, too.

Before rushing over to the CNN studio in Washington, D.C., where I was scheduled to discuss the election results with my good friend Wolf Blitzer and the other election night specialists, I made a quick dash to my home on Capitol Hill to get something soothing to eat. I was running on an empty stomach (I'd been too tired to walk down the street for a salad or soup during lunchtime). My staff was scattered throughout the country doing election protection work, and I stayed in Washington, D.C., to help with other problems.

Chip, my little Pomeranian, greeted me at the door when I arrived. He wanted to play fetch. Chip ran around the living room as if nothing was happening. Well, he's a dog, and it was time for him to use the outside facilities.

Back inside the house, I noticed my refrigerator was empty. Just half-empty jars of mustard and pickles. No meat. No eggs. No bread. And no time to thaw out some seafood gumbo or leftover red beans. But I did find something way in the back of the icebox that made my mouth water. I saw a full jar of my sister Lisa's pickled okra and took it along with a bag of potato chips and drove myself to the CNN Washington Bureau. Thank God for family members who sent me care packages every month with tasty treats and goodies from Louisiana.

The election news did not get any better as I sat there in front of CNN's TV monitors and ate my cold pickled okra with salty potato chips. New Hampshire, which voted in 2000 for Bush, flipped for Kerry, but things did not look so good in the rest of the country, especially in the South. Not one state was coming our way.

I hated losing the South to Bush again. But the reality is that we have conceded the entire region, with the exception of Florida, to the

Republicans since the 2000 campaign. Still, I was praying for an upset in Virginia or in Senator Edwards's home state of North Carolina.

Suddenly, my mood shifted and became somber as more states
like Missouri went into the red, or GOP, column. Unless we captured
Ohio, I kept thinking to myself, it's over. How could this be?

The Democratic Party in 2004 was in its best shape ever. Even
with the new campaign finance reform laws limiting the amount of
money we could collect from the so-called rich and famous, the
party's donor base had nearly tripled. In my opinion, we had former
governor Howard Dean and the other Democratic candidates to
thank for energizing and motivating ordinary people to reclaim their
party and government.

Although turnout was extremely high throughout the day with so
many new voters showing up at the polls, Bush and the Republican
Party managed to pull out more people and swamp election offices
across the country with local volunteers willing to do whatever it
took to get out the GOP vote.

But the awful, sorrowful news kept coming in from exit polls and
from the official tabulations from the states: Bush was winning the
electoral vote by a slim margin, and it appeared from the early tabulations that the president's popular vote margins were also increasing.
This caused me to worry. I thought we did everything right in 2004
in targeting our base in key battleground states, enlarging the electorate and engaging young people to rally to our side.

What went wrong for the Democrats?

How could Kerry be losing when every poll conducted in the final
weeks had the Democratic nominee ahead by two points or more?

Just as I was beginning to withdraw emotionally from the terrible
news, I saw one of the producers walking toward my interim desk.
CNN has lots of producers. Normally, I am familiar with the folks
involved in programming one of my regular shows like *Inside Politics* or
American Morning. This was a new face, and I did not know his name.
He seemed in a hurry and just looked at me as he walked to my little
cubicle.

"Donna, you're on in the next segment," he said. Live TV. I was
exhausted from a long election season and temporarily at a loss for

words. After years of being quoted and spinning everything in sight, I was no longer interested in talking about the election or commenting on what was happening to Democrats across the country. Part of my unease came from an earlier experience I had had on another cable network. Back in the 2002 cycle, when I had to stay on live TV for hours explaining how Democrats lost control of the U.S. Senate, I was so wasted that I wanted to walk home in the rain. The problem was, I was in New Jersey and D.C. was hundreds of miles down the highway. But the awful experience stayed with me. I could not find any good political news to report. I kept saying that the results were still being counted, and meanwhile some of our candidates were conceding before all the votes were in. I did not have a clue why they lost. Why Democrats were losing another close race.

The producer must have read the look on my face, because as I sat there clueless, staring at the tube, he walked away and never returned. So I sat there in the studio, hiding for over four hours until 3:00 AM. I wanted to get home to play with my puppy and go to bed. But first I had to get permission.

I called New York, where Lucy Spiegel, CNN's vice president and one of my buddies, asked me if I wanted to go on or go home. After all, it was late. Senator Edwards was about to come out and make a statement. I knew what was happening because I was still linked up via email to the Kerry folks and their constant chatter and analysis.

"Donna, what is he going to say?" Lucy asked. "We're not giving up until all the votes are counted," I told Lucy. Edwards went out to address the large crowd in Boston and the even larger crowd watching on TV from across the nation and the globe. Edwards, who appeared rested and upbeat, said the following:

> It's been a long night. We've waited four years for this victory, we can wait one more night. Tonight, we are keeping our word, and we will fight for every vote. You deserve no less.

The night no longer seemed so grim. I like it when Democrats fight back and stand up for every vote to be counted. I needed to get out of the CNN studio. There was nothing more to be said, and even if there was, the range of raw, conflicting emotions left me too exhausted to communicate effectively, let alone spin the eventual outcome.

I had to find a way to disappear. Before anyone could notice, I sneaked out the side door past the security desk and slipped into an elevator to go home. When I arrived at home, Chip was waiting for me by the door, and he stretched as if he was planning on another walk. No way. I pulled out a treat and convinced him to follow me upstairs, where we watched TV for the next two hours in silence.

Three hours later, with hardly any sleep, I was summoned back to CNN. I had no time to read the morning papers or review my emails. My BlackBerry was still down, having broken months before. The Kerry campaign talking points, which were delivered overnight, were not helpful. Feeling strangely subdued and groggy, I headed to CNN to comment on the election results and debate the Black conservative GOP consultant Reverend Joe Watkins.

Hearing Reverend Watkins brag about the Bush victory and resulting mandate before all the votes had been counted allowed me to regain my voice. What hubris, I thought to myself.

I was ready to spin what was happening in Ohio and to argue strongly why Kerry should not concede to Bush until all the votes had been counted across the country. (New Mexico and Iowa were still in contention.)

Just minutes before we went on the air, CNN had called the race in Ohio as too close to call. All of the emotions I had felt in Florida 2000 suddenly resurfaced, and I drew on the strength gained during that experience. I felt like a wounded soldier returning to the political battlefield. Deep down inside I knew I had to keep my composure in the shadow of defeat. I did not work directly for the Kerry campaign, but as a staunch Democrat the pain of losing was still the same.

When I left the studio the night before, the votes were still trickling in from Ohio and I just knew we could pull off an upset. But the clock was ticking and many of the large counties in the state—including Cuyahoga (Cleveland) and Franklin (Columbus)—had finally come in and Kerry was still behind by 150,000 votes. I knew from experience in 2000 that some of the so-called provisional ballots would overwhelmingly break for the Democratic candidate, providing Kerry with enough votes to come from behind and claim a victory.

So that morning on national TV, I mentioned that results were still coming in and the prospects of Kerry holding on for eleven days before conceding. At the same time, Kerry was still looking strong in other key battleground states—New Mexico, Iowa and Nevada. We expected to win all those states, but it was becoming increasingly clear that the Bush team had dominated those states with strong local grassroots support. The truth was, Kerry did not have enough gas in his tank to stay in the race for the long haul. If he did not win the popular vote, as Gore did in 2000, the public would instantly sour on his candidacy. He was just doomed. So hours later, the word came down that Kerry would concede before 1:00 PM.

One day after the most important election in our lifetime, the Democratic nominee called it quits. Kerry, like former vice president Al Gore in his 2000 concession speech, was statesmanlike and passionate.

> In America, it is vital that every vote count, and that every vote be counted. But the outcome should be decided by the voters, not a protracted legal process. I would not give up this fight if there was a chance we would prevail.

Many of my activist friends and civil rights leaders thought Kerry had conceded too soon. Harvard law professor Charles Ogletree and civil rights leader Mary Frances Berry sent strong emails telling me to tell the Kerry folks to "hang in there."

But it wasn't just a matter of votes not being fully tallied. My office began receiving hundreds of emails and angry phone calls from those on the ground reporting massive election irregularities, from polling stations opening late in some areas to young people having to wait up to ten hours to vote in others. Most of the disputed provisional ballots were cast in predominantly Democratic precincts in the state, a disproportionate share in minority or urban centers.

Some of us wanted to find out what all of this meant, and we needed time to figure it out before a formal concession by Kerry. However, after Kerry's speech, the gavel went down and the handwriting was on the wall. Even if there were legitimate challenges to the election, Kerry had all but pulled the plug on them.

This time, Bush would win. It was the smallest election victory of any incumbent since Woodrow Wilson, in 1916. But it did not matter. Democrats and progressive voters all across America were suddenly depressed.

In the days and weeks that followed the 2004 election, I had to come to grips with the hard reality that America was becoming socially and culturally more conservative. Although the Democratic Party was more unified and better funded than ever before, the conservatives were clearly more prepared to take their battle to the heartland using culturally divisive issues like same-sex marriage.

On the other hand, liberals, progressives, moderates and new Democrats put aside any differences they had with each other to work extremely hard to put Senators John Kerry and John Edwards in the White House. This was not an easy task for any of us to accomplish without the full support of the American people, who remained divided over the war in Iraq and whether it was an extension of the war on terror or a distraction. I personally thought the war had become a distraction from the perpetrators of the horrific attack on our country on September 11, 2001.

Bush sought to convince the electorate that Iraq was an extension of the war on terror and it was "risky" and unwise to change leaders in the middle of a war, and he succeeded. The message voters sent was that fear trumped hope. In the end, Bush managed to do for progressives what no other politician had done in a long while: unify the progressive forces.

Ultimately, even with all our new money and strong grassroots support, we did not manage to get out more people to vote than the other team. Elections are won based on turnout. And the Republicans and their conservative, evangelical base simply outhustled progressives and Democrats on the ground. This is something that rarely happens in American politics.

The 2004 election was a sore disappointment for me personally. This time we had no excuses as in past campaigns where we chalked up our losses to lack of money. In 2004 we matched the Republicans in fund-raising but clearly failed to connect with people on an emotional level.

Although I went out there almost daily on talk radio or cable TV defending every Democratic proposal, including Kerry's honorable service in Vietnam, the GOP kept churning out more negative sound bites. To the dismay of many, the Kerry campaign was often late in responding to the attacks.

I worked hard to remain a loyal, disciplined soldier. I sucked it up, bit my tongue, suppressed my disappointments and fell in line as a supportive Democratic surrogate. I avoided public quarrel with the Kerry folks and focused on defeating Bush and the Republicans.

In all, I had traveled to forty-six states since the 2000 presidential cycle. I went to places no one would think of sending a Black woman: deep into the heartland of Iowa, New Hampshire, Utah and even North Dakota. I often felt as if I were doubling the Black population in those states just by being there. I did traditional campaigning in churches, campus rallies and last-minute rallies in urban centers. It was rewarding, but I long for my old days as a warrior inside the trenches looking for new potential voters to rally to our side. For whatever reason, I am now a power player and a surrogate, which can be somewhat humbling given my need to be of service.

Now when I go outside, I must watch what I wear and of course what I say even when I'm not on TV. Whenever I get inside a cab, walk into an airport or even walk down the street, strangers now come up to me and say, "Are you the Democratic lady?" I have become one of the many faces of my party, and with that comes great responsibility, which is what inspired me to continue traveling and pounding the pavement.

The Bible teaches that there is a time for mourning. I continue to grieve over the loss of the 2004 election. So many people depend on the viability of the Democratic Party to stand up and defend civil rights and civil liberties. We are the voice of the powerless and those without a seat at the table. We are the champions of the disenfranchised and those who seek to have full and equal rights. We cannot waver from the looming battles ahead as a reelected president attempts to implement his brand of conservatism.

In going forward, millions of Americans will depend on Democratic politicians and leaders to lead the fight for them. By standing up, they will rally to support us in every election. This is why the party that I have dedicated my life to since 1968 cannot go into hiding until we are back in power and cannot roll over and play dead. Every American who believes in justice, equality and opportunity for all must seize this opportunity to rebuild our progressive movements for social change—one day at a time.

I know that some people believe our first order of business after an election is to form a circular firing squad. Birds gotta fly, fish gotta swim, and I'm sure we'll have plenty of time to replace the current leaders with new thinkers and organizers.

But until we get there, I think we should start by recognizing that we did get some things right in this election.

After the 2000 cycle, we knew we would be up against an opponent with unlimited funds and unlimited resources. And we knew the Democratic Party needed to make some major structural changes in order to compete. In addition to rebuilding the donor base, our party's activist base quadrupled. I can tell you personally that there was far more passion at the grassroots level, and more activists lined up to meet up, stand up and turn out our vote targets this time around than in 2000. Together with our strategic and political allies, Democrats mobilized more voters for Kerry than for any previous nominee in our party's history.

And there's no doubt that had we taken our campaign into the heartland, more Americans would have given us their trust and their vote. But we had a battleground-state plan that involved a limited number of states—mostly in the Midwest and Northeast. The Republicans played all over the electoral map and went after some traditional Democratic voters just to prove a point.

I believe President Bush won this election not because most

Americans believed in the direction he would take us, but because they did not have a clear understanding of where Democrats would lead them in the future. We simply did not do a good enough job at setting out what my friend and Cajun cousin James Carville calls "the narrative"—the single compelling story line that explains what we're about and where we're going as a party.

There are a lot of reasons for that, only some of which were within our control. The country was at war, and developments in Iraq and the Middle East were bound to drive the headlines almost every day. Our opponent was an incumbent with a built-in mega-phone and the power to set the national agenda even on a bad day. And as President Jimmy Carter said, this administration has never been shy about ruthlessly exploiting our shared fear of another ter-rorist attack.

Those were some of the things we couldn't control. But there are other factors we should have, and could have, controlled. And that's where we need to focus now.

In order to win future elections at the presidential, congressional and state levels, Democrats and progressives must do more than tune up or turn up the volume. We have to find the music—the language and the words that clearly spell out who we are, where we stand and why we fight for the values we hold dear. I am still proud to wear the liberal label. But I cannot and will not allow the Republican Party to destroy or distort what it is we fight for. This is one of those hard les-sons that we should have learned after the defeat of McGovern, Mondale and Dukakis. If you're a liberal, say it and proclaim it proudly.

But many of us now fear that as Democrats we will give in to the temptation to misread the 2004 presidential election and think we have to become "Republican lite." This would be an error that will cause us to lose even more supporters in the future. Just read any public opinion poll and you'll be amazed to learn that most Ameri-cans still agree with us on the issues.

Those same polls tell us that most Americans dislike President Bush's policies in any number of areas, including his handling of the war in Iraq. His economic stewardship. His judicial nominations. His disastrous positions on health care. His disregard of the environment. On these issues and many others, those polls we're so beholden to actually tell us people prefer Democratic ideas and policies.

And yet we keep losing.

The reason, I believe, can be found on the first page of the Lee Atwater/Karl Rove/George Bush political playbook. The simple answer is that Bush shows leadership.

From day one, George Bush—a president elected by a minority of one Supreme Court justice—has led this country in ways that actively hurt people and are actually unpopular with the public. But he has been very clear in telling the country what his plan is. And he has followed through, no matter how high the cost or how unpopular the cause.

And with another bitter election loss, we know that the American people respect him for it. They may not like where he's taking them. But they know where he stands. And that, I believe, is a very powerful thing. And we could use a lot more of it in the Democratic Party.

I'll never forget the words of former president Bill Clinton during his speech at the 2004 Democratic convention. He said the public would rather have a "leader who's strong and wrong than one who's weak and right." I think that applies to more than just defense policy. In fact, it's a theory about leadership. And the Republicans almost always do it better.

Democrats and progressives don't really have to be strong and wrong, like the president. We can be strong and right. But we need to stake our claim: figure out what we believe in, decide where we want to go and state clearly how we're going to get there. It's not a magic formula. But it's a simple principle of leadership we sometimes lose along the way.

Most years my friends gather to help me celebrate my birthday in December. But in 2004, we found it hard to lock in a good day to sit still and drink some champagne. Yes, I was still blue. But not for long. On Saturday, December 11, 2004, I delivered the Democratic radio address to the nation. My topic: the need for electoral reform. In my short statement, I made the following call to the American people:

I'm Donna Brazile, chair of the Democratic National Committee's Voting Rights Institute.

Our nation was founded on the principle of one man, one vote. Unfortunately, that was literally the case, as only white male landowners were originally given the right to vote.

Over the years, we as a nation corrected our mistakes, granting the right to vote to women, African Americans and eventually all citizens over eighteen.

America's story is one of expanding opportunity and suffrage, and one of our fundamental principles is that every eligible citizen is entitled to cast his or her vote and have that vote counted.

The Democratic Party stands firmly behind that principle, and that is why the DNC and the Voting Rights Institute have supported a number of efforts since the November election.

We joined the Kerry-Edwards campaign and the Ohio Democratic Party in monitoring the recount in Ohio.

We also sent more than a quarter million dollars to Washington State to help finance a full statewide recount in the governor's race, where only forty-two votes now separate the two candidates.

And this week the DNC announced that we would conduct a thorough investigation into various election administration issues that arose in the state of Ohio during the 2004 election.

We are launching this comprehensive investigative study not to contest the results of the 2004 election, but to help ensure that every eligible vote cast is truly counted.

This study will address the legitimate questions and concerns that have been raised in Ohio about provisional ballots, long lines at polling places and questions about voting machines. Our goal is to understand and report back on what happened and why.

In the next few weeks, we will be assembling a team of recognized experts in the relevant fields to conduct this study. This team will be supported by state and national staff members who were involved in Ohio. We expect this study to take several months and hope to publish a final report in the spring of 2005.

We owe it to the students of Kenyon College in Gambier, Ohio, who waited up to ten hours to vote; we owe it to thousands of Ohio voters who wonder whether their votes were counted with the use of new electronic voting machines; and we owe it to countless other Americans.

This is something that is very important to me. I've spent my entire life urging ordinary citizens to get involved in politics and to volunteer to work on Election Day. This is more important to me than ensuring the right to vote, and I am proud that the Democratic Party stands on the principle that, regardless of who wins, every vote should be counted, and every voter is entitled to have a voting experience free of hassles and intimidation, irrespective of where they live.

When Congress reconvenes next January, I hope Democrats and Republicans will work together to fully fund the Help America Vote Act, which was created to upgrade our voting systems and to ensure every voter has equal access to the ballot box.

There is no place in our democracy for faulty voting equipment, long lines at the polls, untrained poll workers and any form of chads. It's time we erase the vast disparities between poor and affluent communities with respect to reliable voting systems.

As a nation, we should not rest until our elections are free from the problems of elections past and until all Americans can cast their ballots on Election Day fully confident that their votes have been counted.

This is Donna Brazile, chair of the Voting Rights Institute. Thank you for listening, and may God bless America.

Soon there will be more elections to strategize and new opportunities in the electoral arena to prevent the Republicans from permanently realigning the electorate.

The battle for the heart and soul of America is not over. Democrats can win the war by displaying new ideas, new leadership and vigor.

I don't believe Democrats can continue to write off the South and portions of the West and expect to become a majority party again. This is the time to be bold, visionary and transformational in our thinking and analysis in moving forward. Now it's time for progressives to focus on rebuilding our state and local infrastructures. Just as Karl Rove used the 2002 election as a dry run for his 2004 get-out-the-vote operations, Democrats should do the same in 2006 in preparation for 2008 and beyond.

As depressed as I am about the 2004 presidential campaign and our losses, I believe as Democrats we can regain the presidency, Senate, House and state legislatures if we abandon cookie-cutter campaigns; in politics, one size doesn't fit all. Campaigns where marginal hair-splitting differences dominate the election season will not allow us to plant the seeds of change and to harvest new voters. It's time we start relighting the fire of change and start cooking with grease so America can get a taste for what we're stirring up for the future.

Author's note: On Saturday, February 12, 2005, members of the Democratic National Committee selected former Vermont governor Dean to head the Party. Dean, a blunt, tough and courageous leader, has vowed to retool, reform and rebuild the Democratic Party in red *and* blue states.

Not since the election of Ron Brown in 1988 have so many Washington insiders expressed concerns about the new leadership. But they should remember that it was Brown's dynamic leadership that led to the internal and external changes that produced a winning electoral ticket in 1992.

If Democrats have a chance at winning in 2008, it will come from leaders like Dean who respect the progressive base while understanding how to court moderates and independents to join our ranks. Truly, Dean is not afraid to stir the pots. Now, if only Democrats can come up with a winning message. The possibility exists to spice up grassroots politics and stir in new ingredients. Stay tuned and get involved.

Our future is at stake.

Jean's Seafood Gumbo

(for a large family)

2	pounds fresh or frozen medium-size shrimp, in shells, if possible, for stock
1	dozen fresh or frozen blue crabs, cleaned and shells removed (substitute: 2 pounds fresh crabmeat, crawfish, oyster or turtle)
4	teaspoons vegetable oil or shortening
4	stalks celery, chopped
1/2 cup	chopped parsley
2	green peppers, chopped
1	large onion, chopped
1 cup	chopped green onions
4	cloves garlic, chopped
3	bay leaves
1-ounce	can tomato paste
2	teaspoons salt
2	teaspoons ground black pepper
1/2	teaspoon dried thyme
1	teaspoon Worcestershire sauce
1/2 cup	all-purpose flour
1	can whole peeled tomatoes, chopped
	All the Tabasco sauce you can handle
1	pound andouille, turkey, kielbasa or smoked sausage, cubed
2	tablespoons filé powder (dried sassafras leaves)
1	pound fresh or frozen sliced okra
1 bag	Louisiana rice or your local brand

Step 1: Pour yourself a glass of something cold. I prefer a glass of wine, but you can make my mama's gumbo while enjoying a glass of lemonade. Start early in the morning or midday. Relax a bit and put on your favorite jazz, rock, rhythm and blues, hip-hop or Cajun music. Bring on your largest 14- to 16-quart pot. Fill it with two quarts of water. Start the fire on the stove. You're about to cook with grease.

Step 2: Separate the shrimp heads and hulls (skins) from shrimp bodies. Devein shrimp immediately and set aside in cold water. In the large "gumbo pot" boil heads and hulls for thirty minutes to an hour. This will give your Creole gumbo the smell of the streets of New Orleans after an afternoon thunderstorm when everyone is cooking something in the kitchen. Strain shrimp heads and hulls from stock and set aside. Discard heads and hulls immediately. Otherwise, the next day your kitchen will smell like Bayou St. John.

Step 3: Clean the fresh crabs. It's hard to find fresh blue crabs unless you're on the coast or have a good friend like me who likes to ship things around the country. If the crabs are fresh, you must take your time to clean them. Discard the hard back shell and some of the so-called "dead man," or yellow insides. Clean and separate crabs and set aside. (NOTE: If necessary, you can use meat from king, Dungeness, snow or stone crabs for your gumbo. It will work. Trust me. I have stirred up seafood gumbo in friends' homes from Maine to California. Just find me some claws, especially king crab claws, and watch me make a delicious, tasty, "out of the way" gumbo.)

Step 4: Before you fire up the stove again, cut up celery, parsley, peppers, onions and garlic, especially if you're alone and there is no one to help you stir the pots. It takes time peeling onions and garlic. With so many kids, Jean gave each of us something to cut up. I loved the smell of onions and garlic—part of the holy trinity along with green peppers. In later years, when we were off to college, we purchased Jean a food processor and she chopped up more than she needed and used the leftovers to make dirty rice or stuffed peppers. Put the celery and parsley in a separate container from the other chopped ingredients and refrigerate until needed to keep them fresh.

Step 5: Fire it up! Place the gumbo pot with the shrimp stock on the stove. Add cleaned crabs and bay leaves. Stir slowly. You don't want your shrimp stock messing up the floor. Add celery, parsley and tomato paste to the gumbo brewing on the stove. Bring to a boil. Turn down heat, cover and let simmer.

Step 6: Here comes the roux—a thick and favorable sauce that has become one of the most important staples of Louisiana cuisine. Pour oil or shortening into a separate heavy skillet (please do not use a thin omelet pan) over medium-low heat. Slowly stir in flour to make the roux. Keep your eyes on the skillet. If the phone rings, let the answering machine pick it up. Cook roux until it has a dark mahogany color. Do not stop stirring until roux appears nutty or grainy. If black specks appear, the roux is burned. Throw it out and start from scratch. A good roux could take thirty to forty-five minutes of cooking time.

Step 7: Now you are ready to add the holy trinity of onions, garlic and green peppers to the roux mixture. Stir ingredients in slowly because the flour is still sizzling. The moisture will begin to disappear. This is when Jean would add another quart or two of water to the gumbo pot. Add roux to the gumbo pot. Bring to a boil, stirring constantly. Lower heat and cover. The kitchen should smell good right now. Pour yourself another cold something-or-other. You're halfway there. Come back to look and stir in an hour or so.

Step 8: Season to taste: add salt, pepper, thyme, Worcestershire sauce, Tabasco sauce and any Creole seasoning you like. Don't overdo it right now. Let the roux work its magic absorbing all the wonderful ingredients. Gumbo is usually very spicy, but you can keep it mild. Remember, if you have decided to use andouille sausage, it is also hot.

Step 9: Fry sausages and okra with a little bit of leftover grease. Sprinkle a little leftover flour if the okra is fresh. Add chopped peeled tomatoes, stirring until well blended. Add more water if necessary. The roux will keep it thick and tasty. Return to a boil and simmer for ten minutes. Reduce heat and let simmer, uncovered, for two and a half to three hours over low heat.

Step 10: Skim any excess fat. Add shrimp. Stir in slowly as you increase the heat one last time. It's time to stir in the filé powder. Cook another twenty to thirty minutes until gumbo is thick. Taste and adjust seasonings one more time. Did I mention the rice? Seafood gumbo is served over Louisiana rice. Of course, you can substitute your own favorite rice. Just plain old brown or white rice will do. Before serving, taste one more time and adjust seasoning. Turn off the heat and remove seafood gumbo from the stove.

To cool down the pot before serving, place it in the sink filled with a few inches of ice-cold water. If needed, add additional salt and Tabasco sauce. If you can see through the gumbo to the bottom of the pot, work on your roux next time.

Enjoy Jean's Seafood Gumbo and remember to constantly stir the pot while you're cooking.

Acknowledgments

WRITING A BOOK is always a difficult task. For the first-time author, it can seem downright intimidating. Yet my family, friends, colleagues and editors were there for me, just as many of them have been throughout my life and career. I am eternally grateful to all of them.

The advice and counsel of Geoff Kloske, executive editor at Simon & Schuster, was indispensable in encouraging me to complete this project and to explain the inner workings of American politics. I am truly appreciative for the opportunity to tell my story. I will always be grateful to author, writer and lecturer Marita Golden, who guided me and inspired me to write with conviction and spirit. Whenever I grew weary, Marita lifted me up and kept me on my path. She was a gift from God.

I am also deeply grateful to my staff and colleagues at Brazile and Associates, LLC, including Stephanie Walker, Adam Harris, Ernestine Blango, Amy Drayer and Kate Henningsen, for their ongoing comments and suggestions. Jill Johnson in Kenner, Louisiana, helped me retrace my old path and Mark Warner of Ginsberg Lahey provided invaluable research and background throughout this project. I could not have completed this book without their professional guidance and assistance.

Betsy Marvin, my dear friend, was always ready to help me organize my thoughts, while Denise Outlaw, my dedicated colleague from the National Democratic Committee, was always willing to offer guidance and assistance with editing. A special thanks to my agent, lawyer, friend and adviser, Robert Barnett, of Williams & Connolly LLP, for his counsel and timely advice.

I have been blessed over the years with many friends. They keep me going, and this project was no exception. Thank you to Minyon Moore, Tina Flournoy, Julia Hudson, Regena Thomas, Sister Charlotte Ellzey, Kristina Kiehl, Debra Hayes, Toni Luck, Diane Chira, Nikki Heidepriem, Fred Humphries, Michael Matthews, Debbie Jansen, Jon Bouker, John Norton, Joyce Aboussie, Julie Gibson, Lezli Baskerville, Bob Friedman, Martha Strong Schlesinger, Marc Johnson, Barbara Covington, Jennie Adams, Cathy Hughes, Santita Jackson, Donnie Fowler Jr., Michael Berman, Bill Carrick, Paul Tully, Craig Smith, Cornell Belcher, Diane Feldman, Jacqueline Jackson, Tipper Gore, Elaine Kamarck, Leah Daughtry, Thomas Atkins and Pamela Grisham for their friendship over the years.

I wouldn't be where I am today without the encouragement of some key individuals who helped me to advance when I was a young woman eager to organize the world and find my seat at the political table. Shirley Chisholm, Coretta Scott King, Dorothy Height, Reverend Willie Barrows, Walter Fauntroy, Bill Lucy, Stevie Wonder, Cathy Long, Benjamin Hooks, Joseph Lowery, A. Z. Young, Sybil Taylor Holt, Rosemary Minor, Ernest "Dutch" Morial, Wilma Irwin and many, many more helped me to learn the art of politics and to serve.

I also have to thank those candidates who have trusted me over the years with their political futures. This roster includes Joseph Yenni, Aaron Broussard, Mary Landrieu, William Billy Guste, Jesse L. Jackson, Dick Gephardt, Michael Dukakis, Eleanor Holmes Norton, Bill Clinton and, of course, Al Gore to name just a select few who took my advice and allowed me to serve. A campaign manager is nothing without candidates, and those I have worked for have truly enriched my professional life.

I wouldn't have been able to compile these memories without the assistance of my family in Louisiana—Lionel, Ethel Mae, Gwen, Cheryl, Trish, Tina, Lisa, Janika, Sheila, Zeola and Demetria. Their input was a real trip down memory lane for me, and the book is better for it.

Politics is ultimately about people, and the people who make up my life are truly amazing, indeed. To each of them I offer a continued life of struggle and service to keep the flame of freedom burning until, in the words of the prophet Amos, "justice rolls down like water and righteousness like a mighty stream."

Index

About the Author

DONNA BRAZILE is a senior political strategist and former campaign manager for Gore-Lieberman 2000—the first
African American to lead a major presidential campaign. She
is currently chair of the Democratic National Committee's
Voting Rights Institute and an adjunct professor at Georgetown University.